Dear Charles

I hope you enjoy the book.

All the best,

John Sullivan

Raised by a
VILLAGE

Growing Up in Greenport

john sullivan

ARCHWAY
PUBLISHING

Archway Publishing books may be ordered through booksellers or by contacting:

Archway Publishing
1663 Liberty Drive
Bloomington, IN 47403
www.archwaypublishing.com
1 (888) 242-5904

ISBN: 978-1-4808-2210-8 (sc)
ISBN: 978-1-4808-2209-2 (hc)
ISBN: 978-1-4808-2211-5 (e)

Library of Congress Control Number: 2015917211

Print information available on the last page.

Archway Publishing rev. date: 11/24/2015

To Mrs. Van, and the class of 1957, the best of what Greenport had to offer

CONTENTS

PREFACE

In 1996 Hillary Clinton wrote a book, It Takes a Village and Lessons Children Teach Us in which she cites an African proverb that posits, "It takes a village to raise a child." If Mrs. Clinton were looking for a village in the United States to make her point, she could not have done better than Greenport.

In March 1999, while attending a funeral in Greenport, I had a conversation with Renee Vallely Carey. Renee was the older sister of one of my classmates, and I knew her and her three siblings, Peter, George, and Diane, pretty well. She and her siblings had been resettled in Greenport after they lost their parents.

During our conversation, Renee said, "John, I thank God every day for ending up in Greenport after our parents died." Having arrived in Greenport under similar circumstances with my mom and older brother, Bill, I told Renee that I felt much the same way, and we spent a few minutes singing Greenport's praises. That conversation got me thinking about writing a book about Greenport.

My idea got legs when, on September 6, 2001, The Suffolk Times, Greenport's weekly newspaper, ran a front-page, feature article on me. The title of the article was, "Secret Agent Man," and was in reference to my career with the CIA.

Ms. Julie Lane, who wrote the article, started her article with a quotation she attributes to me: "I am a poor kid who made good." I am sure that someone interviewed by Ms. Lane for the article more than likely described me as a poor kid who made good, but I am just as sure that I never said those words to her or anyone else. Compared with those with whom I grew up, I saw myself as less well off. "Poor" is not an inaccurate adjective; just one I can't remember ever using in describing myself.

Mom was forever telling Bill and me, as well as anyone who would listen, that we were too poor to buy this or do that, and I found it embarrassing. Anyone who knew me and my family back in Greenport would have to have been deaf, dumb, and blind not to know we were poor, at least in a material sense, and there was no need mention it.

Some of life's necessities, like a "room somewhere, far away from the cold night air," to quote Julie Andrews's "Wouldn't It Be Loverly" from My Fair Lady, three square meals a day, and adequate medical care, to name a few, would have been welcome additions to our daily lives.

There was also a dearth of what I at that time saw as life's niceties, to wit: clothes other than hand-me-downs, a toothbrush and paste, a bathroom with a tub or shower, regular haircuts, and something to eat besides canned food, hot dogs, and hamburger. These things may have been in short supply, but there was no shortage of love or of feelings of being wanted.

The first time I ever heard anyone refer to me as "poor" was when I was in first grade. Bill and I were playing in front of our house when my neighbor's niece and one of her friends were playing in the next yard. When asked by her friend, "Who are those kids?" she replied, "They're poor people." We were all pretty young at the time, and kids say things like that. I understand that now, but back then, it was a bit painful.

In the less-than-halcyon days of our youth, Bill or I could have been the poster boys for the ragamuffin child: much less than elegantly dressed, unkempt, and scrawny. We lived in substandard housing, and the three of us looked underfed. Impoverished image notwithstanding, Bill and I always felt as though we had a pretty good childhood in Greenport.

Last year, I attended an all-class reunion for Greenport High School and subsequently reconnected with Greta Levine Tedoff, a high school friend and one of the people who, along with her parents, made my life in Greenport a trip instead of a trek. She was living in New York City, and during a visit to see my younger son Jimmy and his wife, Mary, I and my significant other, Young, stopped in for a visit with Greta and her husband, Howard.

As we were reminiscing about Greenport, Greta suddenly said, "John, your family was the poorest family I have ever seen." My sense as to what evoked this comment was that the 2013 version of John Sullivan was very different than the boy with whom she grew up, and as pleased as Greta was, she was having difficulty reconciling the two versions.

Considering the scrawny, unkempt seventeen-year-old I had been when I graduated from Greenport Grade and High School in1957, Greta's favorable impression was understandable. I was certainly better dressed as well as better groomed and seemingly well-fed. The person sitting in her living room had undergone a metamorphosis and was projecting an image that Greta had never seen.

As I regaled Greta and Howard with my Greenport tales, Greta commented that I should write a book about the town. Howard added, "You are a natural storyteller and should give some thought to Greta's suggestion."

On my most recent visit to Greenport to attend another all-class reunion, I ran into Greta's younger sister, Linda. We were in a group of alumni discussing mutual friends, and I repeated what Greta had said about my family being the poorest one she had ever seen. When Linda heard that, she said, "How could she possibly tell?" Penny Coyle, one of my brother Bill's classmates, replied, "Believe me, you could tell."

Greta was not the first person to express surprise and plea-sure over how my life had turned out. In June 2007, my wife, Lee, and I were having dinner when the phone rang. Lee answered, and I heard her say, "Yes." She then turned and asked me, "Do you know a Cynthia Pappas?"

I said, "Yes, I grew up with her." Lee then handed me the phone.

Cynthia was the daughter of Peter Pappas, the owner of Paradise Sweets, Greenport's premier ice cream parlor. It served the best homemade ice cream I ever ate, and was a great place for kids to hang out. I don't recall there being a jukebox there, but Cynthia tells me there was one. Jukebox or not, Paradise Sweets was the place to go after Friday-night basketball games, dances, and movies.

Cynthia was a year ahead of me in school, and I knew and liked her. Mr. Pappas was very reserved but always very nice to Bill and me. Mrs. Pappas was very poised and gracious, and Cynthia's two older brothers, Peter and Connie, were good guys. I don't think Peter ever met a person whose name he didn't remember. Connie was the spitting image of his father, in every way, and that was a good thing.

Cynthia told me that she had just seen me on television, discussing my latest book. During our conversation, Cynthia suggested that I was probably the most famous person ever to come out of Greenport. I thought "well-known" was a more accurate description but was also flattered.

It turned out that Cynthia and her husband, John Newton, lived nearby, and we made arrangements to get together. The visit was somewhat of a repeat of my visit with Greta and Howard and very enjoyable. We spent over two hours catching up on old friends, and since that visit, I have kept in touch. John and Cynthia subsequently came to one of my lectures and attended Lee's funeral. John's brother had been in Special Forces and was Missing In Action (MIA) in Vietnam. When the body was recovered, he was buried in Arlington National Cemetery, and I attended the funeral. That was the twelfth funeral I had attended at Arlington since coming back from Vietnam.

My conversations with the Tedoffs and Newtons got me to seriously thinking about writing a book about Greenport, and my first thought was, "Why do I want to write such a book?"

In 2003, Antonia Booth and Tom Monsell's excellent book Images of Greenport came out. It is a beautiful pictorial history of Greenport, and I loved it. The book is essential reading for anyone interested in the history of Greenport, but it is more about places and events than people and is somewhat dated. People cited in Images are historical figures, not people with whom current readers may be able to readily identify or relate. I want my book to be about the people who made Greenport the great place it was for me and my family and with whom the people of Greenport can identify. My history in Greenport is a very personal one, and hopefully, reading Raised by a Village will be a personal experience for those who read it.

The people of Greenport fed, clothed, protected, and encouraged me, and they gave me a sense of belonging that those of my pedigree rarely experience. All of this was done without any strings attached. Strings or not, I owe the people of Greenport a great deal, and Raised by a Village is my way of paying that debt.

If I were to enumerate the individual acts of kindness Greenporters extended to me and my family, the book would be much too long. But in the ensuing pages, I will cite enough of them to make it very clear why Raised by a Village is an appropriate title for the book.

When trying to come up with a title, my first thought was Welfare Brat. Having spent so much of my youth on welfare, I thought this was an appropriate and catchy title. I also thought that there is a lot of misinformation about people on welfare and I could enlighten the uninformed. However, Dr. Mary Childers had already used that title in her well-received book, and although we were on welfare, neither Bill nor I was ever a brat.

It occurred to me that most publishers would consider publishing a book-long thank-you note a less-than-profitable undertaking, and in order to catch the interest of a publisher, I needed an angle or hook. That hook came from a quote attributed to Sidney Poitier, to wit: "Internally, I see myself as an ordinary man who has had an extraordinary life."

If Mr. Poitier sees himself as ordinary, my ego can only allow me to describe myself as much less so, but it also demands that I describe my life as extraordinary. For someone who never distinguished himself while growing up and for whom there were no great expectations, my life has been every bit as extraordinary as Mr. Poitier's.

When I was growing up, the ordinary prospects for a Greenporter of my background was to finish high school, enlist in in the military, serve out the enlistment, return to Greenport, and settle down. Finishing college was step one on my road to the extraordinary. Working for the CIA for thirty-one years and writing two books about my experiences took my journey into the realm of the extraordinary.

There is a "poor boy makes good" aspect to my story, with some differences. The hero of poor-boy stories usually has obstacles other than lack of money to overcome, such as a dysfunctional family, a physical disability, and possibly a villain who makes the hero's struggle even more difficult. When and if the poor boy makes good, there is usually a desire to go back home and tell the hometown folks, "I guess I showed you."

I never had such obstacles to overcome or felt the need to show Greenporters that I had turned out pretty well. However, since the day I left for college in 1957, it has been on my mind that someday I would have to say thank you to the people of Greenport for all they have done for me. That time has come, and at age seventy-five, I am feeling the need to get it done quickly.

On two of my trips back to Greenport, I was stopped by people I had known, but not well, as a kid. The first was Halsey Staples. I had known two of his older brothers, Stuart and Bob, but not Halsey. "You're John Sullivan, aren't you?" were his first words to me.

When I said I was, he said, "Congratulations on your success. It is well deserved, and we are all very proud of you." For someone I had not known to recognize me was very flattering, and I basked in the glow of Halsey's recognition.

The second encounter was with Dorothy "Dottie" Reuther. She was three years ahead of me in school and a very lovely girl. I knew her father, "Fagan," who was always nice to Bill and me, but hadn't known Dottie very well. I was coming out of the local 7-11 when she approached me. Again, it was, "You're John Sullivan, aren't you?" When I said, "Yes," Dottie's face lit up with a smile, and she said, "We are so proud of you." These two incidents gave impetus to my desire to say thank you to Greenport.

The heroes of Robert Ruark's Poor No More and Bud Schulburg's What Makes Sammy Run were obsessed by a desire to be rich. My goal in life has never been to be rich but rather not to be poor, and there is a difference. To become rich, I would probably have to take risks, and I was more averse to losing what I had than I was eager to be rich. In the real world, at least as I saw it, to get rich meant being very competitive, having to occasionally compromise one's values, and not being a nice guy. I couldn't see myself as meeting any of these criteria.

Being a nice guy didn't mean making sure that people liked me, but rather making sure that no one disliked me. I didn't work very hard at the former, but did at the latter, and it seems to have worked.

Kids of meager means who succeed are usually very smart and very driven, with a great artistic talent or exceptional athletic ability that helps pave the way for them. With the exception of a modest ability to whistle, I had none of these. What I did have were the people of Greenport, who were more than enough.

In the following pages, I hope to give the reader a very up-close and personal picture of whom I was and how I became who I am today. In the process, I hope to make it clear that I not only was raised by a village but raised well, and I am so very grateful.

John F. Sullivan
August 4, 2014
Reston, VA

Chapter 1

GREENPORT

My first memory of Greenport is of waking up on a cot, on the deck of a small fishing boat that was taking me, Bill, and Mom from Fishers Island to Greenport. We were being relocated after my father had passed away in July 1940.

Fishers Island is a small island off the coast of Connecticut, seven miles long and two miles wide at its widest point. Although closer to Connecticut than New York, Fishers Island is a part of Suffolk County, New York.

Bill and I were born in New London, Connecticut. Our father had been the sexton for, and Mom the housekeeper in, the rectory at Our Lady of Grace Roman Catholic Church until our father passed away on July 20, 1940, at the age of forty-nine.

I was eleven months old at the time, and I don't know how old I was when we left Fishers Island. I assume it was the fall of 1940 or spring of 1941, as it was pretty cool when I woke up on the deck of the boat, but I never thought to ask Mom. The only memories I have of our time on Fishers Island are of sitting in a high chair, watching Mom beat a water rat to death with a broom, and of an army doctor from Ft. Wright lancing an abscess on my butt that I got as the result of being bitten by a spider.

My early memories of Greenport are mainly of how kind the people were. On one of our first Christmases in Greenport, Mr.Leander Chute, a local plumber, brought Bill and me toy drums. On another occasion, before Bill or I had started school, we were locked out of our apartment because Mom hadn't paid the rent. We were standing in front of the house, Mom was very distraught, and we were wondering what to do when Emelio "Unc" Giorgi, the local garbage man, came along.

He asked Mom what was going on, and when he found out, he went to the landlady, got the key to our apartment, and moved us. He never charged us a cent, and for all our time in Greenport, he never charged us to take our trash away.

I can't recall ever seeing Unc at Mass, but I consider him to be one of the more Christian people I have ever known. He also hired a lot of the local boys to work on the truck with him. In addition to paying the boys, he took them to breakfast and would buy them sodas during breaks. One of the things I liked best about Unc was that he never mistook me for Bill, as many people in Greenport did.

Another true benefactor during those early days was Julia DeBenedetto Aanstead. Bill and I started going to Mass on Sunday before we started school. Occasionally, when Mom had to work, we would go by ourselves. On many of those occasions, Julia would take us to her house after Mass and give us eggs and fresh vegetables from her garden to bring home.

Eventually, Julia became our landlord, and that was very fortuitous. She was one of the kindest women I have ever known and without a doubt the best cook I have ever met. Aunt Julia, as I came to call her, came to typify how kind Greenport could be, and I loved her dearly.

Her husband, Don, was equally great but not as demonstrative as Julia. Don also had a very dry sense of humor. He was well read, had a lot of common sense, and I loved being around him. My most memorable moment with Don occurred after I got back from Vietnam and was telling him that I wished Mom had lived long enough for me to make life better for her. Don paused and said, "John, you never gave your mother a minute of grief and were her pride and joy. Don't beat yourself up."

Once World War II started, Greenporters became totally invested. Seventeen young men from Greenport lost their lives in the war, and gold star flags in the windows of those who had lost family members were a constant reminder of those sacrifices.

My most poignant memory of WWII comes from a story told to me by John Montgomery, a football teammate and very good friend. John's father, Chris, was the person who delivered the telegrams from the War Department notifying families that their son had been killed or was missing in action.

On one of those occasions, John was in the car when Mr. Montgomery pulled up in front of a house where he had to deliver a telegram. He put his head on the steering wheel and said, "John, I know these people, and I just can't deliver this one. Will you please do it?"

John had to go around to the back of the house and walk up a flight of stairs to deliver the telegram. He knocked on the screen door, and a young woman came to the door. He handed her the telegram, and as he did, an older woman came out of another room. As soon as she saw the telegram, she broke down.

For a six-year-old boy, this was pretty heavy stuff, and when John told his mother what had happened, she blew her top at Mr. Montgomery. Mr. Montgomery's job was one I could never have done.

A harsher memory is of the week when Mr. Widertsky got word that his two sons had been killed, eight days apart, on the island of Saipan. When he got the second notice, he ran out in the street screaming.

There were scrap iron drives, paper drives, war bond rallies, victory gardens, and blackouts. Rationing was strictly enforced, and there was a pride in our military that I have not encountered since leaving Greenport. When I started kindergarten in 1944, there were pictures of Greenport boys who were serving in the military posted on the wall of the main corridor. Each time another boy went off to war, his picture was posted. Those pictures are still there.

Patriotism was almost palpable, not, "the last refuge of the scoundrel" of Thomas Jefferson. Each time a young man was drafted, there was a huge send-off, with most of the town at the station to see him off. Some of that must have rubbed off on mom. From as early as I can remember, she made it clear that serving in the military was the way one paid his dues for living in America and that I would be paying those dues.

Draft dodgers, or "slackers" as they were called, were scorned. There were those who had legitimate reasons to seek a deferment and were hesitant to do so for fear of being stigmatized. There were also some who claimed deferments in order to work on family farms, and some of them were seen as less patriotic.

Postwar Greenport had a brief economic letdown. The largest employer in Greenport was Brigham's Shipyard, and the end of the war brought a huge reduction in the workforce as well as a concomitant loss of business for many of Greenport's merchants. On a bitterly cold Sunday morning in early 1946, the largest fire in the history of Greenport pretty much put the shipyard out of business. There were rumors that the fire was arson and set to cover up huge thefts of materials, but no investigation was undertaken.

There were no slums in Greenport, but there were quite a few substandard houses, ours among them. Among the bad memories of my life in Greenport, none is worse than the memory of how cold it was in our house during the winters. We would wake up with ice on the insides of the windows, and we could see our breath when we exhaled.

We didn't have central heating, and the wood- and coal-burning stove in the kitchen was our only source of heat. The wood never lasted through the night, and the coal gave off an unhealthy odor. Both fuels gave off smoke, and the walls and ceilings were smoke-stained, reminding me of the dreary slum housing of *Angela's Ashes*, the wonderful book written by Frank McCourt. There were so many things in that book to which I could relate and identify; most of them are not pleasant, but all are part of the fabric of who I am.

Greenport was a hardworking, hard-playing, and hard-drinking town. Farming and fishing were how most of the people made a living, and making a living in these venues was not for the weak. The hours were long, the work arduous, and the pay low. The best-paying job was working on the deep-sea scallop boats, but it was also the most difficult and dangerous way to make a living. The movie *Perfect Storm* reminded me of the Greenporters who went out to sea in scallop boats.

Respite from the daily grind was found in one of the many bars in town. I remember delivering papers to one of the bars on a hot, summer Sunday morning. The smell of stale beer and cigarettes was overwhelming, and was a factor in my never becoming a smoker or drinker.

On Saturday nights, heels were kicked up, and wild oats were sown. On Sundays, seven churches and a synagogue were available to those who wanted to pray for crop failure. I never had to pray for crop failure or confess that particular sin of the flesh, but had I done so, it would have been at St. Agnes R.C.C. The confessions I made assuaged my guilt for whatever sins, minor as they were, that I committed. The prayers provided solace and hope, and being an altar boy gave me some status. For Mom, St. Agnes's was so much more. St. Agnes's was an occasional source of income and comfort, and her membership in the parish was a significant part of Mom's identity.

St. Agnes's was also the site of The Lot, a fairly large piece of land across the street from the rectory. After a house on the corner of The Lot was torn down, the foundation was filled in, and the empty space became the site of the parish's annual block party as well as a place where many of the neighborhood kids played pick-up games of football and baseball. From the time I was in fifth grade until the Catholic school was built on that property in 1952, I and the neighborhood kids spent most of our free time playing there, weather permitting.

During that time, Dick Corazzini formed a neighborhood football team, and all games were played on The Lot. Playing on that team was my first experience playing football, and I liked it very much. When not playing games, Don Hunton, Nathan Goldin, and I would spend hours playing a game we made up called "Official Quarterback," in which one of us would be the quarterback while the other two would be opposing receivers.

On one of my visits back to Greenport, I was talking to Mrs. Hunton, Don's mother, when she brought up The Lot. "John," she said, "From sunup to sundown, we never had to worry about where our kids were. You were on The Lot."

My most memorable moment on The Lot was when Bill came over to tell me that the Giants had beaten the Dodgers in the 1951 playoff game during which Bobby Thompson hit the "shot (home run) heard around the world." That was a devastating announcement for me, a die-hard Dodger fan.

Another very memorable moment occurred while playing in a pick-up football game and tried to tackle Bill Dinizio. Bill ran right over me and, in the process, knocked me out cold. That was the first time in my life that had happened. I came to with Don Hunton asking me, "Are you okay, John?" Among my many Greenport memories, times spent on The Lot are among my best.

Compared with the two nearest neighboring towns, Southold and Mattituck, Greenport was much more of a melting pot. The two largest ethnic groups were the Polish and Italians, followed by the Irish and Germans. There were five Greek families, the Pappases, Moscoveys, Drossoses, Proferes, and Pouloses, as well as a Greek Orthodox church. The only Russian family I can recall was the Bondarchuk family. There were two Portuguese families, the Claudios and the Glorias, and Claudio's restaurant is the oldest family restaurant in the United States. The Aansteads, Hanffs, and Norkeluns were Norwegians, and the only Asian family were the Reyes family, who were Filipino. I don't recall any Latinos or Hispanics, and about 10 percent of the population was African-American. The Jewish population was small but significant.

On my most recent visit to Greenport, I stopped in at Greenport Grade and High School to do some research in the GHS library. Joan Heaney Dinizio, a member of the Heaney family, who were great benefactors to the Sullivans and who had helped me on past visits, was again very helpful. On the way out of school, she said to me, "John, why don't we stop in and say hello to Kathy?"

Kathy was Joan's cousin, Kathy Heaney Wallace, the daughter of Jack and Helen Heaney and one of the third-grade teachers. When we went into the classroom, the first thing I noticed was that over half the class were Latinos. After saying hello to Kathy, I began speaking Spanish with the kids and had a lot of fun with them. Greenport's ethnic balance had changed dramatically since I left.

Greenport was less genteel than Southold and Mattituck; it was more blue-collar and less straight-laced, and there was some crime. Gambling, prostitution, domestic violence, and barroom fights accounted for most of the crime, but I recall three murders, one of which launched the criminal career of Greenport's most infamous former resident, Bobby Waterhouse. Bobby earned his infamy by murdering two women and spending more time than any man in history on death row (thirty-five years) before being executed.

There were two bowling alleys in Greenport, Santacroce's and Schiavoni's. Santacroce's was the more popular of the two and had a lot more business. Schiavoni's had three pool tables in addition to the four bowling lanes and was a place where the local kids hung out.

When I first started setting up pins in Santacroce's, I wasn't a good enough pin setter to work the league matches and went to work at Schiavoni's. The money per game I earned was the same in both places, but I learned to play pool at Schiavoni's, and that was a real plus. After a year at Schiavoni's, I was able to go back to Santacroce's, where I worked until my freshman year in high school. During the summers of my junior high school years, I worked on a couple of the local farms picking potatoes, beans, peas, and so on during the days and at the bowling alley at night.

Gambling was big in Greenport, and three bookies that I knew of flourished, as did a numbers operation. I didn't know anyone in Greenport, except maybe Mom, who didn't know what a bookie was, let alone who they were. Two were barbers and one a store owner. They were friendly, active in the community, and accepted. There were supposedly organized crime ties to the bookies, but I never heard about any organized crime violence in Greenport. On one occasion, the biggest bookie in town noticed Bill's worn-out shoes and took him to Brandi's shoe store and to buy him a new pair.

Sportsman's cigar store was located next to Santacroce's bowling alley and was an integral part of the local scene. There was a section of the store that was set aside as a TV room, and when I wasn't setting up pins, Al Marttoccia, the owner, would let me come in and watch television. I saw most of the big boxing matches of that time as well as the *Ed Sullivan Show* and other programs; 90 percent of the TV I saw in Greenport was seen in Sportsman's cigar store. There was also a card room upstairs where some pretty high-stakes poker was played, and I saw more than a couple of locals leave broke.

I was an eleven-, twelve-, and thirteen-year-old kid when all of this was going on, and I was spending a lot of time in the company of adults, most of whom treated me very well. This was an aspect of growing up that most of my contemporaries never experienced. The language I heard in this environment was not fit for a church social, and the day-to-day dramas discussed by the men I was around gave me a broader perspective on life in the raw. This, in conjunction with my own experiences, helped me mature a little sooner than many of my contemporaries.

Mr. Martoccia managed the local football and basketball teams and was involved in local politics as well as all other civic activities. He was definitely one of those who made Greenport a good place in which to live, and I thought that he was one of the smartest men in Greenport.

He was an avid New York Giants baseball fan, and when Bobby Thompson hit his home run off Ralph Branca to win the 1951 pennant, Mr. Martoccia put a big sign in the front window of the store with a sickle. The sign said: "Looking for Branca?"

Mrs. Maureen Van Popering, my eighth-grade English teacher, benefactor, and mentor, knew that I spent a lot of time there, and I can remember her saying to me: "John, the high point in the lives of so many of these men was a game they played years ago, and I find that very sad."

I think it was Lee Trevino, the golfer, who coined the phrase, "The older I get, the better I was," and I saw this with many of the guys who hung around Sportsman's cigar store. I agree with Mrs. Van that it was sad.

There were two houses of ill repute in Greenport: Len Jones's on Third Street and Madam Pam's on Sixth Street. Their clientele was primarily the crews from the bunker boats who sailed out of Greenport in the summers, but there was some local patronage. The "ladies" would arrive on the three-o'clock train on Friday afternoons and depart on the Sunday afternoon train.

On Sunday mornings, there would be a parade of customers walking past St. Agnes's to and from Madame Pam's, and I can remember Father Holland railing from the pulpit on this "blight on decency." Indecent it may have been, but it was also one of the reasons bunker boats used Greenport as a home port and a positive factor in the economy.

There is a tale in Greenport about a raid on one of the houses. The state police had called the Greenport police station to notify them that there was going to be a raid that evening. At the time of the call, the chief of police was availing himself of the services of the house. The officer who took the call called and warned the chief. When the state police arrived, the chief was leading the ladies in a Bible study session.

When the Menhaden bunker fish disappeared from Long Island waters, so too did the bunker boats and their crews. The bunker boat exodus, in conjunction with the passing of Len Jones and Madam Pam, resulted in the closing of the two houses of ill repute.

The police force was small, and I knew all of its members pretty well. Bud Goldsmith was the one I knew the best. He was a pretty mean cop, but I got along well with him, and he always called me "Dick Tracy." Neither Bill nor I ever got in trouble with the police, and I left Greenport thankful that I had never had a run-in with Bud.

I am sure that there had been some corruption in the Police Department, but the only firsthand knowledge I have of it was a very minor incident. Frank Swiskey was a good friend of Harry Bubb (one of my best friends), and occasionally we would hang around together. On one of those occasions, Frank told us about having gotten a speeding ticket and having it fixed by Irv Levin, his boss in Levin's clothing store. During my time away from Greenport, the police department was dissolved and policing responsibilities were taken over by the Southold Town Police Department.

The volunteer fire department was outstanding and was the center of much of the social activity in Greenport. The event of the year was the Washington's Day birthday celebration sponsored by the fire department. There was a huge parade followed by firemantic contests (as the firemen competitions were called) and a dance at the American Legion hall that night, where Victor Zembruski, the Polish drummer boy, and his polka band played the night away.

Two young firemen, Bruce Bellfountaine and Rich Sycz, died while trying to rescue a child from a burning house. They were told that a little girl was in an upstairs bedroom, and they went in to get her. The fact that the little girl was not in the house in no way vitiates their heroism. Their funeral was the biggest in the history of Greenport, and a beautiful statue in front of the firehouse memorializes their sacrifice. Members of the fire department were the backbone of Greenport's citizenry and an asset to the community.

Greenport's medical community consisted of five doctors and Eastern Long Island Hospital. "The doctor" in Greenport was Dr. Kaplan, and he was our doctor. There were four other doctors in Greenport, Dr. Sperling, Dr. Tuthill, Dr. Olson, and Dr. Heath, and there seemed to be enough business to keep them busy.

Dr. Kaplan seemed a bit gruff to me, and I was a bit intimidated by him. There are two contacts I had with Dr. Kaplan that I remember very well. The first of these came about when I badly sprained my left ankle during track practice in 1956. Two teammates took me to his office, where he taped my ankle and told me to come back the next day so that he could take me to the hospital for an x-ray.

The next day, he took me to the hospital. When Katherine Droskoski, the x-ray technician, saw the tape around my ankle, she told Dr. Kaplan that she couldn't x-ray through the tape, he just tore it off. There was a little skin, a lot of hair, and some blood on the tape as well as a lot of pain.

When I came home for summer vacation after my first year in college, I had a cast on my left leg, from hip to ankle. It had been on for nine weeks, and I needed to have it cut off. I went to

Dr. Kaplan's office, where he told me that he would take me to the hospital the next day and cut the cast off. The next day, Dr. Kaplan took me to a treatment room, where he had me take off my pants and sit on an examining table. He picked up a vibrating saw and began cutting.

The blade hit my leg, and I yelped. "This saw can't cut you. Don't be so jumpy!" was Dr. Kaplan's admonition. The blade hit my leg three more times, but I managed to control myself. Dr. Kaplan made two hip-to-ankle cuts in the cast, put the saw on another table, turned, and walked out, leaving me to peel the cast open, get dressed, and leave.

When I opened the cast, there were three fairly long cuts on my leg, oozing blood: one on the outside of my upper thigh and the other two on the outsides of my left and right calves. I hadn't bent that leg in over nine weeks, and the going was very slow. I hobbled down the hall to a pay phone, where I called Mrs. Bubb, the mother of one of my best friends, who came and picked me up.

Dr. Kaplan never charged me a cent for removing the cast, and I am grateful. But these two interactions left me with less-than-warm feeling for a man who had given his professional life to Greenport and was a legend.

Dr. and Mrs. Kaplan had four children, Herschel, Sybil, Hilda, and Micah. Micah was a good friend and my teammate on the 1956 football team. On one of my trips back to Greenport, he told me a story that gave me a bit of a different perspective on his father.

Micah had been home from the University of Buffalo medical school when his father woke him up to drive him to the hospital. Stanley Tamin, a good friend of Micah's and mine, had been in a bad accident. Stanley died on the table, and on the way home, in words as I can best recall, Micah told me, "On the way home, my father said, "Sometimes you want to just want to reach inside and make them live, and you can't do it. I delivered that kid, and I had to tell his mother that he was dead." And I had the audacity to wonder why Dr. Kaplan might be a little insensitive, on occasion!

Dr. Kaplan and the rest of the medical community served Greenport very well, as did the school, churches, and police and fire departments. Greenport wasn't the "Mayberry, RFD" Of TV's *Andy Griffith Show* but a real town with real people, good and bad. Fortunately, there were many more of the former than the latter, and that made Greenport an ideal place in which to grow up.

Everyone knew everyone else, and living in Greenport was, at times, like living in a fishbowl. On occasion, this could seem intrusive, but there was also a degree of protection, especially for the kids. Neighbors looked out for each other's kids, and any potential child molester would have to navigate through a minefield of concerned citizens to get to potential victims.

Straying from the straight and narrow without being found out was not an option for kids. If a kid got into any kind of trouble, the news would, more often than not, get home before the kid did.

I recall one of my high school classmates, Sharon Lellmann, telling me that one evening her father came home from work and confronted her with an accusation that she had been seen smoking with Diane Woodward, another of our classmates. Sharon and Diane had been sucking on lollipops as they walked down the street. This was Greenport.

In 1982, I returned to Greenport to celebrate the twenty-fifth anniversary of the graduation of the class of 1957. During that event, I reconnected with a lot of friends, and since then I have tried to get back there as often as possible. Recently, I brought my significant other, Young, my daughter-in-law, Kristen, and my two grandchildren, Katie and Andrew, out to Greenport. On our many walks around town, I had few encounters with people I knew when growing up. But those that I did have were great, and Greenport was still home to me.

There has been a significant decrease in Greenport's population since I left. When I lived in Greenport, the population was around three thousand people. In 2011, the population was 2,198. A more significant change in Greenport has been an astronomical increase in real estate values. As of 2009, the median price of a house was $442, 874. I can recall one of my boyhood friends telling me his mother had paid $6700 for their house. A few years ago, that house sold for $412,000..

Greenport is becoming more and more like the Hamptons, with more and more city people buying weekend getaway houses, and buying a house is pretty much out of the question for the kids who stay in Greenport. Jack and Helen Heaney take care of mom's grave site, and I always stop in to say hello to them when I go back. On one of my recent stops, Jack told me that three houses had been sold on his street in the previous year, all to New York City dwellers who were buying weekend houses.

Among the problems that go along with the population drain is that Greenport is having difficulty finding people to do the menial jobs that keep towns functioning. The supply of volunteers for the fire department is diminishing, new teachers can't afford to raise a family in Greenport, and there is no reason to think this will change any time soon.

Currently, the real estate boom continues. As time goes on, there will be fewer and fewer residents whom I recognize, but I will go back. Greenport is a part of who I am, and that is something I don't want to forget.

Chapter 2

LITTLE THINGS
MEAN A LOT

In 1954, Kitty Kallen sang a song, "Little Things Mean a Lot," that became a big hit and, based on many of my experiences in Greenport, is a fitting title for this chapter. When Mom worked at the local theater, she used to go into the Park Diner to get a cup of coffee and became friends with John Moscovey, the owner. On many occasions, Mr. Moscovey lent Mom money that he probably knew he would never get back, and he was a real benefactor.

In addition to lending money to mom, Mr. Moscovey helped Bill and me. Mr. Jaeger, the owner of Jaeger's department store, was a frequent customer in the diner, and on one occasion, Mr. Moscovey ordered snowsuits from Mr. Jaeger for Bill and me. Mr. Jaeger, thinking the snowsuits were for Mr. Moscovey's two daughters, Athena and Adrienne, ordered girls' snowsuits. Bill and I were not fashion conscious, and we wore them with gratitude

The Goldin family—Oscar and Eva, the parents, and Louis, Joyce, and Nathan, the three children—lived around the corner from us, adjacent to St. Agnes's church. Louis and Joyce were more than twelve years older than I, and Nathan was a year younger than I. Bill and I both played a lot with Nathan.

All of the Goldins were very nice to Bill and me, and in the summers Mr. and Mrs. Goldin would take Nathan, Bill, and me for rides up to Long Island Sound to watch the sunset. On the way home, we would usually get ice cream. To someone who, prior to those rides, had never seen Long Island Sound, this was a very big deal. Those rides were also my first recollection of riding in a nice car. I am sure Mr. and Mrs. Goldin didn't realize the effect these little things had on me, but such unsolicited acts of kindness have allowed me to be predisposed to see the good in people before looking for the bad.

Louis and Joyce played tennis, which was not common among kids in Greenport at that time, and Nathan and I used to go up to the tennis courts behind the school to watch them play. Occasionally, Joyce would hit with Nathan and me, and I got to like tennis. Seeing that I was interested in tennis, Joyce gave me an old tennis racket. That simple act had some great unintended consequences.

Once I had a racket, Nathan and I would go up to the courts and play, but I never came close to being a good tennis player. I spent a lot of time hitting and returning tennis balls off the rear wall of the school, and I did get pretty good at doing that. While stationed in Vietnam, I took some tennis lessons and started playing tennis.

When our older son, John, was six, I began hitting with him, and he became a pretty good player. The first time I took him to the tennis court to use the hitting wall, he hit and returned the ball 209 times before he missed a ball. In 1989, during his freshman year in high school, his team, the South Lakes Seahawks, was playing in the regional finals. The match score was 0–2. John and his doubles partner, Ryan McInerney, were down 0–5, with John serving at 0–40, match point.

Coach Kaplan told the team to start packing up the gear, but

Matt Rosner, one of John's teammates, yelled that it wasn't over. John won that game with four straight aces, and they went on to win the championship. During the last game of the final set, John's teammates were chanting, "Johnny, Johnny," and when he hit a winner to seal the victory, they carried John off the court on their shoulders. Only a father who has been there can identify with the pride I felt on that day.

The next year, John led his team to a state championship. He was subsequently recruited by the Army, Navy, and Air Force Academies as a tennis player and by Vanderbilt and Stanford as a minority (Hispanic) rather than a tennis player. John chose the U.S. Naval Academy. Before graduating in 1996, he was the captain of the navy tennis team and was also elected company commander by the midshipmen in his company. More recently, he was inducted into his high school's athletic hall of fame. It all started with Joyce Goldin giving me a tennis racket.

Another of those little things that had a profound effect on me was an occasion when Joyce Goldin and a neighbor, Mrs. Ann Kalabacker, took me and Bill to see a stage play at the John Drew Theater in East Hampton. Although I didn't see it as such at the time, I ultimately saw this as an effort on Joyce's and Mrs. Kalabacker's parts to bring some culture to the Sullivan brothers. The play they took us to see was *The Fourposter,* and I think the stars were Hume Cronyn and Jessica Tandy. Both Bill and I enjoyed the experience very much, and stage plays are one of my favorite forms of entertainment.

Mrs. Goldin was a very cultured lady, and I remember very well Saturday afternoons playing in and outside the Goldin house as Mrs. Goldin listened to the opera. On one occasion, the opera to which she was listening seemed so dreary to me that after it was over, I asked Mrs. Goldin what it was. She told me it was by Wagner, and I knew that I would never be a fan of his operas. If I can't tap my foot to or whistle the melody, what I am hearing isn't music.

On another occasion, I heard someone singing "La donna è mobile" and loved it. I had the same reaction to "The Grand March" from *Aida*. I never discussed opera with Mrs. Goldin, but she did explain to me how opera attendees were given a book called a libretto to help them understand what was going on.

I am sure that Mrs. Goldin knew that most of what she was saying fell on deaf ears, but the fact that she was willing to take the time to do this says a lot of good things about her. There was another thing Mr. Goldin did that, although not for the Sullivans, had a very positive effect on me. He had his store manager, Eddie Copin, install a basketball backboard and hoop on their garage. This was no cheap peach basket hoop and backboard but a fancy piece of work. The driveway leading to the garage and the area in front of the garage were smooth concrete and made a great basketball court. Some of my happiest hours as a kid were spent playing basketball with Nathan and the other kids who came over there to play.

During the summer between fifth and sixth grades, I was the bat boy on the local baseball team, the Seals. My favorite player on that team was Bill Norkelun. One night at practice, an older kid who used to pick on me a lot, Lenny Moerland, was giving me a hard time until Bill intervened and ran Lenny off the field.

That same summer, Joe Buckin, the center fielder on the team, gave me my first baseball glove. It was old and beat up, with two strands of the webbing missing, but receiving it was better than my first kiss, and another mindless act of kindness that I won't forget.

Some other examples: On some nights I would finish working in the bowling alley just before the first show at the movie house got out, and on the way home, I would mix with the people exiting the first show and sneak into the second show. I know Jim Quatroche, the manager, saw me on many of these occasions, and on one occasion I actually saw him laugh, but he never did anything about it. I know it didn't cost him anything, and he probably didn't give it any thought. But I saw a lot of movies that I wouldn't have otherwise seen, and it was a big deal to me.

The one expense I had to incur when I played football was for football shoes. Before our first football practice in my freshman year, Cliff Utz gave me a pair of his old shoes. I used those shoes for the four years I played football. On another occasion, in the summer before I left for college, Mr. Utz, Cliff's father, gave me a very good suit. That gesture was great, but so was that of Mr. Kraal, the local tailor. He practically had to rebuild the suit, and he didn't charge me a penny for it. That suit lasted me through college.

Greenport was not well known for its cultural outlets, but there was a program of community concerts in which well-known artists would be brought to Greenport for performances. Tickets were hard to come by and beyond my budget. Mrs. Diller, the French teacher and guidance counselor, arranged for me to work on the stage crew for these performances, and I got to see and hear Eugene Istomin, a very fine pianist; The Oberkirchen Children's Choir (who had a very successful record, *The Happy Wanderer),* and Rey and Gomez, a Spanish dance duo.

I enjoyed all the performances, but the one I remember most was the Rey and Gomez performance. I was dust mopping the stage when Rey, the male partner in the dance duo, showed up. He was very pleasant and asked where there might be a good hotel. I referred him to the Townsend Manor.

As I dusted, he began limbering up. I could not believe how hard he was stretching and gyrating and at one point asked him, "Won't you be too tired to dance?"

"Young man, if I didn't do this now, I wouldn't be able to walk after the performance." From the performance, I got a taste of how beautiful dancing could be, and from his comment, I understood the importance of stretching before any serous exercise.

When I was twelve, I was picking string beans on Brown's farm in East Marion. I was the only male among the other pickers, who were all Polish ladies in their fifties, sixties, and seventies, with one exception, Annie Bondarchuk, who was a year older than I.

Annie was someone I had known from school, and I liked her very much, simply because she was always nice to mom and me. She was the ninth of ten children and the second girl. Annie was born with a hare lip and cleft palate, and the family couldn't afford the surgery necessary repair Annie's affliction. To that end, Annie was put in foster care in western Long Island, where her hare lip and cleft palate were repaired. Annie eventually returned to the family, where she had a difficult time readjusting and was a bit rebellious.

The Bondarchuks were the toughest family in Greenport, though not in any kind of criminal sense. They were very hard working and prone to fighting. They were honest as a day is long but not known for their sociability. That being said, Annie's difficulty in making the transition is understandable.

Scholarly pursuits were not a part of the Bondarchuk agenda, but work was, and that is why I ended up picking string beans with Annie. Those ladies worked like machines as they chattered like magpies, leaving me in the dust. Each picker had a basket to fill, and once it was filled, the picker had to take it to the head of the row, where a truck would pick it up.

Throughout the day, Annie would empty some of her baskets into mine, to help me keep up. She was embarrassed when I thanked her for what she was doing and blew it off as being nothing. To some this might not mean much, but at the end of the day, Mr. Salminen, the foreman, asked me to come back the next day. Without Annie's help, that wouldn't have happened.

To me, Annie was not an unattractive girl but a diamond in the rough. I saw parallels between her and the character played by Betty Hutton in the movie *Annie Get Your Gun*. She never wore makeup or dressed to please guys, and I thought that was more of a case of her not knowing how than not wanting to.

Annie married Walter Klotz, and they raised five kids. When she recently passed away, I was deeply saddened.

Along that same line of "Little Things Mean a Lot," a couple of days before I left for college, I took my trunk to the Railway Express office to send it to Albany. Mr. Frank "Sparky" Coyle, a member of the Board of Education, worked there and greeted me warmly. He asked, "What can we do for you, John?"

I showed him my trunk, filled out the address form, and handed it to him. "That's it, John. Good luck." Mr. Coyle refused my offer of payment. Again, this is another example of how very well the people of Greenport took care of me.

Among the many commodities that "went to war" during World War II was Fleer's bubble gum, and when it came back on the market, stores that had it sold out quickly. I remember running into Chris Montgomery coming out of Johnny's Market. He told me that he had just bought the last two pieces of bubble gum in the store and gave one of them to me. Six-year-old kids aren't usually that generous, but Chris was and still is. That gesture from almost seventy years ago still sticks in my mind.

Among the more difficult little things to articulate are those that weren't present in my life and yet made such a difference. Number one among those was the fact that neither Bill nor I ever invited any of our friends into our house. I was always too ashamed and embarrassed to do so, not so much by the fact that our living quarters were dilapidated and substandard, as by the way they were kept up. Plaster was falling from the walls. There was one small toilet, in a very small closet, and the walls and ceilings were always covered with soot. Bill and I were told by Mom never to invite any of our friends into the house, and we didn't.

On my first vacation from college, Thanksgiving of 1957, two of my classmates drove me home, and there was no way I could avoid inviting them in. They were both very nice to Mom, which I expected, but one of them, when we got back to school, told my roommate what an absolute dump I lived in.

This wasn't done out of malice, and I didn't see it as such. But until that incident, my college friends, with the exception of those from Greenport who knew me, thought I came from the same background as they.

I never hid my background, but neither did I advertise it, lie about it, or pretend to be someone I wasn't. My background was nothing of which to be ashamed, but Albany was a fresh start for me. I not only wanted to keep that way but also wanted to see how well I would do without the support and encouragement to which I had grown accustomed.

Chapter 3

M O M

Mom was Helen Frances Rowan Sullivan, who was born in Dublin, Irish Free State, on May 23, 1900, and emigrated to America in August 1929. She worked as a domestic. While she was the housekeeper in the rectory of Our Lady of Grace R.C.C. on Fishers Island, she met my father, William J. Sullivan, who was the sexton. They were married on November 29, 1936.

On July 20, 1940, my father died, without me ever knowing him. Mom always told us that dad had died of ulcers, but as it turned out, he died of carcinoma of the stomach. Back in those days, cancer was almost a forbidden word.

With two children under the age of two, Mom couldn't work or stay on Fishers Island, and we had to go on welfare. I was too young to understand the stigma attached to being on relief, but that would come. Suffolk County Social Services relocated us to Greenport.

With no family contacts and not knowing a soul, I can only imagine how frightened Mom must have been when we arrived in Greenport. Being an Irish immigrant with a third-grade education, two children under the age of three, and totally dependent on a social welfare system with which she was unfamiliar were daunting obstacles to overcome. But overcome them Mom did, through hard work, an absolute belief in God, and the incredible goodwill of the people of Greenport.

Mom's faith was unquestioning and the only thing that took second place to her love for Bill and me. From as early as I can remember, morning and bedtime prayers were an integral part of our daily routine. There was a small, plastic font of holy water near the back door of our apartment. Each day, before we left the house, Bill and I would have to dip our fingers in the holy water, make the sign of the cross, and say our morning offering before we went outside.

On one occasion, in late August 1944, Mom had already left for work, and Bill and I were in a hurry to go out and play. Bill had already left, and I ran out to catch up with him, without saying my prayers. I had a toy pop gun in my hand when I saw Bill, who was playing with a friend, Gil (Bubby) Raynor. When they saw me, Bill said, "Let's get him!" They chased me into the path of an oncoming car that hit me. I wasn't hurt badly but was very shaken up, and it did cross my mind that God was sending me a not very subtle message: Say your prayers.

As big a stickler as mom was about saying our prayers, she was even more so about our saying "please" and "thank you." Neither Bill nor I could get a scrap of food passed to us, permission granted, or anything else unless each request was preceded by a "please" and followed by a "thank you."

Of all the things I learned or inherited from mom, none has been more beneficial than her insistence on being polite. We may have been short on etiquette, but we were not on manners. When I was the company clerk for my unit in Ft. Bliss, Texas, my company commander, Captain Anderson, decreed that I was to answer all incoming calls. I had taken a call from the regimental commander, who had been favorably impressed by the way I handled the call and commended me to Captain Anderson.

My colleagues in the CIA used to joke about how polite I

was with the subjects I tested, saying I was the "Pollyanna of polygraph." Being polite has always worked for me, and in my professional life, I found that in dealing with some pretty nasty people, my soft approach was effective.

In an interrogation, you have to be who you are. If I had come on like Andy Sipowitz, the hard-nosed detective in the very successful television show *NYPD Blue*, I would have had to wait for my subject to stop laughing before I continued the interrogation. Mom didn't leave an estate of one red cent, but the good manners she instilled in me were as good an inheritance as any parent could leave an heir.

As good a Catholic as mom was, she was also a bit of a paradox. She borrowed money from everyone and, as I saw it, had no intention of ever paying it back. I think the people who lent Mom money knew they wouldn't be getting it back and tolerated it because they knew the money was for Bill and me. I saw this as generosity typical of so many Greenporters, and also a bit of paternalism on the part of the lenders which was neither intrusive nor unwelcome.

Mom had her flaws, but she was very friendly and always upbeat, with never a bad word to say about anyone. Her brogue couldn't have been thicker, and in conjunction with her very strong Catholicism, it endeared her to the Catholic community. Just as important was a very strong work ethic that earned her the respect of all those who knew her. Greenporters wanted to help Mom, and they did.

Of all the people in Greenport who were kind to mom, none was more so than Edie Klipp Kudlinski. She was one of those larger-than-life people whose positive personality affects everyone around them, and Mom loved her.

At eighty-five, Edie does not seem to have a lost a step, and a trip back to Greenport is incomplete without a visit with Edie. She not only helps me with information for my book but always lifts my spirits. She is one of Greenport's real treasures.

I believe that Mom literally worked herself to death. She died at sixty-six, of natural causes. Given that she was a chain smoker, I thought she might have had lung cancer, but I ultimately concluded that she was just worn out. Mom never refused an offer of a job to clean a house. I remember a Christmas Day when Mr. Bill Clark, the owner of the Clark house on the North Road, came to our house at about seven in the evening and asked Mom to come out to the house and clean up after a large party. Mom didn't get home until almost midnight, and she worked in the rectory the next day.

I can't recall Mom ever spending a cent for an article of clothing, cosmetics, entertainment, or anything else. She was, in modern-day parlance, almost a bag lady. On one occasion, she was put out of a local restaurant for trying to cadge a cup of coffee, and as good as most of the people of Greenport were to her, she was also the object of some derision.

I remember one occasion in particular when I was in Santacroce's bowling alley and heard the mayor of Greenport jokingly refer to mom as "Old Lady Sullivan" in a very derogatory way. I knew and liked the mayor very much, and if he had known I was there, he wouldn't have said what he did. I didn't make my presence or displeasure known, and on occasion, I still feel bad about not having done so.

Clayton Harrell, one of Greenport's barbers, was always teasing Mom about the fact that Eamon DeValera, the president of Ireland, had worked in the Fulton Fish Market in Brooklyn before going back to Ireland and becoming president. Every time Mom brought us there, and after Bill and I started going there by ourselves, he would always bring this up. I found him a lot less than funny and almost boorish. On one occasion, when I was about ten years old, I went in to get a haircut and told Mr. Harrell, "Mom will pay you later." Mr. Harrell turned to the rest of the customers, paused for effect, and then laughingly said, "Where have I heard that before?"

When I started playing football, practice lasted until after the barber shop was closed, and it was difficult to make time for a haircut. One evening, we got out of practice early, and I went to get a haircut. My hair was still wet from the shower, and Mr. Harrell asked me why. I told him I had taken a shower after football practice, and he said, "Who are you kidding? You don't play football." He then turned to the other two customers and said, "This squirt is trying to tell me he plays football." Comments like these are one of the things one has to put up with from buffoons like Mr. Harrell when living on the lowest rung of the social ladder.

In school, one of the kids nicknamed Mom "The Old Gray Mare," and anytime I was around him, he would start singing "The Old Gray Mare." This was very mean-spirited, and I saw myself as cowardly for not doing anything about it.

On two occasions, I actually did get in a fight as a result of someone calling Mom a beggar. The first was in the lobby of the Greenport Theater. In one of the few fights I ever won, I knocked him down, grabbed him by the hair, and beat his head on the tile floor. I was in third grade at the time and not strong enough to do serious damage, but he did bleed, and I knew I had hurt him.

On the second occasion, four years later, the same kid skated by me at the skating rink and yelled that my family was nothing but a bunch of beggars. I was punching him as hard as I could when his older brother and another kid pulled me off him. The fact that there was some truth in the insult convinced me that unless I accepted that reality, I was going to get in a lot more fights. I chose to accept the reality.

There were rumors that Mom was stealing money from the poor box in St. Agnes's. I was pretty sure the rumors were true but didn't want to believe it, and I had to confront her before she got into any real trouble. At twelve, this was a tough thing to do. As I had thought she would do, Mom denied it, but not very convincingly, and I knew she had done it. After my talk with her, there were no more rumors, and I think she stopped.

The food that Mom bought with the money she borrowed, and perhaps on occasion stole, was less than abundant or gourmet, but I had no trouble eating it. Friday nights we had cod fish cakes, Kraft dinner, or grilled cheese sandwiches. On Sundays, it was usually chicken, and we never had turkey on Thanksgiving. During the week, it was hot dogs and baked beans, which I still love, canned spaghetti with meatballs, and occasionally pork chops. All of our meals were one course, but occasionally we would have canned fruit for dessert.

I knew that there were many who had less to eat than we did, and in my travels I have encountered so many who were much worse off than we had been. But when I was a kid, my perspective was much narrower, and I just knew that I was hungry more often than I was full.

When Mom was working, breakfast was whatever we could buy with the quarter she gave Bill and me before she left for work. For me, it was a marshmallow candy bar. I never ate three square meals on any kind of regular basis until I was in the army.

Stella Rempe, the wife of a local farmer and a very lovely lady, frequently gave us fresh vegetables, strawberries, and on one occasion, some calf liver. The food she gave us provided a temporary nutritional boost, but we lived on canned food.

To this day, I have never eaten a salad, cauliflower, celery, eggplant, spinach, broccoli, sprouts, asparagus, or drunk a cup of coffee. It was meat and potatoes, and a meal isn't a meal without potatoes. There was never a drop of alcohol in the house, nor was there an ounce of anti -drinking fervor. Drinking alcohol was something we didn't do, but drinking soft drinks was another matter. I drank more Coca Cola than milk, and if ever I had an addiction, it was to Coca Cola.

Such a diet left Bill and me malnourished, and I attribute the Type II diabetes I have today to my soft drink consumption.

Another of the long-term effects of what I saw as a less than adequate diet was that until very recently, whenever I ate at a restaurant, I would always order the biggest steak or prime rib and often double up on the dessert. In bakery shops, I never ordered just one jelly doughnut or apple turnover. I wanted to make sure to satisfy my hunger.

The cafeteria at the CIA training facility was outstanding, and I went a bit crazy during training. I started out at 134 pounds, came out of there at 152 pounds, and eventually ballooned up to 171.

When I was diagnosed with Type II diabetes, I started to diet. I now weigh 144 pounds and eat less than half the calories I used to consume each day. I exercise every day, drink no soft drinks other than an occasional ginger ale, still don't smoke or drink, and am probably healthier now than I was fifty years ago.

Mom passed away at sixty-six, and my father at forty-nine, and I seem to have exceeded my genetic lifespan. Life is pretty good, and I pray that it continues to be so.

What Mom did, she did out of necessity and love for Bill and me. I can never remember Mom taking a bite of food until she was sure Bill and I had eaten. That didn't excuse Mom being a deadbeat, but it did make it understandable and not something for which I could, in good conscience, criticize her. There were, however, other aspects of Mom's child-rearing skills, or lack thereof, about which I was less understanding.

In the summer of 1943, just before Bill started kindergarten, Mom was working at the Wyandanch Hotel as a chambermaid. There was a small strip of beach across from the hotel, and one afternoon, Mom took us there and just left us. Neither of us could swim, and there was no one else on the beach. No one ever swam at this beach, as it was too dirty. I remember looking down into the water, looking up, and not seeing Bill. Suddenly, there was a lot of commotion, with people running toward the water, and the police car showed up with its siren blaring.

I saw Frank (Shake) Stanislaus, a Road Department laborer, holding Bill in the front seat of the police car, with Bill's head out the window. The car took off, again with siren blaring. Joe Turner, a local teenager, had gone into the water and pulled Bill out before he drowned. Someone had gone to the hotel to get Mom, and when she showed up, she was pretty distraught.

Bill was brought home from the hospital that night and seemed okay, and no more was said about his near-drowning. I don't know whether or not the town was protecting Mom over this incident, but today a mother who left two very young children, neither of whom could swim, on a deserted beach would be seen as criminally negligent.

I never saw a doctor until I was hit by a car in 1944, just before I started school. Every illness Bill or I had was diagnosed by mom as "a cold." In third grade, I was on the way home from school when I fell down and hurt my left wrist. It hurt quite a bit, and when I showed it to m om, she said, "It's a cold. Pull on the doorknob, and it will be okay." I did as she directed, and it got worse. When I went to school the next day, my wrist was pretty swollen, and I couldn't use my left hand.

Miss Brooks, the school nurse, came into our class to see Mrs. Cox, our teacher, and happened to see my wrist. "John, what happened to your wrist? It's all swollen." Miss Brooks sent Mom a note telling her to take me to the doctor. If Miss Brooks hadn't written that note, Mom wouldn't have taken me. The note made it "official," and that sealed the deal.

Mom took me to see Dr. Kaplan, who told Mom to take me to the hospital. The next day, Mrs. Santacroce took Mom and me to the hospital for an x-ray, which showed I had some chipped bones in my wrist. What I remember most about that incident was that when the bill for the x-ray came (nine dollars), Mom tossed it aside, saying she would pay it. Even then I was aware of mom's propensity not to pay bills. I told her to give me the nine dollars, and I would take it to the hospital to pay it.

Surprisingly, she did, and I walked up to the hospital and paid it. Mrs. Hartung, the lady who ran the business office, seemed very surprised to see who was making the payment, but she took my money.

Bill and I used to run around barefooted. On one occasion Bill was playing on the railroad dock and got a large splinter in his left foot that ran from the ball of his foot to his heel. Mom told Bill, "It will work itself out."

Three days later, Bill woke up early in the morning, complaining of the pain in his foot. The foot was very swollen, and Bill couldn't put his shoe on. Pus was oozing out of the wound, Bill was crying, and Mom thought it was time to take him to the doctor. Mom took him to see Dr. Heath, who opened the wound, removed the splinter, drained the pus, taped the foot, and gave mom some antibiotics for Bill. The cost: two dollars. Dr. Heath also told Mom that Bill had been within a couple of days of losing his foot.

Dr. Heath was a nice old man, and he did the school vaccinations as well as the physicals for those going out for sports teams. I liked him, but I remember one vaccination session when he put a needle through the arm of one of those being vaccinated.

Bill and I were both frequently told that we need to have our tonsils out. Mom honestly didn't believe in having this done, and we both still have our tonsils.

My first visit to a dentist was when I was in seventh grade. I tripped over a desk and fell flat on my face without breaking my fall with my hands. I was knocked out cold and came to with Miss McCollligan, the art teacher, holding me and a piece of one of my upper front teeth in my hand.

The nerve of the broken tooth was exposed, and the pain was excruciating. It took more than a week of pleading to get Mom to take me to a dentist. The dentist to whom Mom took me was a St. Agnes parishioner, Dr. Schaumburg, the brother of Mrs.

Schaumburg, my first-grade teacher. In a rather long and painful process, Dr. Schaumburg put a porcelain cap on the tooth.

The cap fell off during my freshman year. Mom didn't see any need to have it replaced, and I went through high school with one of my upper front teeth missing. This, in addition to my inability to dance and other factors, not only diminished my self-esteem but also inhibited my social maturation.

Medical and dental care were unknown quantities in mom's upbringing, and she neither saw the need for them nor felt that we could afford to make them a part of our lives.

Until two members of the PTA, Mrs. Herr and Mrs. Rhinehart, gave Bill and me toothbrushes when we were in sixth grade, neither Bill nor I ever brushed our teeth. This was not one of those little things that mean a lot but something that made a real difference in my physical well-being. Bill never brushed his teeth, and when he was sixteen, he had to have all of them removed because they were so rotten.

From as early as I can remember, I had poor eyesight. In second grade, I couldn't see the blackboard very well, and I remember how this inhibited my attempts to learn addition. Miss Ging would put a column of figures on the board, and I would add the decimal points as well as the numbers. In fourth grade, I had an eye test in conjunction with an annual physical examination, and Mom was told that she needed to take me to an eye doctor. My vision was 20/400, and I had astigmatism. Dr. Wiesen told mom that I should have been wearing glasses since I was old enough to read an eye chart and that I needed an operation to correct my "lazy eye." I never got the operation. During two subsequent annual physical exams, Dr. Heath told me that I had bronchitis and to have Mom bring me to see him. I did, and she didn't.

Sex was never discussed in the Sullivan house. I was curious and read a lot on the subject, but at home, the only thing I heard was, "Sex is bad, until you get married." From mom's tone of voice, I inferred that even then it wasn't that good.

There was an old, dilapidated, empty house across the street from the rectory when mom first started working there. Father Kelle, the pastor at that time, had it torn down. When I asked Mom why, she said, "Because of the rottenness that is going on there. Boys and girls are committing mortal sins there." I later found out that what she meant was having sex.

I was reading the *Daily News* one day when I read a headline, "Cop Cleared in Rape," and asked Mom, "What is rape?"

Mom got all flustered and said, "You're too young. I will tell you when you are older." I looked it up in the dictionary. "Illicit carnal knowledge" was what I read. I had to look up two more words, but I finally got it.

In high school, I never had a girlfriend or so much as "made out" with a girl. I had five dates in four years, with five different girls. I used to tell my friends that every girl I took out told me she had a good time, but they also told me not to spoil the night by asking them out again. When I got to college, I was totally unprepared for any kind of romantic relationship. To me, there was no such thing as a causal relationship, and that inhibited my social maturation.

Mom's only advice to me regarding marriage was, "I don't care who you marry, so long as she is a good, Irish, Catholic girl." My first love after leaving Greenport was not a Catholic, and I think that my being a Catholic was a factor in the failure of that platonic, and unfortunately unrequited, but very intense, infatuation.

My next "love," also not a Catholic, dumped me because she knew she could do better. My third venture in the pursuit of true love was a Lutheran, and a very good one. She asked me if I would be willing to change religions, and, of course to me, that was unthinkable. I don't think that was the main reason she dumped me, but dump me she did.

Nothing had prepared me for the emotional part of relationships with girls. From "guy talk," some great advice on the facts of life from Jim Heaney, reading *Playboy,* and seeing some pornographic pictures, I had some ideas about the mechanics of romance but nothing about the dynamics of a relationship. Unfortunately, neither did Mom, and there were times when I wondered how Bill and I came to be.

One of the positives to being raised by Mom was that, at least in my opinion, I never became a male chauvinist pig. I saw, first-hand, how tough, resourceful, and compassionate a woman can be and had nothing but respect and admiration for the gender, even though Mom always said a woman's place was in the home.

In a case of writing what I thought the professor wanted to hear, I wrote an essay for my college English composition class in which I posited that denying women equal opportunity in the job market was inhibiting our country's ability to compete in the world market by neglecting a gifted labor pool. I got an A on the paper.

Any doubts I may have had about the capabilities, courage, and potential of women was dispelled by the contacts I had with Viet Cong females during my two tours in Vietnam. I remember one woman biting off the tip of her tongue and spitting it in the face of an interrogator and another who was a prisoner in the National Interrogation Center being sent a note that read, "Kill yourself. They will break you." She hanged herself with her bra.

Being raised by mom and never knowing my father also had unforeseen, long-term effects. Most kids learn to drive by being taught by their father. We never had a car, and although I learned to drive by taking driver's education when I was a senior, I didn't get a driver's license until I was thirty-four. During my first two years at the agency, I never had a date, mainly because I didn't have a car. Most boys learn how to fix things from their fathers. I didn't, and throughout my life, I have had to ask other people to help me with the most minor of repairs or pay to have them done.

Another aspect of growing up without a father was that I never experienced the marital dynamic. Mom did everything, and I expected my wife, Lee, to do the same. Until I got married, I had never had an argument with a female and didn't know how to handle arguments. As far and few between as arguments were with Lee, I managed to survive them, and Lee put up with me for forty years. Most importantly, I had no frame of reference for the father/son relationship. My sons seem to have turned out rather well, and I have to say so much of that was due to Lee.

There was another aspect of growing up as I did that left its mark. During my youth, money was the panacea. Any of my problems, real or perceived, could, or so I thought, be solved by throwing money at them. Not having enough money to throw at my problems left most of my problems unresolved, and that left some real scars.

During my Greenport days, I spent a lot of time looking in the windows of Jaeger's department store and Levin's men's clothing store, coveting things I was seeing and knowing that I couldn't afford them. It is very difficult to articulate what it has meant to me to know that I can afford to buy things that I coveted as a child.

Because I didn't want my sons to have similar experiences, I may have overdone it in throwing money at my their problems. The lesson I learned from this was that it is easier to say no to your children when you can't afford to accede to their wishes than it is when you can.

As uninformed, outdated, and even dangerous as mom's attitudes about nutrition, health, hygiene, and sex were, her attitude about education, at least for me, was more of a problem. To mom, school was a place kids had to go until they could get a real job. I cannot recall Mom ever asking me how I was doing in school, or if I had any homework, and she never suggested that it was important to do well in school. Bill had to stay back in two grades, first and fifth, and Mom expressed neither displeasure nor concern. College was an unknown entity to mom and not any part of our future.

Mom didn't read my report cards; she just signed them. Most of my classmates took their tests home to show their parents. I didn't, not because they were so bad but because the first few times I did, Mom didn't show any interest.

For part of sixth grade and all of seventh and eighth grades, I was working most school nights in either Santacroce's or Schiavoni's bowling alleys. I have to think that if I had spent more of those nights at home, I would have gotten more sleep, done some more studying, and enjoyed school more. I am pretty sure that the idea that my work schedule might impede my academic progress never entered Mom's mind.

In first grade, I got in a fight before school started, and the boy I was fighting with said he was going to tell the principal. I got scared and took off. The truant officer, Mr. Welden, saw me on the street, and I ran away from him.

I went to the movie house where Mom was working to tell her what had happened, and Mom was sweeping out the aisles when she saw me. As I later found out, Mr. Welden had already been there. When Mom saw me, her first words were, "Stay right there, and don't you move!" She got a cane that someone had left in the theater and beat me black and blue with it. She then dragged me, screaming, back to school. Skipping school wasn't the issue; bringing negative attention to her was.

There was also an incident in first grade in which Mom disappointed me. On this occasion, I really had to go to the bathroom, and I raised my hand to ask Miss Schaumburg's permission. She very cursorily told me, "No." The third time I asked her, she saw the desperation on my face and said, "If you have to go, go." It was too late. That evening, Miss Schaumburg came over to our house to apologize to mom. Mom was very gracious, but I wanted her to really let Mrs. Schaumburg know that what she did was unacceptable.

On a very memorable occasion, when I was in second grade, Mrs. Gardiner, Mr.Nye, the school principal's secretary, came into the classroom and handed Ms. Ging an envelope. At the end of the day, Ms. Ging handed me the envelope and said, "John, take this home to your mother."

When I gave Mom the envelope, she opened it, read the letter, and confronted Bill and me. "Mr. Nye wants to see me tomorrow morning. What have you two done?"

We swore to her that we hadn't done anything, and Mom's answer was, "God help you if I find out you are lying."

Mom went to school the next day, in her maid's uniform, and had a meeting with Mr. Nye. Bill and I were home when Mom came home from work, and both of us were pretty nervous.

"Mr. Nye wanted to see me because he wanted to meet the mother of the two politest kids in the school," were Mom's opening words. Her follow-up was, "That had better not change."

On another occasion, it had started pouring rain while we were in school, and I hadn't brought my galoshes with me. Suddenly, Mom came through the door, dripping rain, carrying my galoshes. She came to my desk, handed me the galoshes, and gave me a big kiss and hug. All the kids laughed, and I was embarrassed.

Mom loved music and was a member of the church choir. In the last apartment we lived in before I left Greenport, there was an old piano that a previous tenant had left. When I was a senior in high school, Mrs. Lindsay, the choir director and organist, was visiting and noticed the piano. She said, "Helen, why didn't you tell me you had a piano here? I would have given the boys piano lessons." I would have sold my soul to take piano lessons, but it never occurred to me to ask Mom to get me piano lessons or to her to think I would want them.

I remember the uproar when Elvis Presley came on the scene. His performances were viewed by many as sexually suggestive and immoral, but not Mom. "There is a thread of gold in that voice. He sings as well as Bing Crosby or Frank Sinatra ever did, and he will make more money than both of them."

One of the standard tests we had to take in school was the Kuder Interest Inventory. I think I took the test two or three times. On each of those tests I scored higher in music than any of the other interest categories, and it was suggested that I pursue a career as a musician. As an adult, I have taken guitar lessons and tried to self-teach myself piano when the kids were taking lessons, but it just didn't work out.

As a dyed-in-the-wool member of the servant class, Mom was very respectful and almost obsequious when she met authority figures or any of my teachers, which was very seldom. There was one of those occasions that I remember well. We were in the A&P and ran into Mr. Calvin, my sixth-grade teacher. I introduced Mom to him, and she asked, "How is John doing?"

Mr. Calvin answered, "John is no problem, but he would do better if he tried harder."

"Who wouldn't?" was Mom's answer which caught me, and by the look on his face, Mr. Calvin, by surprise. Mom was not known for her wit, and I was very impressed by her comeback.

As sweet and nice as mom was, she could be feisty. One day I was playing in a yard with some kids, and I got in an argument with one of them. It was getting close to fight time, and the father of the kid with whom I was about to fight came out of the house and told me to "Go back to where you belong."

By coincidence, Mom happened to be walking by and saw what was going on. She was on this man like a mongoose after a cobra. "Where John belongs is wherever he wants to be," she told him. She never asked if I had started the trouble, which I may well have, but she saw some adult going after her little boy, and she wasn't having any of it. I was a bit surprised and a bit embarrassed but also proud of her.

Too often, I had allowed myself to be embarrassed by the way Mom would shamelessly bargain with Mr. Brandi and Mr. Sturm, Greenport's two shoe store owners, over the price of a pair of shoes or over her public displays of pride in and affection for me. Two of the long-term effects of these things on me have been that I don't bargain, but I do publicly and emphatically demonstrate my pride and affection for my children and grandchildren.

If I don't have enough money to buy something, I don't buy it, and if I have enough money but think the price is too high, I don't buy it. For the forty years Lee and I were married, we never paid a cent of credit card interest, and since Lee passed away, I have only paid interest once, that being when I just forgot to pay a bill. I am sure my unwillingness to bargain has cost me money, but I find it to be demeaning and too much of a reminder of when Mom had to bargain to survive.

At seventy-five, I have yet to meet anyone who loved me as much as mom did, and she deserved so much more than my embarrassment. In 1966, while I was stationed overseas, Mom passed away. My biggest regret is that she never lived long enough to see her grandchildren or to allow me to provide a better life for her. I am who I am because of her, and I am very grateful.

Chapter 4

B I L L

Bill and I were "Irish twins." Bill was eleven months older than I, we looked a lot alike, and people were always mistaking us for each other. But in terms of personality, we were completely different.

Growing up in Greenport, Bill was more popular than I, and I can't remember him ever getting into any kind of fight, verbal or physical. He was well-spoken and seemed to do well at getting along with people. I, on the other hand, was a very mouthy, wiseguy, know-it-all kind of kid who had a propensity to rub adults and kids the wrong way. Mom once told me, jokingly, that I had been vaccinated with a phonograph needle, and she was more correct than she knew.

Bill was also a puzzle, in that I could never understand why he didn't do well in school. Bill's near-drowning left him with a phobia about going near the water, and it wasn't until he was in his fifties that he learned to swim, but I saw no outward signs of any kind of learning disability . Throughout his school days, Bill always ranked pretty close to the bottom of his class, and I have concluded that his near- drowning had to have affected his learning functions. .

When Bill had to repeat first grade, he didn't seem upset, and I didn't understand that. I caught up with Bill in first grade, and when he had to repeat fifth grade, I passed him. Neither mom nor Bill seemed upset. There was no, "You have to do better" from Mom or "I will try harder" from Bill.

Compared with Bill (but not with many of the kids in my class), I was a very good student, but mom never made an issue of that with Bill. By that time, I had already become Mom's favorite, but it had nothing to do with me doing better in school than Bill. Rather, it concerned Bill's attitude about the Catholic Church. Bill had never bought into the church the way I did, and for mom, that was a negative.

Bill took real exception to the church's censorship, and when we were told from the pulpit that we couldn't go to see *The Outlaw*, starring Jane Russell, he was very angry. The diocesan newspaper was *The Tablet,* and each week it would rate movies. Mom made sure that if we went to the movies at all, it would never be to an X-rated movie. This really upset Bill. Actually, it upset me too, but I never said anything.

When we were in the fourth grade, Father Carmody, the new assistant pastor, conducted a class for altar boy candidates, and Mom made both of us take the class. From day one, I knew Father Carmody was someone with whom I would never get along. That being said, I did well in the class and became, by at least two years, the youngest altar boy in the parish. Bill didn't make the cut, and I think he was relieved, but a couple of years later, he did become an altar boy.

A commonality shared by many Irish immigrant mothers was a hope that a son would become a priest. For mom, if there was going to be a priest in the Sullivan family, it would more than likely be me and not Bill. I think this was the factor in making me Mom's fair-haired boy.

Bill and I had different interests and different friends. We didn't compete with each other on any level, and we rarely fought.

I read voraciously and Bill hardly at all. On occasion, he would ask me to read to him. We attended school together for thirteen years, and in all that time, I can't recall Bill ever bringing a book home, either for homework or just to read, nor do I remember him ever going to our local public library.

On one occasion, Greta Levine invited Bill and me to go to a kids' play that was being put on at Tiffeth Israel, the local synagogue. Mom asked Father Holland if it would be okay for us to go, and Father Holland told her that a synagogue was no place for two young Catholic boys. Bill went, and I didn't.

A more significant difference between Bill and me was our attitude about work. For whatever reason, from a very young age, I was always able to find a way to make a dollar. In the summer between fifth and sixth grade, I began setting up pins in Santacroce's bowling alley. Although I wasn't making a lot of money, it was money we needed. When I offered to get Bill a job there, he worked one night and quit.

One work-related incident I remember occurred when Bill was given an opportunity to earn a Boy Scout uniform by doing some yard maintenance at the Townsend Manor, a very fine local hotel. Bill took the uniform but didn't do the job.

There wasn't any money for luxuries, and I recall an occasion when I had been saving money to buy a baseball glove. The glove I wanted was a Wilson Ball Hawk, which cost $12.95 at Jaeger's department store. I had accumulated a little over ten dollars when Mom came to me and ask me to lend her money to buy Bill a pair of shoes. I reluctantly gave her the money, knowing I would never get it back. And I didn't.

That incident forever changed the family dynamic. That was the first time I can recall resenting mom for "borrowing" my money and Bill for not being willing to work and earn his own money. Physically, Bill weighed less than I, and even though he was a little taller, I was stronger than he. He did no exercise whatsoever and had no interest in sports, either as a player or spectator. It did occur to me that maybe Bill wasn't cut out for manual labor.

A trait that I have to believe Bill inherited from mom was borrowing money without any intention of paying it back. In eighth grade, on two or three occasions, kids would come to me and tell me that Bill had borrowed money from them and not paid it back. On each occasion, I would go to Bill and ask him to make good on his debt. I don't know whether or not he did, but there were no more complaints to me. I resented Bill for putting me in this situation.

During this time frame, the Parent Teachers Association (PTA) hired a local dancing instructor, John Piccozzi, to give dancing lessons. The lessons were on Monday nights, and I worked in the bowling alley every night except Tuesday, so I couldn't take the lessons. Bill did, and I resented him for it.

In high school, Bill was Mr. Nice Guy, and it was a well-deserved title. He played the records at the high school dances, worked on the stage crews for all the plays and musical performances, and was a good guy to have around. Bill's teachers liked him, and I think this helped him get some Ds that probably should have been Fs. My impression was that Bill enjoyed his popularity and found high school to be a good experience.

Bill also had a girlfriend, which I never did. She was a lovely girl from Southold, and I didn't meet her until one of my class reunions, when her husband, John Moore, introduced me to her, saying, "Here is the girl I stole from your brother."

I graduated a year before Bill, and Mom and I went to his graduation, during which he was presented with a Rotary Club loan in order to attend Albany Business School. Bill had finished at the very bottom of his class, and I found it strange that he had gotten the loan. A few days after graduation, I ran into Mr. Martoccia, who was a member of the Rotary Club. "John, Bill's grades were pretty bad, and we're just hoping that our loan will give him the kick start he needs" was what he said to me. As it turned out, this was another loan that Bill had no intention of repaying.

Bill had begun working in Bohack's during his junior year and was still working there when he graduated. Just before I returned to Albany for my sophomore year, I ran into Eddie Copin, Bill's boss at Bohack's. I had known him for most of my life, liked him very much, and was a bit surprised by what he said to me.

"John, the only reason Bill is going to Albany is to be around you. He is a hustler. Don't let him bring you down." Unfortunately, Eddie's words were a harbinger of things to come.

At the time Bill enrolled at Albany Business College, you couldn't transfer credit from there back to high school. He lasted a month before quitting and getting a job at a local supermarket. Once Bill started working in Albany, he rarely came back to Greenport. Bill did come back for mom's funeral, but he has never visited her grave or attended any of the Masses for her. He didn't come to the funerals of Mr. and Mrs. Heaney or Don and Julia Aanstead; all of whomlies who had been so critical to our survival in Greenport..

I introduced Bill to many of my college friends, among them my roommate and his uncle and grandmother. The uncle got Bill a job with the state health department that he held for thirty-eight years, and the grandmother lent him money that he never paid back. This caused me some problems with my roommate and was very embarrassing.

The night before I enlisted in the army, I took Bill out for dinner. I had just received my last paycheck from Cohoes High School, where I had been teaching and coaching, and I hadn't had time to pay a local store sixty-eight dollars that I owed them. I gave Bill a hundred dollars to take care of it.

While at Ft. Bliss, Texas, three months later, I put in for a security clearance. Two weeks later, an investigator called me in to tell me that I had an unpaid debt of sixty-eight dollars that had to be resolved before the processing could proceed. I took care of it and got my clearance, but not before I had a long talk with Bill.

Things were never the same between Bill and me after that, but we did stay in touch. I didn't see Bill again until Mom passed away. It was a very nice funeral, and I gave Bill four hundred dollars to buy a tombstone for mom's grave. Six months later, Julia Aanstead wrote and told me that Mom's grave did not have a headstone. I wrote back and told her to get the price of a tombstone but not to buy it until she got my check. She did, and Mom's grave has a headstone.

Bill couldn't make it to Lee's and my wedding. His excuse was that he didn't have a passport, which made sense, but I didn't believe that was why he didn't come. Before he retired and moved to Albuquerque in 1997, he did manage to visit us on a few occasions. On one of these visits, he totaled my car, and on another, he got drunk at a restaurant in DC, and I had to go pick him up.

Bill has never sent either of his nephews a Christmas or birthday present, but on one occasion, just after my younger son, Jimmy, got out of the hospital, Bill called him and invited him to take a trip to Canada with him. Jimmy told him that he would like to go but would have to ask me. "F—k him, we'll just go," was Bill's answer. Jimmy was very upset when he came and told me what Bill had said, and so was I. I immediately called Bill. He said he didn't remember what he said, and I told him never to speak to either of my kids that way again.

When Jimmy got married, Bill couldn't attend the wedding, although I offered to pay all his expenses. When Lee passed away in 2009, I again offered to pay Bill's expenses to attend the funeral, and he rejected my offer. That was the last straw.

Since then, our contact has been sporadic. In 2012, his landlord contacted me to tell me Bill hadn't paid his rent. I paid it, and the next time it happened, I paid it again, but subsequently I paid him an unannounced visit. I found him living in absolute squalor as well as in poor physical and mental health. I offered to bring him back to Virginia and live with me, and I confess to feeling somewhat relieved that he refused my offer. I did take him to a doctor for a physical and a psychologist for an evaluation. He weighed ninety-seven pounds, and the doctor said he was severely malnourished as well as being in the early stages of dementia.

The psychologist didn't think he needed to be an assisted living facility, which I found strange, and at the psychologist's suggestion, I made arrangements to have someone periodically look in on him.

A couple of months later, he was evicted from his apartment. He is currently living in an assisted living facility. When I speak with him, he sounds in good spirits, and I was relieved to know that he is being cared for.

Recently, I was contacted by Dennis and Gwynne Whitcomb, who are good friends of Bill's. Dennis has been taking Bill out to lunch and advocating with the staff for better care of Bill. They have been a godsend.

About a month ago, Dennis called me and said that Bill wasn't doing well. He suggested that I might want to come out and see him, which I did.

Bill was delighted to see me, and I was able to take him out of the facility. On our first outing, Bill fell and couldn't get up. As I picked him up, it was obvious that he has very little strength in his legs.

On the second day, I met with Dennis and his wife as well as with Bill's Social Services case worker and his doctor. I had bought some vitamins for Bill, and the doctor said she would get orders written for Bill to take them. With his case worker, I made arrangements for Bill's funeral, when the time comes, and that went well.

Most importantly, during this visit, I saw Bill in a context I had never seen before: that of a frail, feeble, and very sweet old man in need of help. There was no sign of the hustler or scam artist. The urge to take him in my arms and tell him I loved him was very strong, and I gave in to it.

As anxious as I had been about the visit, I am so glad I went and am planning to try and get out there more often. Bill's short-term memory is gone, and our conversations are pretty one-sided (as are most of my conversations). But Bill is a big tile in my life's mosaic, and in his lucid moments, I see someone of whom I want to see more. Hopefully, in the time we both have left, I can do that.

Note: Bill passed away on December 5, 2014.

Chapter 5

THE HEANEY FAMILY

O f the many positive experiences we had in our early years in Greenport, none was more significant or more enduring that our connection with the Heaney family. About two years after we arrived in Greenport, Mom decided to go off welfare and get a job. In order to do that, she would need to find someone to take care of me and Bill. That person was Julia Heaney. Over the next several years, she and her family became the closest thing Mom, Bill, and I had to an extended family.

When Mrs. Heaney began taking care of Bill and me, her three older sons, Bill, Jim, and Joe, were in the army and overseas. Her younger daughter, Julia, and the three younger boys, Bernie, Jack, and Jerry, were at home. There was another daughter, Mary, whom I never got to know, and Bernadette, who died in infancy.

Mr. Heaney was working in the shipyard, and I didn't see all that much of him. He ran a tight ship and did not spare the rod. There was a razor strop hanging by a mirror near the kitchen sink, and it wasn't for honing razors. On one occasion, Mr. Heaney chased Bernie up a tree with the strop.

One of my best memories of those early days with the Heaneys was of their dog, Ted. He was a mutt, very friendly to me, and when I got older, he would follow me wherever I went. As gentle as Ted was, he did have some fight in him.

I was playing in the front yard one afternoon when I saw Ted chasing a very large rat. He caught the rat, and a long fight ensued. How long the fight lasted, I don't know, but many of the neighbors came out to watch it. Ted finally killed the rat, and everyone cheered.

Having three sons overseas was a constant source of worry for Mrs. Heaney, but she handled it well, and the whole family rejoiced when mail from any of the boys arrived. I was in the kitchen with Mrs. Heaney when Bill, the oldest boy, came home, and the relief and joy expressed by the family were something to see.

After Bill and I started school, Mrs. Heaney no longer took care of us on a regular basis, but the Heaney house had become a second home to me, and I spent a lot of time there. The Heaneys were avid sports fans, and to my everlasting pleasure, that rubbed off on me. All the Heaneys were Dodger fans, and I became one too. Mrs. Heaney taught me how to keep box scores of baseball games, and I learned to read by going through the sports pages in the *New York Daily News* with her.

One of the perhaps unintended consequences of this was that I could hold my own in talking (but not playing) sports with anyone. This gave me a bit of status with the school's athletes, many of whom became teammates and friends.

Reading the *Daily News* also led to doing crossword puzzles, at which Mrs. Heaney was very proficient. In teaching me how to do crosswords, Mrs. Heaney gave me a life-long avocation that served me very well on my world travels and gave me a pretty good vocabulary.

When I was in fourth grade, I was having great difficulty learning long division. On the Wednesday before Thanksgiving,

Miss Sinsebaugh, my teacher, kept me after school to give me some help.

As hard as she tried, Miss Sinsebaugh couldn't get long division across to me. She screamed, yelled, and was almost in tears as she tried to pound it into me. In a final gesture, she wrote down the correct answer to the problem on which I was working and said, "Just copy the answer so that I can say you got the right answer!"

The day after Thanksgiving, I went over to Mrs. Heaney's and told her what had happened. She got a pad and pencil, and within an hour, she had shown me how to do long division. I have never forgotten.

Jack and Jerry were the closest in age to me, and they treated me like a little brother. Jack was the best athlete in the family, and it isn't a stretch to say he was my first hero. Jerry also was an athlete, but he was not as good as Jack. Still, on more than one occasion, he kept me from getting picked on.

I never really got to know Joe well. He left Greenport after getting out of the army, and I didn't see much of him. When he and his family moved back to Greenport, I got to know him better and came to like him very much.

Bill, the oldest brother, was somewhat of a role model for me. He was the first in the family to graduate from college and went to Hofstra on the GI Bill. During the summers, he would work on the deep-sea scallop boats, and between trips he always found time to have a catch with me.

The football team banquet in 1953 was a father/son affair, and Bill took me. When I had some misgivings about leaving Greenport and going to college, Bill's advice was, "John, this may be your one chance at having a better life. You have earned the right to go to college. Don't pass it up." I didn't. The age difference between Bill and me was such that we weren't "buddies," but in every other way, Bill was one of the people who made Greenport so good for me.

Bill may have been a college graduate, but I saw Jim as the smartest of the brothers. I didn't get to know Jim until I was in the seventh grade. He was the dock master at Mitchell's Pier, and Bill and I would wrap squid that was used for bait for him and also run all kinds of errands. On many occasions, Jim lined up jobs for me cleaning boats docked at the pier or cleaning fish that the boaters had caught.

On one of those occasions, Jim told me that there was a boat tied up at Tyler's dock that seemed to have lost its propeller. They needed someone to go under the boat and see if it was there. I did the job and found out that the propeller was missing. The boat's captain paid me ten dollars for about five minutes' work. When I told Jim, he said, "Bill is never around when there is money to be made."

During slow times, Jim would talk about sports, history, Greenport, sex, religion, and anything that came up. Of the brothers, Jim was the one I saw as a father figure. He took a real interest in my football happenings and encouraged them, rather than disparaging my playing as many others did.

On one of those occasions, a local named Woody Dean got on me about playing football. "John, are they using you for a tackling dummy? Do you have any splinters from sitting on the bench? What position do you play, left out?" Jim saw it was upsetting me and, in no uncertain terms, told Woody to knock it off.

During our 1953 championship season, I was discussing some incidents that I saw as dirty playing on the part of some of the players I played with and against. "John, as small as you are, hard, rough play may seem dirty, but it is just hard, aggressive football," Jim told me. "If you don't understand that, you shouldn't be playing." He also told me that dirty players are a liability for any team. "When teams come looking for revenge on a dirty player, they don't care whose door they knock on."

Mom clearly couldn't discuss the facts of life with me, but

Jim gave me one piece of advice that I have never forgotten, to wit: "John, a stiff p—k has no conscience." That message was delivered in the vernacular, and I appreciate the fact that Jim used the language he did, as it enhanced the effectiveness of the message and made it easier for me to retain. I have passed that message on to both of my sons, in the vernacular. Jim was not a profane person, nor were any of his brothers, but in discussing a sexual event (not experience) with me, I think he got it just right.

Probably the hardest lesson I learned from Jim was that idols can have feet of clay. I admired Jim and learned a great deal from him, but he did have a serious drinking problem. On a few occasions, when he was drunk, he went off on me in a very mean way.

These occasions occurred when I was thirteen and fourteen and really hurt. I got over it, and learning to deal with Jim when he was under the influence was an important part of my maturation. When I started making visits back to Greenport in 1982, spending time with Jim was an essential, and very pleasurable, part of each visit.

Bernie, brother number four, is the brother with whom I developed the closest relationship. He had biceps the size of softballs and was as gentle as a lamb as well as being the brother I would want with me if I were in a tight spot.

In fact, although Bernie denies it, there was an occasion when I was in a tight spot, and he may have saved my life. In the summer of 1954, I was trying to swim the perimeter of Southold Town Beach. Each leg of the perimeter was about two hundred yards long, and I was on the third leg when I ran out of gas.

I hadn't begun to panic, but I was getting weary and worried. My strokes had slowed considerably, and I was pretty far from shore. Suddenly, there were Bernie and Ken Miller, another friend.

Each of them took one of my arms and pulled me in to the beach. Bernie had been watching me, noticed my distress, and got Ken to help him pull me in. I am pretty sure that I would had been in real trouble had they not helped me.

Bernie and his lovely wife Maria had four children, Tim, Shawn, Maria, and Kerry. Tim was murdered by the Long Island Sniper, Shawn went down with his ship in the Bering Sea, and Kerry died in his sleep. I don't know how they ever got through these ordeals, but the fact that they did is a tribute to their faith, love for each other, and the support of their entire family.

At eighty-one, Bernie is the older of the two remaining siblings, Jack being the other. I am in almost daily contact with Bernie and Maria, and he has been so very helpful with providing family and local history data for the book. He and Maria have also been buffers against cynicism and a constant reminder of how good people can be.

Mom, Bill, and I were analogous to passengers on a rowboat, adrift in some rough seas. The Heaney family was an anchor that stopped the drift and helped us get through the storm.

Chapter 6

THE CHURCH AND I

Since Bill and I were old enough to walk, we attended Mass every Sunday and holy day of obligation. I was very much hooked on Catholicism, and although I am not as devout as mom was, at seventy-five I still am a practicing Catholic and wouldn't have it any other way.

St. Agnes was the only Catholic church in Greenport, and it was our parish. The ethnic makeup of Greenport was such that Catholics were the largest religious denomination. That gave Mom, Bill, and me a lot of exposure. A single mother with two very young children in tow at Mass was a novelty in St. Agnes, not in a negative sense, and the parishioners welcomed us with open arms.

The Golden Age of St. Agnes's was during the tenures of Fathers Holland and Carmody, 1949–1955. Father Holland had been a Navy chaplain during WWII and was a very outgoing, dynamic man. Father Carmody was much more reserved, spoke with a New England accent, and in my opinion was humorless. I always felt that Father Carmody was looking down his nose at me, and I couldn't warm up to him.

Mom was elated with the arrival of Father Holland. Mom

had been working as a housekeeper in the rectory in Forest Hills when one of the priests assigned to the parish asked her if she could go out to Fishers Island and take care of the pastor there. That priest was Father Holland.

Fathers Holland and Carmody were a dynamic duo and complemented each other very well. The parish grew under their leadership. A Catholic school was built, the parish became much more cohesive, and I can't recall the morale in the church ever being as high as it was during their tenure.

In Father Carmody's altar boy class, the emphasis was on learning Latin, and not much time was spent on learning the rituals. I had no problems with the Latin but had a rocky start learning all the rituals.

I took being an altar boy very seriously and on occasion visualized myself being a priest. All Irish Catholic mothers, especially Irish immigrant mothers, dream of having a son who becomes a priest. I know that was Mom's dream for me, and for a while I shared it. Surprisingly, Mom never pushed me; I think she just assumed that a priest was what I was going to be.

Not long after I began serving Mass, I had my first run-in with Father Carmody. It was a very cold morning, and the church was chilly. I had just finished serving the seven thirty Mass when he came into the sacristy and immediately started yelling at me: "Don't you ever touch another electrical switch in this church. Do you hear me?"

"Father, I don't know what you are talking about, but yes, I hear you. And if you ever lose your voice, you will find it in my left ear," was my answer.

Without pause, Father Carmody then said, "You broke the furnace."

Then I knew what he was talking about. The day before, Albert Dinizio, who had been substituting for Alex Giorgi, the regular sexton, asked me if I knew where the switch for the furnace was. I told him that I didn't know, but he must have found it. I didn't tell Father Carmody this. He had just confirmed my initial impression of him, and that was enough.

As I got the rituals down, I became a very good altar boy, but my tendency to reply in kind occasionally got me in trouble. One of the most memorable of those occasions occurred just before I started seventh grade. Every Tuesday night, there was a Novena that required one altar boy. I was alone in the sacristy with Father Carmody when he said, "John, you and your brother have remarkably good manners."

The correct response would have been, "Thank you very much, Father." My response: "Father, good manners in poor kids is like humility in priests: often expected, seldom found." As mouthy as I was, this was still way out of character for me, and to this day I don't know why I answered as I did. I suspect that it was because I didn't like Father Carmody, and I interpreted the tone in his voice as being condescending and patronizing.

Father Carmody's reaction was to get red in the face and very tight-lipped. For a second, I thought he was going to hit me. I had seen him slap Bobby "Boots" Doucette in the face when we were taking altar boy classes and knew he was capable of doing it, but the moment passed.

There were two other incidents with Father Carmody that made an impression on me and very much affected my thoughts about becoming a priest. On the first occasion, I had served an early Mass for him and was clearing the altar when a lady approached the rail and asked if I would ask the priest to give her communion. Father Carmody was still in the sacristy, and when I told him about the lady he got visibly angry, but he did give her communion.

The second occasion was similar and involved me. From the time I started going to Mass on Sunday until I was in the army, almost twenty years later, I had never missed Mass on Sunday. And from the day of my first communion, I never attended Mass without receiving communion.

I was in eighth grade and came down with the flu. I was throwing up and had a fever and chills, but Mom thought that as long as I didn't sneeze or cough in anyone's face, I should go to Mass. I went to the eleven o'clock Mass, at which no one received communion. I was a little bit out of it, and the part of the Mass when communicants approached the altar passed before I realized what was happening.

Father Carmody had been the celebrant, and I wasn't looking forward to asking him to give me communion, but I did. Although he did give me communion, he did not do so willingly. Providing communion to communicants is a primary function of priests, and I saw Father Carmody as being derelict in his duty.

I got along with Father Holland pretty well, but I had a few bones to pick with him. Back in the day, a communicant had to fast for at least eight hours before receiving communion. As previously stated, I never served a Mass during which I didn't receive communion, and on school days when I served Mass, I always went to school without eating breakfast. There were a lot of weeks when I went to school without breakfast. At the time this was happening, it never occurred to Mom that this might not be healthy

Altar boys were scheduled to serve Mass a week at a time. There were two masses each morning, one at seven and the other at seven thirty. One morning as I was leaving for school, Father Carmody and Father Holland were talking in the sacristy. Father Carmody paused in his conversation with Father Holland and said, "John, why don't you go into the kitchen and tell Dora (the housekeeper) to give you a piece of cake or something to eat?"

Without waiting for me to answer, Father Holland said, "He doesn't need it. Let him go to school." I would have declined Father Carmody's suggestion but was very upset at what Father Holland did. In those days, I always needed something to eat, and Father Holland knew I hadn't had breakfast. More importantly, I couldn't understand how a priest could do something like that.

On another occasion, Bill Mallett and I were the altar boys for a wedding. Bill and I were in the sacristy with Father Holland, the groom, and the best man when the best man asked Father Holland, "Is ten dollars each enough for the altar boys?"

"That's too much. Give them five." Father Holland certainly knew what my financial situation was, but didn't have a clue as to what an extra five dollars meant to me.

At another wedding, this one at three in the afternoon, the best man gave Father Holland ten dollars for me and Henry Carlozzi, the other altar boy. Father Holland, after the wedding, handed the ten dollars to Phil Proferes, the church sexton, and said, "Phil, split this up with Sully, you, and Henry." Phil got paid a salary for being there, and I just couldn't understand Father Holland's reasoning.

On one Good Friday, there was a ceremony during which the altar boys had to take off their shoes as they approached the altar. There were eight altar boys in the sacristy when Father Holland asked me if I had on clean socks. I was the only one he asked, and I thought his question was insulting. Therefore, I answered in kind, to wit: "No, Father, but I did polish my feet with black shoe polish." A couple of the altar boys laughed, but Father Holland didn't.

It was slow in coming, but I came to a conclusion that Father Holland, and almost all of the priests I had met, didn't have much of an idea as to how real people lived. They went off to the seminary at a very young age, rarely, if ever, had a real job, and never knew a day of want. Most, if not all, parish priests (at least all of those I met), were from functional homes and knew nothing about marital discord. Priests, for the most part, left home before sex became a part of their lives and had no frame of reference for giving counseling on sexual matters or marital discord.

Compared with many other parishes I have visited, St. Agnes's was well off. The priests lived better than most of their parishioners (a fact that was not lost on me when I was considering being a priest), and I had trouble identifying with or relating to them. I remember Mrs. Van, my eighth-grade English teacher, telling me that on the previous Saturday, Father Holland had called Mrs. Van's husband, Bernie, to ask if he could get a couple of men to help move some furniture. Mr. Van and another member of the Holy Name Society went to the rectory, where Father Holland asked them to take a new TV up to the sun room. Mrs. Van commented that being a priest did have its perks.

Parishioners were forever bringing fresh fish, scallops, clams, vegetables, lobster, freshly killed beef, and other edibles to the rectory for the priests. One night, when I was working in the bowling alley, my boss, Mike Santacroce, asked me, "Do you ever get any of the food that people bring to the rectory?"

"Not a bite," was my answer. Mom would cook the food, and I don't know if she was ever offered any or forbidden to take it, but I know she didn't bring any of it home. On the occasions when I visited Mom in the rectory, she never offered me anything to eat or drink.

Father Carmody would arrange trips to the Barnum and Bailey circus for the altar boys, which were great, and there were a couple of summers when he and Father Holland would take me, Phil Proferes, and Harry Bubb to Southold Town Beach almost every day. For me, those days were as good as it ever got in Greenport.

On one of those days at the beach, Harry Bubb and I were discussing how deep the water was at a float about a hundred yards off the beach. I had dived off the end of Mitchell's pier, where I knew the water was seventeen feet deep at high tide, and reached the bottom. On several occasions, I had tried to do that at the float, and although I could see the bottom, I couldn't reach it. That led me to conclude that it must be at least twenty feet deep.

Father Holland heard me and said, "Sully, don't be silly. Swimming pools are only ten feet deep, at the deep end."

I answered with, "But Father Holland, Long Island Sound isn't a swimming pool. Ten yards from the beach, the water is over my head." I thought my logical response to Father Holland's non sequitur was logical, but it didn't sit well with Father Holland.

My thoughts of becoming a priest peaked in the summer of 1952. Two priests who were assigned to Chaminade High School, the premier Catholic high school on Long Island, would come out to Greenport to go fishing. One of them approached me one day after Mass and asked if I had ever thought of becoming a priest. I told him I had, and he told me that I would have to leave Greenport and go to the minor seminary and that I shouldn't wait too long before I made a decision.

I never mentioned this to mom but did give it some serious thought. My decision not to pursue the priesthood was based primarily on the fact that Fathers Holland and Carmody had known me for three years, and neither had ever suggested that I should think about becoming a priest. If they didn't think so, who was I to disagree? I don't think they questioned my devotion but rather my pedigree.

At that time in my life, pastoral pedophiles were pretty much in the closet and an unknown entity, at least to me. Given the number of priests with whom I had had contact, one might think that strange, but it was a fact. As it turned out, I had had such a contact but just didn't know it. In 2007, I attended my high school class's fiftieth reunion. I was telling the story about the priest who had asked me if I wanted to be a priest, and when I finished, one of my classmates told me that the priest who had posed that question to me was her brother's first homosexual contact. Her brother died of AIDS.

During my sophomore year, Sharon Lellman, a diamond in my crown of friends, dubbed me "Father John." I didn't use profanity, drink, lie, or steal, had had only one date in my life, and was sure that I didn't give off any gay vibes. I couldn't dance, and I was at the top of the "worst dressed" list in school. Given that I was a totally celibate young man who neither swore nor drank and who was also very devout, "Father John" was not an inappropriate appellation.

On Christmas Day 1954, Bill and I were serving a Mass that Father Holland celebrated. He was in a lot of pain and couldn't bend over to tie his shoes, so I did it for him. Over the next few months, his problem didn't get any better, and in the spring of 1955, both he and Father Carmody were transferred to St. Peter's parish in Port Washington. Father James Mooney, who had been the pastor in Port Washington, became our pastor.

Father Mooney was old, very frail, and an old-school Irish priest. He changed a lot of the way altar boys did things, and not liking the changes, I decided to quit. That was a big decision, and one that Mom didn't like, but in retrospect, I don't regret it. Not being an altar boy did not bring about any diminution in my religious fervor, and I was getting more sleep, which was not a bad thing.

Father Mooney's first assistant pastor was Father Heffernan, and I think Father Mooney drove him to drink and out of Greenport. Father Heffernan's replacement was Father Ray Shashaty. He became an instant favorite with the kids but eventually left Roman Catholicism to become an Eastern Rite priest.

In the spring of 1958, just before the spring break, Mom wrote and told me that Father Holland was terminally ill with cancer. I was saddened by the news and decided to stop in and see him on my way home from Albany.

I hitchhiked from Albany to Port Washington, found the rectory, and knocked on the door. When the housekeeper answered the door, I told her I would like to see Father Holland. She told me that Father Holland was in the hospital, but she would get Father Carmody.

Father Carmody greeted me by saying, "John, this is a surprise. I know Father Holland will want to see you." He then invited me to have lunch, after which he took me to the hospital.

As we were going in, we passed Perry Como, who was coming from a visit with Father Holland.

It was painful to see Father Holland. He had lost a lot of weight and was very pale. Even so, he was well enough to smile and greet me. "Sully, it is good to see you. Thank you for stopping in."

The three of us talked for about a half hour, and when a nurse came in to give Father Holland some medication, I took the opportunity to say, "I guess I had better be going." Father Holland thanked me again, asked me to say hello to Greenport, and me to pass the word that he wasn't seeing visitors.

Father Carmody then drove me to Rte. 25 to resume my hitchhiking to Greenport, and his last words to me were, "Please, John, tell the people back in Greenport that Father Holland is not seeing visitors."

My first stop when I got to Greenport was the rectory. I went to the kitchen door, where Dora greeted me warmly and asked me to come in. I was telling her about my visit with Father Holland when Father Tennant came into the kitchen.

"What do you want?" were his opening words.

"I just came from seeing Father Holland, and he asked me to say hello to Dora" was my answer.

"You've done it, and you can leave," was his answer. Dora was embarrassed, and I was in the mood to kick Father Tennant right where it would hurt the most. He was one of the rudest men I ever met, devoid of humility, and as poor a messenger of Christ as I have ever seen.

There was one more trip down the St. Agnes Memory Lane. In July of 1967, I had just gotten out of the army and was staying with Mrs. Heaney until I left for Michigan State. A few days after I got home, I went over to East Hampton to visit a college classmate, Dr. Chuck Fowler. While there, I attended Mass in Bridge Hampton, where Father Carmody was the pastor and, coincidentally, the church where Mom and Dad were married.

After Mass, as Father Carmody greeted parishioners in front of the church, I approached him and introduced myself. "Oh yes, John, what you are doing over here?" were his first words. I told him I was visiting a friend in East Hampton, had heard he was the pastor in Bridge Hampton, and decided to come over.

We exchanged bland pleasantries, and I went back to Greenport thinking that my visit with Father Carmody had been anticlimactic. I don't know what I had expected, but Father Carmody didn't let me down and was just as I expected him to be.

When I reflect on growing up in Greenport, the out and out charity of the St. Agnes parishioners to me and my family comes to mind. Being an altar boy is the first thing I ever did well, and it gave me confidence as well as a modicum of status. Priests I met in Greenport showed me a spiritual side as well as a human side to being a priest, and in so doing, they kept me from making the mistake of trying to become one.

Currently, I am a Eucharistic minister in my parish, St. Thomas a Becket, and have found that very rewarding. A couple of years ago, the church secretary called me and asked if I would be interested in just visiting a blind, wheelchair-bound, 91-year-old man named Bill Carmichael. I said yes, and thus began one my most rewarding experiences.

Bill had been a speechwriter for five presidents and was a great raconteur as well as a very good man. I took him out to eat and shop, and in the time he had left, we had some great times. Bill was a big man, as well as a gourmet eater, and loved the Korean restaurants to which Young and I took him. He had some great stories about his time in the White House, and we spent hours comparing our life stories. There were occasions when I had to help Bill change his catheter and clean up spills in his kitchen, and the satisfaction I got from doing that can't be measured.

My favorite gospel in the Catholic liturgy is Luke 10–25,

the parable of the good Samaritan. Bill Carmichael was the best opportunity I ever had to be the Good Samaritan of whom Jesus preached. So many of the people of Greenport were good samaritans who prepared me very well to go and do likewise. I know I made a positive difference in Bill's life, and there is nothing I have ever done that has given me more satisfaction.

With all the negatives about priests that I have cited, it would be logical to question why I am still a Catholic. My answer is that I have no problems with the message of Catholicism, just with some of its messengers, clergy as well as laity.

Recently, one of my fellow Eucharistic ministers, Kate Buschelman, commented that she felt it is was more important to be a good person than to be a Catholic. That resonates with me and pretty much sums up my current attitude about the church.

Chapter 7

ON THE DOLE

Of the many humiliating experiences I encountered while growing up in Greenport, none was worse than being "on the dole," the term Mr. Gibbs, my seventh- and eighth-grade history teacher, used in reference to those on public assistance or relief. Arthur and Lucia Tasker were the first people I ever told that I grew up on welfare, although I am sure everyone with whom I grew up knew it, and I never mentioned it to Lee, my wife of forty years.

Paul Harvey, a well-known conservative radio commentator, once read a list of things every child should have to undergo before reaching maturity, one of which was being humiliated. I would agree that being humiliated can help build character but also suggest that a daily dose of humility is more than any child should have to endure. Being on the dole was a public acknowledgment of being in need and a 24/7 experience.

In the eyes of God, we may be equal, but that is the only place. Feeling less than equal diminishes self-esteem as well as self-confidence and makes each day more of a challenge than it should be. For the most part, the people of Greenport were very kind, but there were those who weren't. The first time I heard the term "welfare brat" was when I was playing with Bill at our friend Gil "Bubby" Raynor's house. Bubby's mother, Martha, was talking to a friend, Rose Dawson, when Mrs. Dawson asked, "Who are these kids?"

"They're a couple of welfare brats," Mrs. Raynor answered, and the tone of her voice made it clear to me that welfare brats were a lesser species. That was the first time I can recall feeling stigmatized by being on welfare.

On the occasion of the twenty-fifth anniversary of the class of 1957, I was speaking with Grover Thompson, one of my classmates. When I told him I was working for the government, he said, and not in a joking way, "Still on the dole, huh, John?" Grover was a friend and had been great baseball player. His comment, and the tone of it, caught me by surprise. My brilliant retort: "That may be how you see it, but I pay more taxes in a year than you earn in a year." That may have been a slight stretch, but I just had to say something.

My first memory of being on welfare was when our case officer, a Mrs. Chase, came to visit us for the purpose of determining whether or not Mom would be able to keep us. Consideration was being given to having Bill and me put in an orphanage or foster care.

What I remember most about that incident was how Bill cried when Mrs. Chase asked him if he would like to go live with another family. Mom was also crying, and I wasn't really sure of what was going on. Mrs. Chase didn't remove us from mom's care, and that was a good thing, but that incident had long-term effects on her. She was always aware of the fact that we could be taken away from her, and that terrified her.

Another way in which that incident affected Mom was that she maintained a very low profile with Social Services, in that she never asked them for anything. Welfare recipients, if they needed anything not covered by the monthly payment, could petition the case officer for a supplemental payment. Mom never did that.

I remember so well serving midnight Mass on a Christmas Eve with my socks showing through the holes in my shoes. Mom just didn't want to bring any attention to her or us and wouldn't ask our case officer for money to buy me a pair of shoes.

There have been fleeting moments when I thought about what it would have been like if we had been put in an orphanage, placed in foster care, or put up for adoption. I am quite sure we would have eaten better, had a more comfortable home, and received better health care, but Mom's love for us and the thought of being separated from her or Bill trumped all of these things.

Welfare cheats are a problem not only for the taxpayers who fund them but also for those in genuine need who try to play by the rules, as both groups are tarred by the same brush. The common image of the typical welfare cheat is either that of an unmarried or otherwise single female with children, living the high life on the government's tab, or a drunk man or woman, too lazy to work, who uses a welfare check to sustain his or her alcoholism. Mom was neither of these, and it was not right for her to be lumped in with the cheaters. With the lone exception of a glass of wine at Jack and Helen Heaney's wedding, on August 22, 1953, I have never seen Mom take a drink, nor was there ever any type of alcohol in our house.

Mom worked herself to death. I never saw her turn down an offer of work and often witnessed her come home bone tired. On some of those occasions, she would make a cup of tea, sit down, and cry. There were occasions when her arthritis was very bad, and she would still go out on a job. Mom's work ethic and desire to better provide for us made her, at least in the eyes of the powers that be, a welfare cheat. It occurs to me that there is something inherently wrong with a system that would classify her as any kind of cheat.

In Dr. Childers' book, she addressed this issue and claimed that her mother often worked in a department store, "off the books," in order to survive. I know the feeling. There was no way that we could live on the monthly welfare check we got. For us, there wasn't enough to pay the rent and keep enough food on the table. I can recall one occasion when I read the breakdown of the allowances in our welfare check. Five dollars was allotted for clothing and one dollar for school supplies.

Any income we obtained would be deducted from our check, and we couldn't let that happen. We never knew when a bit of extra money would come in, and when it did, we were not going to share it with anyone outside the family. Making a couple of extra dollars wasn't the only reason I worked, as I always felt that being on welfare made it incumbent on me to show the people of Greenport that I wasn't lazy.

Asking people for anything has always been a problem for me, and that applied to asking for a job. One of my biggest problems was that until I graduated from college, I thought anyone who gave me a job was doing me a favor.

With a college degree, for the first time in my life, I felt as though I was bringing something to the table that a prospective employer might want. The very first interview I had after graduating from college resulted in me being offered a job. I had another interview scheduled and wanted to do that one before making a decision. During that interview, I was also offered a job and took it.

As a kid, my self-image was such that I didn't see myself as having anything to offer a prospective employer and lacked the self-confidence that would allow me to think that anyone would actually want to hire me. Combining this attitude with my scrawny physique, unkempt appearance, and lack of driver's license didn't help.

As it turned out, every job I got during my four years in high school was unsolicited. During the summer after my freshman year, Archie Kaplan, a neighbor and owner of the Colonial Pharmacy, approached me and asked me if I would like to work in his store that summer. He said I looked like a kid who needed a job.

That was the first salaried job I ever had, and I enjoyed it very much. There were two events I remember vividly about the job: the hurricane just after Labor Day and the suicide of Bill Mallett. First, the hurricane: The wind was howling and there were torrential rains coming down when Mr. Kaplan knocked on our door and told me we would have to go down to the store and drill holes in the floor to let the water run into the basement. That short trip down to the drugstore was one of the scariest things I have ever done. Branches were falling from the trees and high-tension wires were falling on the streets. The hiss they made scared the bejesus out of me.

As I passed Kaelin's Florists, a huge gust of wind lifted the greenhouse off its base, and hundreds of panes of glass were shattered. I saw a tree branch blow through the window of Hoppy's Cleaners. I saw a rowboat tied up to a parking meter.

By the time I got to the store, I was drenched to the skin. There was no electricity, and we had to work in the dark, but I helped Mr. Kaplan drill holes in the floor, moved a lot of merchandise off the floor, put the stuff that was destroyed in one corner of the store, and went home.

The next day, I went back to the store to clean up the mess created by the hurricane. At about four o'clock that afternoon, Bill Mallett came in to buy some film. As he was paying for the film, he asked me to serve Mass for him the next day. I declined, and Bill went home and committed suicide.

My next job, during the summer of 1955, came about as a result of one of my football teammates, Henry Myslborski, asking me if I wanted a job. Henry would be graduating in June and enlisting in the navy. He had done the grounds maintenance at Sage's Cabin Rentals and was offering me his job.

I had a great summer working there. At the end of the summer, I told Mr. Sage I would like to come back, and he told me that would be fine with him. When I went to talk with Mr. Sage in June of 1956, he told me he had given the job to someone else. I was very disappointed, not only because I wouldn't be working at a job that I had liked but also because Mr. Sage hadn't let me know and, to put it not so nicely, had gone back on his word.

In either case, it was the middle of June. I was without a job, hadn't been looking for one, and was almost in a panic mode. One Saturday morning, Jim Heaney got me a job cleaning a boat, and after I finished, he asked me if I would run over to the diner and get him a sandwich and cup of coffee.

The diner was the Park Diner, which was a Greenport institution. While I was waiting for my order, John Moscovey, the owner of the diner and one of our benefactors, asked me what I would be doing that summer. When I told him that I didn't have a job, he offered me a job washing dishes and keeping the diner clean. I accepted his offer, with a huge sigh of relief.

This turned out to be one of the tougher jobs I have had. I worked from five in the morning to three in the afternoon, six days a week. On weekends, from five until seven in the morning, we were swamped with weekend fishermen, and it was chaotic. I made good money, but it was a tough job. I did get two good meals a day, and that helped.

That fall, Mr. Bubb, Harry's father, asked me if I would be interested in working on weekends at the gas station. I said yes and worked there until I left for college. At that time, I was also delivering the New York Times to students and teachers in high school who had subscribed to it.

One morning, on my way to school, Mr. Bubb pulled up in his truck and said, "John, I really need you to work today. I have a really bad hangover." I got Bill to deliver the papers, and skipped school.

Summers were very difficult. Welfare checks were cut because there was no heating expense That left us in pretty bad shape,and even with the money I was making, we were always behind.

Most people in that situation have to find a store where they can buy food on credit. For us, that was Johnny's Market, a store owned by Johnny "Doc" Carbone. Without that credit, we would have been much worse off, but it was a very unpleasant experience. On almost every occasion when I would go into the store, Doc would remind me that Mom was getting further behind on her bill every month. "No matter how hard she tries, she just can't get caught up" was his constant refrain, and it got old very quickly.

This went on from junior high school through high school, and it was not a situation in which I could demonstrate my rapier wit with a wise-guy reply. Often, I just wanted to say, "Doc, what do you want me to do about it? I know we owe you money, and if I had it, I would give it to you," but I held my tongue.

The one positive that came out of this experience was that I have an aversion to owing anyone anything. In my life, I have borrowed money on two occasions. One of those was in college, when tickets went on sale for a concert and I didn't have enough money with me to buy a ticket. I borrowed five dollars from my roommate and paid him back when we got back to the dorm. On the other occasion, I was teaching school and someone stole my wallet. I borrowed five dollars to hold me over until payday, when I repaid the money.

There was no question that we owed Johnny's Market money, and I had an almost perverse urge to repay him. I didn't like him, and if there was anyone to whom I didn't want to owe anything, it was he.

During graduation week, I was given just over four hundred dollars in gifts. The next day, I approached Doc and asked him how much we owed him. He checked, and told me $368. I handed him the four hundred and told him to keep the change. Mom got real upset when I told her what I had done, but I have no regrets and would do it over again.

My last contact with Suffolk County Social Services occurred after Mom passed away. Unbeknownst to me, mom had taken out a life insurance policy on herself with Bill and me as her beneficiaries. A couple of months after the funeral, I got a letter from SCSS notifying me that the insurance had been bought with welfare funds and requested that I sign the policy over to them. I had no problem with that, and thus ended a necessary, but very difficult relationship.

Dread of ever again having to live as we did when growing up has been the driving force in my life, a force that has kept me almost continuously employed since the day I left Greenport.

Alexis de Tocqueville, the French philosopher, was a strong advocate for the impoverished and disenfranchised peoples of the world. He posited that nations should be held accountable for, as well as rated on, how humanely they treat their poor.

From my perspective, America ranks pretty highly, and I am so grateful for all that she has done for me and my family. I have worked in forty countries without finding one where I would rather live.

Chapter 8

FRIENDS

In profiling those with whom I grew up and whose friendships meant so much to me, I will focus on those whom I feel I knew as well as they knew me and who had the most profound impact on me. I have known each of them for over sixty years, and with one exception, Don Macomber, we have kept in touch over the years. They are Greenport to me, and *Raised By a Village* would be incomplete were I not to acknowledge their roles in my life.

My Greenport friends have done much to help get me to where I am today, and profiling them is part of my thank you to Greenport as well as an attempt to give the reader another perspective on me.

I hope none of my former classmates feels slighted by not being profiled in this chapter, but I don't have enough current, or past, information about them to do justice to a profile of them.

Diane

I have known Diane Woodward Sawyer longer than any of my other friends. We met in September 1944, when we started kindergarten. We were classmates from kindergarten through college. Since college, we have stayed in touch, and since we both became authors, our contacts have been more frequent.

It didn't take long for the teachers, and the rest of the kids in the class, to realize that Diane was very intelligent. It took even less time for the boys to realize that she was also the prettiest girl in the class and, by the time we got to high school, the prettiest girl in the school.

Not wanting to be different from all the other boys in the class, I worshiped Diane from afar. Diane handled her potential suitors very well and was never dismissive of any of us. She was never aloof but always poised, and I never heard her say an unkind word to anyone.

The traffic around the Woodward house would get a little heavy with suitors, and on one occasion, Mr. Woodward accidentally ran over a bike belonging to one of them, Dick Banker, who, in his eagerness to press his suit, had left his bike in the driveway.

I never really got to know Mr. Woodward and don't know from which of her parents Diane inherited her intelligence, but I am certain that she inherited her personality from her mother, Mrs. Monica Woodward. From my earliest days as an altar boy, Mrs. Woodward seemed to take a very special interest in me, and I reveled in her attention. Mom was a very good Catholic, but Mrs. Woodward was just as good, if not better. She was my catechism teacher, and she was a very good one.

Diane's brother Jimmy was two years older than I and an altar boy until he came down with polio. Jimmy was in St. Charles Hospital in Port Jefferson for quite a while, but he made a great recovery. He was very intelligent wore a perpetual smile, and I got along with him very well. After graduation, Jimmy enrolled in Villanova, became an engineer, and worked for many years at Pratt & Whitney in Connecticut. Both Diane and Jimmy turned out to be good, accomplished, and very decent adults, a feat I attribute to Mrs. Woodward's efforts and the example she set.

Diane was one of the most focused and disciplined students I have ever met as well as very fun-loving. She was very intelligent but earned her grades the hard way, that is, by studying more than the other kids.

I once asked Diane, "Who motivated you more, your mother or father?"

Diane told me, "Neither. I competed with Jimmy, but I was self- motivated."

Until high school, Diane and I were good friends. In high school, we became better friends. During our freshman year, our class put on a dance called the Blarney Ball. I didn't know how to dance and was very reluctant to ask her to go to the dance, but my hormones got the better of me, and I did. Diane's agreeing to go with me was the highlight of my high school social life. That doesn't say much for my social life, but that's the way it was.

We kissed (my first, ever) near a replica Blarney Stone at the dance, and I wouldn't recapture that moment of bliss until more than halfway through my first year of college. That first kiss was chaste, as platonic as a kiss between two fourteen-year-olds can be, and a magic moment I have never forgotten.

Not long after that, Diane was babysitting for her aunt, who lived two houses away from ours. She was out in the yard, and I went over to talk with her. We talked, over the fence, for over two hours, until Bill came to call me for supper. That was the first in-depth conversation I had ever had with a girl. As great as it was, it highlighted some of our differences and led me to conclude, even at the age of fourteen, that Diane was destined for great things. I wasn't going to college and probably would end up in Greenport. The only thing I had to offer was the ability to make her laugh, which wasn't, and shouldn't have been, enough.

My prospects changed during our senior year. Diane and I were awarded regents scholarships, and we both applied for the Lillian Ging Memorial Scholarship. Although Diane was much more deserving, I got it. No one was happier for me than she.

A lesser person would have been justifiably angry at not being awarded that scholarship, and this was just another example of the powers that be bending the rules to help me. That this was done at the expense of one of my dearest friends has always bothered me.

Another of my many good memories of Diane is of our senior trip to Washington. During that trip, we took a moonlight cruise on the Potomac that included a dance. When the band played "Blue Tango," Diane and John Tasker went out on the floor, and within two minutes, they were alone on the floor as about five hundred kids watched. They got a huge ovation when the dance ended.

I don't know what contact Mrs. Sperling, the mother of Jonathan Sperling, one of our classmates and another of my best friends, had with Diane, but I remember her telling me, "Diane Woodward is such a wonderful girl. I think she is the smartest, as well as the best-looking, girl in the school. I expect great things from her."

Diane and one of our classmates, Bill Lieblein, dated for a while. They were Ken and Barbie dolls, with a lot more class than their Mattel replicas, and my good friends. Having them as friends did a lot for my self-image, and their friendship was one of my most positive experiences in high school.

One of my more poignant memories of Diane and Bill occurred over the Christmas break during our freshman year in college.

Bill was working at the family marina and had to drive to Northport to pick up some equipment. He invited me and Diane to go with him, and I remember that occasion as quality time with two of the best friends I had ever had.

It was the first time just the three of us had socialized. Our past contacts were in groups or one on one, and in those group contacts, Bill and Diane were nice to me because they were nice people. On this occasion, they chose to have me with them because they genuinely liked me. They still do, as do I them.

In college, Diane and I became even better friends. I believe I was the one who introduced Diane to one of my fraternity brothers, J. Robert "Buzz" Sawyer. Diane's sorority hosted a coffee hour for our fraternity, and I introduced them. Subsequently, at O'Heaney's bar, Buzz approached me and said, "Tell me about Diane Woodward." I told Buzz that Diane was the best thing that ever came out of Greenport and as good a friend as I have ever had.

At the end of our junior year, Buzz and Diane got married in Albany. In marrying Buzz, Diane had chosen wisely. Her brother, Jimmy, escorted her down the aisle, the reception was great, and to watch Buzz and Diane dance was to conjure up memories of Fred and Ginger.

At the wedding reception, I met Diane's cousin Barry, who was in the seminary at St. Norbert's Abbey in DePere, Wisconsin. At the reception, Barry approached me and said, "Aunt Monica thinks you'd be a good priest." I told him there was a time I had thought so, too, but I was no longer so sure. Barry told me that if I wasn't absolutely sure, it would be a big mistake to go down that path. That was the last time I ever discussed becoming a priest with anyone.

In the small world category, when I was in the Army Language School in Monterey, California, I met another soldier who told me he had attended St. Norbert's College. When I asked him if he knew a Barry Sinnott, he looked at me a bit strangely and said, "I gave him his tonsure" (the shaving of the crown of the head prior to becoming a priest or monk).

After Diane graduated, she and Buzz moved to Tallman, New York. Buzz taught at Westchester County Community College and Diane at a local high school. When I was working in Bangkok, I worked with one of Buzz's students from WCCC.

We went separate ways after graduation, but always stayed in touch. As I traveled around the world, I would send her and her family a postcard from wherever I happened to be, and we exchanged Christmas cards.

Shortly after coming back from Vietnam, I attended a get-to-gether of college friends in Trumbull, Connecticut. Tallman wasn't very far away and Buzz and Diane drove over/ We re-connected and have stayed in much closer contact over the last forty years. .

When Buzz and Diane retired, they moved to St. Petersburg, Florida, where I visited them. Kirk and Barrie turned out very well. Kirk graduated from Georgia Tech and Barrie from the University of Virginia. Kirk is an engineer and Barrie a lawyer. As yet, I haven't met Kirk, but I have met Barrie, and she is, fortunately, her mother's daughter.

Diane is an accomplished author and a confidante with whom I can share my ideas as well as discuss my failures and successes. Everyone should be blessed with such a friend. Without being redundant, I can't overstate the importance of Diane's friendship. At a time in my life when my self-esteem was very low, the best-looking and one of the most popular girls in the school was one of my best friends. I can't put a price on how much that meant to me. I learned two of life's great lessons from Diane: Beautiful girls can be nice, and having a heartfelt, platonic friendship can be more rewarding than a hormonally driven infatuation.

Jonathan

My friendship with Jonathan Sperling had an interesting beginning. Jonathan's father, Dr. Nathaniel Sperling, and his family had moved to Greenport after World War II, and Jonathan started school a few days later than the rest of the class.

On his very first day in first grade, during lunch hour, I picked a fight with him. Although he denies it, I am pretty sure he won the fight. Regardless, both of us went back to class disheveled and dirty. Mrs. Schaumburg, our teacher made both of us stand in front of the class as she chastised and berated us. Not long thereafter, Jonathan invited me over to his house to play. That "play date," to use today's terminology, was the beginning of a wonderful friendship that continues to this day.

There was a hiatus in our friendship between the time we both finished college and when we reconnected in Bangkok in 1972. I was stationed in Vietnam at the time but occasionally worked in Bangkok and had heard that Jonathan was there on an assignment with the United States Agency for International Development (USAID). On one of my trips to Bangkok, I showed up at his house and knocked on the door. His wife, Nancy, answered.

"I'm John Sullivan. May I please speak with Jonathan, if he is home?" I asked.

"So you're little Johnny Sullivan! Please do come in."

Our reconnection was great, and I have been knocking on his door ever since. Of the many things Jonathan did for me, the one for which I am most grateful was his taking me to Floyd Memorial Library, where he introduced me to Mrs. Gertrude Pemberton, the librarian, and got me a library card.

Mrs. Pemberton was very kind to me, and my library card opened my mind to new people, places, and events where it had never been. Over the years, the library became a refuge for me. On rainy or cold days when there was no school, I would head for the library. One activity I engaged in at the library was reading the *New Yorker* magazine. The articles were very well written, and I know reading them helped my own writing and speaking.

Jonathan and I would read the same books and discuss them, and I became hooked on reading. My reading interests initially centered on any and all books about sports, and I saw reading as entertainment more than as a learning exercise. In time, I came to see reading as both, and any academic success I had was due in a large part to my love of reading. I owe that to Jonathan.

I was a bookworm, but I didn't have good enough grades to be called a geek. By the time I finished high school, I was pretty sure I had read more books than any kid in the school and had acquired a habit that would serve me well for the rest of my life.

A more subtle, but no less significant benefit of Jonathan's friendship was the influence his attitude about college had on me. No discussion of college ever took place in the Sullivan house, and Jonathan's constant "when we go to college" comments aroused a curiosity in me. College was not for the likes of me, I believed, and then, as now, I never allowed my reach to exceed my grasp. By the time I got to high school, more and more kids were going to college, but higher education for a kid on welfare was still not a realistic goal.

When Jonathan's older brother, Ken, left for Williams College, Jonathan began to talk seriously about college. That was just as we started junior high school, and I can remember Jonathan saying to me, "John, this is where we have to start getting serious about school. If we are going to get into a good school, we have to get good grades." Jonathan absolutely assumed that both of us would go to college.

I never disabused Jonathan of that idea, because I knew that he meant well and he genuinely had my best interests at heart, but in my heart I knew he was dreaming. Even so, he planted the seed, and it bore fruit.

Jonathan's family was also part of the friendship, and they were great. Dr. Sperling had been awarded the Silver Star for heroism during the battle of Huertgen Forest. He was one hard-nosed man, but he was also a fine doctor and great role model for his two sons. (Coincidentally, my father-in-law was captured in the same battle as the one in which Dr. Sperling earned his silver star.)

Mrs. Sperling was the epitome of poise and gentility and always made me feel welcome in her home. Not being very scholarly did not mean that I was stupid, and as much as I read books, I also read people. There were those in Greenport who treated me patronizingly. Mrs. Sperling never did.

Unlike the rest of the freshmen who took Latin, Jonathan took French, over the very strong objections of Mrs. Diller, the French teacher. She vented her ire and spite on Jonathan and made life in French class miserable for him. I think this is one of the reasons Dr. and Mrs. Sperling decided to send Jonathan to a prep school, Wilbraham Academy, for his last two years of high school. Mrs. Diller's shabby treatment of Jonathan colored my opinion of her.

A more tangible benefit of Jonathan's friendship was that when Jonathan left for Wilbraham Academy after our sophomore year, Dr. Sperling would hire me to answer the phone while he and Mrs. Sperling went out. More important than the money was that during those phone-sitting sessions, I had access to the Sperling's record collection and got to listen to some of the best music I have ever heard.

There was an incident that occurred one night when I was manning the phone that was rather memorable. I was using the bathroom just off Dr. Sperling's office when the phone rang. I went over to his desk and answered the call. As I wrote down the message, I noticed a medical journal and opened it. Therein were the first pictures of a naked girl I had ever seen. There was nothing sexually arousing about the pictures, and the incident was just a case of curiosity being satisfied.

While attending the Army Language School, I ran into an alumnus of Dartmouth College named Pat Moorman. In playing "Whom do you know that I know?" with him, Pat knew Jonathan very well and thought highly of him.

Our careers took Jonathan and me to Washington, and we have lived within fifteen miles of each other for many years. Jonathan still travels a lot, but we still see each other, and when I go out to Greenport, I stay in the Sperling house. We don't pick our parents, but do have some choice as to who our friends are. In choosing Jonathan to be my friend, I couldn't have done better.

Jonathan and Nancy have two lovely daughters, Alex and Victoria. I do a lot of substitute teaching in Langley High School, the school from which they graduated, and both are still remembered by their teachers. Someday Alex will be running some big government agency, and Victoria will be making wherever she is better for her being there.

Lee passed away in December 1999, and Jonathan came to the funeral. I, and some friends were in the vestibule of the church talking with Father Moretti, who would be saying the Mass, when Jonathan came through the door..

As Jonathan and Father Moretti made eye contact, surprise lighted up their faces. They had served together overseas when Father Mark was working for the State Department, and he had babysat for Alex and Victoria. Father Mark had nothing but good things to say about Jonathan, as do I.

None of my other friends had the effect on me that Jonathan did. My life's lesson, derived from that friendship, is that one true friend is better than a hundred friendly acquaintances.

Harry

Harry Bubb is another of my friends with whom I am still in touch and also the only friend I am profiling who was not a classmate. I had known Harry for several years before we became friends as a result of seeing him in church on Sundays, at catechism classes, and in school with mutual friends. Our friendship started when we were both in Father Carmody's altar boy class.

In the summers of 1952 and 1953, we became closer when Fathers Holland and Carmody would take Harry, Phil Proferes, another altar boy, and me swimming at Southold Town Beach. On days when Fathers Holland and Carmody didn't go to the beach, I would hang out with Harry, and we would either hitchhike to Town Beach or find something to do around his father's gas station.

During those two summers, I worked at Santacroce's bowling alley at night and usually had my days free. On some days, I would get a job picking beans, peas, or potatoes. On others, Jim Heaney would find some work for me to do at Mitchell's Pier. There was never any guaranteed income or any status attached to any of the jobs I did, but I was making some money, and that was always a good thing.

However, as scrawny as I was, jobs were hard to come by. Working on a charter boat was one of the better jobs, and I knew a lot of the captains, but those jobs took a lot more strength than I had. On the occasions when I did get such a job, I always had trouble pulling in the anchor, and that was an impediment.

Harry worked at his father's gas station during both of those summers. Business was usually slower in the afternoons, and Mr. Bubb would give Harry three hours off to go swimming. The work wasn't that physically demanding, and yet Harry had no body fat and more muscle than any of the kids I knew.

There were six in the Bubb family: Mr. and Mrs. Bubb, Bobby, Harry's older brother, Colette, his younger sister, and Dennis, the younger brother.

Bobby was a bad kid: mean, nasty, and always in some kind of trouble. He never did anything to get himself in trouble with the police, but he was always on the edge and was a constant source of anxiety for Mr. and Mrs. Bubb. I lost track of him after I went off to college, and the last I heard of him, he had passed away while living as a hermit in the Maine woods.

During one of Mrs. Van's eighth-grade English classes, Bobby walked in, threw his book on her desk, and announced, "I just quit."

Mrs. Van said, "How nice. Now, get out of my class."

Bobby had bought a bottle of dandelion wine to class and gotten a couple of his classmates drunk. He was expelled.

I remember an occasion when Harry, Phil Proferes, and I were raking leaves in the church yard discussing one of Bobby's escapades, and Father Holland overheard us.

"I could get Bobby to do anything I want, "said Father Holland. My immediate thought was, *Are you that naïve or just arrogant?*

Harry and I just looked at each other and smiled, and then Harry said, "I don't think so, Father."

Father Holland had grown up at a time, and in a place, where priests were respected and feared. Bobby had neither respect for, nor fear of a priest.

In fall of 1953, Harry would be starting his third year on the football team. Just before school started, the football coach, Dorrie "CJ" Jackson, called a meeting for all the players and those wanting to try out for the team. Harry asked me to go with him, and that turned out to be one of the more fortuitous events of my high school years.

There were only about twenty kids at the meeting, and most of them were already on the team. When CJ saw me, he said, "John, do you want to try out for the team?"

I don't know exactly why I said yes, but at the back of my mind was the thought of someday becoming a football coach. If I were going that route, I figured I should play the game.

To this day, I think that decision was not only one of the more impulsive things I ever did but also one of the best decisions I ever made. I weighed 105 pounds, not much of which was muscle, but I loved football and wanted to give it a try.

Over the next two years, Harry and I became very good friends. He played football, basketball, and baseball, and I was on all three teams with him, playing on the football team and managing the basketball and baseball teams. When not involved in games or practices, we hung out together. He included me in parties to which he was invited and expanded my social horizons.

This was not a symbiotic relationship, as I have no idea what Harry got out of our friendship. Wherever we went, Harry paid my way. Not once did I ever ask him to do this, and not once did Harry even suggest that I owed him anything or was in any way "mooching" off him. There were times when I was embarrassed by Harry's charity, and that is what it was, but I also appreciated that what Harry was doing was charity at its best, and it made Harry the fine person that he was.

In July of 1955, Harry enlisted in the army. He and John Montgomery, another teammate from the football team, had decided to enlist together, and at the very last minute, on a whim, Harry's brother Bobby also enlisted.

While Harry was in the army, we stayed in touch, and after basic training, he sent me a pair of spit-shined jump boots. After his discharge, we drifted apart. A few years ago, we reconnected and have rekindled our friendship. Last year, Young and I visited with him in New Hampshire, where he now lives. He looks great. He has visited me here in Virginia, and I am looking forward to more visits.

During the fall of my senior year, I began working part-time in the gas station and worked there until I left for college. On Saturdays, Mr. Bubb would let me take off for football games. It was a great job, and Mr. Bubb was one of the best bosses I ever had.

Growing up without a father left me one of the least handy people I know. Working in the gas station gave me some exposure to doing minor maintenance on cars as well as some great experience in dealing with good and bad people.

On one Sunday afternoon, when I was alone in the station, two of the local lowlifes pulled up to the pumps. The driver held up two fingers, indicating, or so I thought, that he wanted two dollars' worth of gas. They then got out of the car and went into the station.

I had pumped about $1.80 worth of gas when the driver said, "Hey, I meant two gallons." I finished putting the two dollars' worth of gas in the car, went into the station, and said, "Two dollars, please."

An argument ensued, and Mr. Bubb's sister-in-law, Stacia, who lived behind the station, opened the connecting door and said, "John, are you having a problem?"

I told her no, turned back to the lowlife, and said, "Two dollars, or I call the police." When they continued to argue, I picked up the phone. One of them threw two dollars on the counter, called me a little prick and they both stormed out.

At the time of that incident, it never occurred to me not to do what I did. When Mr. Bubb found out about it, he didn't get angry. But he did tell me that if anything like that happened again to wait and let him handle it, saying, "John, you are a good kid. Those two guys are assholes and not the kind of people you should give a hard time."

A few years ago, Harry wrote a book of poems about Greenport, and in some of these poems, he has captured the essence of the town. Each time I read one of the poems, I am back there roaming the streets, and it is as if I never left. There have been occasions when I wished that were true.

Harry is also one of my primary sources for information for this book as well as a constant source of encouragement. From Harry I learned that a friendship doesn't have to be symbiotic to be meaningful. There are people who do good things not because they are getting something out of it but because it is the right thing to do. Harry was, back in the day, one of the latter.

BILL

Bill Lieblein was, and still is, one of my best friends. We weren't all that close in school, but we were good friends. We were first-generation Americans, classmates, altar boys, and, for our last two years in high school, teammates on the football team. These commonalities were the basis for our almost seventy-year friendship. If I were to pick one aspect of Bill's character that defines him, it would be his sense of responsibility.

Like Diane Woodward's and Jonathan Sperling's mothers, Bill's mother was someone with whom I was enthralled. She spoke grammatically perfect English, with a beautiful German accent, and always found time to have a conversation with me, not just say hello but to actually speak, whenever we met.

Bill was not what I would call a good athlete, but he had the size, strength, and toughness to be a good football player, and he was. Bill also succeeded at everything he did and it didn't take him long to become a starting tackle on the team.

The only time I was ever jealous of Bill was when he dated Diane Woodward, but they were two of the best, and, as far as I was concerned, that was as it should be. From eighth grade through our senior year, Bill was the president of the class of 1957, and he was a very good one.

After high school, Bill earned a degree in engineering at Villanova and then fulfilled his NROTC commitment by becoming an officer on a nuclear submarine. Bill's mother passed away in July of 1967, after a long battle with cancer. Bill was deployed at the time and couldn't attend the funeral. In another "Whom do you know" conversation, Admiral Charles "Chuck" Larsen, the superintendent at the U.S .Naval Academy when my older son was there, told me he had served on the nuclear submarine *Nathaniel Green* with Bill and spoke very highly of him.

I had gotten out of the army two days before Mrs. Lieblein passed away and was staying with the Heaneys until I left for Michigan State. Mrs. Lieblein, in her final days, had been writing to me in German, and I knew she was very ill. On my first day home, I paid a visit to the Lieblein house and got to see her. She recognized me but was in terrible pain and heavily sedated. It broke my heart to see her in that condition.

The next morning, Mr. Lieblein and Bill's younger brother, Peter, came over to the Heaney house to tell me that Mrs. Lieblein had passed away. Both he and Peter were weeping, and they asked me if I would be a pallbearer for Mrs. Lieblein. Needless to say, I was extremely honored.

Mrs. Lieblein is buried very close to Mom, in a beautiful site overlooking Sterling Creek, in sight of the Lieblein house. Each time I visit Mom's grave, I stop and say a prayer at Mrs. Lieblein's.

At Mrs. Lieblein's funeral, I had a long talk with Bill's younger sister, Marlene. Marlene was a few years younger than I and one of the most naturally beautiful girls I have ever known. During our conversation, Marlene commented that Bill was the rock on which the whole family leaned.

Since our twenty-fifth class reunion, Bill and I have become closer, and I treasure his friendship. When Bill's father needed his help to run the family business, the Port of Egypt Marina, Bill gave up a very promising career in the navy to do the right thing and turned the business into a very successful enterprise.

Bill married Kae Cottrell while he was still in college. They raised five children, but the marriage ended in divorce. I attended Bill's second wedding to his very lovely Barbara, who has become a wonderful friend.

While I was having a conversation with Marlene at the reception, she mentioned that when her marriage fell apart, Bill was there for her as he has always been for the family. Marlene said that Bill had literally saved her life and she didn't know what she would have done without him.

A little over a year ago, I took Young, my daughter-in-law, Kristen, and my two grandchildren, Katie and Andrew, out to Greenport. As we drove into the marina, Andrew said, "Grandpa, I have never been in a boat. Do you think your friend might take us for a ride?" I told Andrew that I didn't know and that Mr. Lieblein might be too busy.

As always, Bill was glad to see me, and as usual, he was very busy. "John, I would love to spend more time with you guys. I am just about to close a sale on a half-million-dollar boat, but I think I can make time to take you guys for a ride in the boat."

Bill proceeded to take all of us out on the water, where he actually let Katie and Andrew pilot the boat. He was so painstaking with Andrew that Andrew still talks about that event.

Next month, two of our classmates, John and Arthur Tasker, will be celebrating their seventy-fifth birthdays. I am hoping to attend and to see Bill and Barb, as Bill was a prime-time player in the drama that was my life in Greenport.

The most important thing I learned from Bill is that regardless of the circumstances, when your family is in trouble, you help them. In this day and age, there are too many who have forgotten that.

Sharon

From first grade, through eighth grade in GG&HS, each grade was divided into two classes, and A class and a B class. Sharon Lellmann was in the B class until we got to high school. Up until then, there were two commonalities we shared: our friendship with Diane Woodward and our Catholic faith. We were in the same first communion and confirmation classes and attended the same catechism, or Confraternity of Christian Doctrine (CD), classes, during which we became good friends.

During the summer before we started high school, Sharon threw a surprise birthday party for Diane, to which she invited me. That was my introduction to what would become "The Porch Gang."

Sharon lived adjacent to the school, and during our freshman year, we started meeting over the lunch hour on her front porch. There was Sharon, Diane, Bill Lieblein, Joanne Sturm, Arthur and John Tasker, Bob Adams, Sue Hudson, Holten Brandi, Kathy Gloria, Bill Dinizio, and eventually Rich Brooks, whom Sharon would marry.

I knew of no requirements for inclusion in the gang, and there were those who called it a clique, but I felt that word had an inaccurate connotation. Regardless, inclusion in that group enhanced my self-esteem and meant very much to me.

Sharon's father, Gus, was very prominent in Greenport's athletic community, and I was the batboy on the local baseball team when he was the manager. Each year, Mr. Lellmann would organize a trip to New York to see a Giants baseball game. On two occasions, Mr. Lellmann took Bill and me to see the games and paid our way. Those trips were the only times I had ever been more than twenty-five miles west of Greenport or been to New York City until I was in high school, and they were a very big deal to me.

Mr. Lellmann would also hire Bill and me to put coat and shirt hangers together in his dry cleaning business. We didn't make a lot of money, but every cent helped.

On my first summer home from college, Mr. Lellmann hired me to be a bar waiter for a party at the Shelter Island Yacht club where he was bartending. I made more money that night than I had ever made in one day, more than eighty dollars.

One of my best memories of Sharon was when she, Rich, and I attended the wedding of two of our classmates, John Moore and Jane Cowan. Rich gave Jane away, and at the reception, Sharon and I danced to Jerome Kern's "The Way You Look Tonight." That was the best dance I have ever had.

Rich

Richard "Rich" Brooks joined our freshmen class in 1953 and is another classmate I didn't really get to know until the re-union in 1982. Since then, I have gotten to know him better and been amazed by him. He is a genuine Renaissance man: a great teacher, a fine painter, a great genealogist, a good athlete, and a carpenter. I recently told Rich that I had practically no knowledge of my ancestors. Rich asked me to give him the places and dates of birth of my parents, and within two weeks, he had more information on my family that I had learned in seventy-five years.

Sharon and Rich are, and always have been, there when someone needs them whether it is sitting with a friend dying of cancer (Edwina Green Skrezec), driving to upstate New York to try to help an alcoholic classmate, driving three hundred miles on a moment's notice to attend the funeral of a friend (Bob Adams), or giving away a classmate and bride whose family didn't attend her wedding (Jane Cowan).

They are both very busy, and I don't know how they do it.

At their fortieth anniversary, I gave a little talk and ended it by paraphrasing something from an anniversary card: "There are days when you two don't have it all together, but together, you two have it all." They still do.

Sharon is, for all intents and purposes, the class mother hen. She is the focal point for interclass communications, a primary mover in organizing our annual mini-reunions, and one of the most giving people I have ever known.

What I have learned from Sharon and Rich is that the definition of friendship is determined by how one responds to friends in need. No couple I have ever met responds to the needs of friends as do Sharon and Rich.

Charlie

Charlie is Charles Calvin Burnham, and of all my friends, he is the one I envy most. This is not only because of his accomplishments but also because I don't know anyone who goes to bed at night with a clearer conscience than he.

Charlie was one of the first ham radio operators I knew and was really into radio and audiovisual activities. He did all the audiovisual things that needed doing in high school and in some ways was the Thomas Edison of Greenport.

On one occasion, Harry Smith, another of Greenport's finest, came to Charlie's house and told him that there was a mysterious light flashing in Long Island Sound. He asked Charlie to go with him to take a look at it. As it turned out, a sailor was using a searchlight to send Morse code messages. Charlie replied to the message, telling him to shut down as he was alarming people.

Mr. and Mrs. Burnham ran the Manaton House, which was a rooming house where some of the teachers lived. The Burnhams were wonderful people, and Mrs. Burnham, who worked in the Levine's Arcade, was always very kind to mom.

After Charlie graduated, he enlisted in the navy, where he became an electrician. When his enlistment was up, he joined the naval reserves and stayed on at the Brooklyn navy yard, where he taught electronics to naval reservists.

During that time Charlie enrolled in the RCA Institutes for TV Production and Studio Operation. Prior to graduating, he was asked to teach a course on television to a group of television executives. After graduation, Charlie was hired by ABC as a video tape operator and editor. Subsequently he was nominated for several Emmies and awarded two, one for videotaping and editing the 1976 Olympics and the other for his coverage of the New York City Marathon.

Charlie is the only person I know who is the absolute best at what he did, not in his opinion but in the opinions of his professional colleagues. While Charlie was still working with ABC, he and his lovely wife, Penny, moved out to Southold. He got involved with the audiovisual department run by Don Fisher at Southold High School. Through his connections with ABC, Charlie obtained a lot of used equipment and began training students the art of filming TV programs and running a TV studio.

After Charlie retired from ABC, he began working with Don on an almost full-time basis. I have been videotaped on two occasions by Charlie's protégés, and I am in awe not only of their expertise but also of their genuine respect and admiration for him.

Charlie conducts the classes and mentors his students pro bono, and he engages his students on a personal level that is rarely attained in a classroom. His gift for teaching, knowledge of the subject matter, and devotion to his students is only surpassed by his humility.

At our most recent Class of 1957 get-together, hosted by Charlie and his lovely Katrena, Sharon Brooks, Ken Mosby, and I were singing Charlie's praises. We concluded that if there is a more innately decent person anywhere, we haven't met him or her.

Dale

Dale is Laura Goodale (Corwin) DeCastro. If there is anyone

in the class of 1957 who had a tougher row to hoe than I, it was Dale. She lost both of her parents under traumatic circumstances, and she and her younger brother, David, could be perfect models for a poster promoting kids who overcame tremendous obstacles to attain success. Dale became a well-known and respected nurse and David a veterinarian.

For as long as I have known her, Dale wanted to be a nurse, and she became a very good one, graduating from Brooklyn Hospital in 1960 and working at Eastern Long Island Hospital for forty-one years. She is a certified alcohol and addiction counselor and received her degree from Pace College in 1992. By the time she retired, she was considered an expert in her field and well-known throughout Long Island.

In 1969, Dale was widowed and left with three children aged three, five, and six. Currently, one of her sons is a detective and another an electrician, and her daughter is a registered nurse. Dale's seven grandchildren light up her life.

During her senior year in high school, Dale was dating a great guy from Sag Harbor named Pete DeCastro. They drifted apart after high school but subsequently reconnected and were married in 1992. Pete is a very successful builder, and he and Dale are living the good life. It couldn't happen to a nicer couple.

Dale and I also drifted apart during that time but reconnected at the twenty-fifth reunion, and since then we have kept in touch. The last time I saw Dale was a month ago, and she looked stunning. I will be seeing her and Pete next week at the party for John and Arthur and am looking forward to it.

Ken

Kenneth Arthur Mosby and I were in kindergarten together, and I got to know his mother before I got to know him. One day, when I was in kindergarten, she saw me struggling to get my galoshes and put them on for me. On other occasions, she would see that my shoes were untied or that my shirt wasn't tucked in and make the necessary adjustments, and I came to like her very much.

When we started first grade, Ken went into the B class and I into the A class. Even so, Ken was a presence; big, athletic, articulate, and very well-mannered. All the kids and teachers liked him. In my opinion, Ken was second only to Dick Breese in terms of athletic ability and potential. He had speed, legs like fire hydrants, upper body strength, and smarts. Ken played all sports prior to high school, and in high school he focused on basketball.

After graduation, Ken enlisted in the air force, where he served on a K-135 tanker. Upon his discharge, Ken embarked on a career with the New York Police Department, where he was promoted to detective. As a detective, Ken investigated more than five hundred homicides and was ultimately recruited by NYPD's elite Intelligence Division.

Ken is a great storyteller, and one of his favorites is of his summer Sundays as a youth, when he would buy newspapers at Ging's store and sell them to the "ladies of the night" at the two local brothels. Ken told me that seeing many of the scantily clad women as he sold papers was an unexpected benefit of the job.

During my most recent contact with Ken, he told me that his most poignant Greenport experience took place on our class trip to Washington. On that occasion, Dudley "Mr. D." Vail and Fred Randle took Ken out to dinner because, as a black, he couldn't go on the Potomac cruise.

Ken was denied admittance to the restaurant, but Fred and Dudley said, "If he doesn't eat, we don't." The restaurant still wouldn't serve them, so they went to the Howard Theater, Washington's version of Harlem's Apollo Theater.

One of my most poignant memories of Ken is of a call he made to me on 9/11. Ken's office was in the line of sight of the Twin Towers, and he called to tell me that he could see people jumping out of the buildings. Ken was almost in a panic mode, and that conversation, in addition to the fact that I knew the copilot of the plane that flew into the Pentagon, are my two most vivid memories of the day.

Since retiring, Ken has done a lot of security work for private concerns and is pretty much an expert in his field. He works with Habitat for Humanity helping build houses, and it is tough to keep in touch with him, but when you need him, he is there.

When Lee passed away, Ken and Jonathan Sperling were the only two of my Greenport friends who were there. This is in no way meant to be a criticism of those who didn't come, just a statement of fact. Jonathan drove ten miles and Ken more than four hundred. I have never forgotten that gesture. Ken is also a bit of an enigma, in that some of us in the class of 1957 (Sharon, Dick Breese, Dale, and I) have trouble getting in touch with him until we need him.

The Twins

John and Arthur Tasker were the only twins in the school, and one rarely heard the name of one without hearing the name of the other. From day one in school, Arthur was the brightest kid in the class, and if he hadn't been such a nice guy, he could have been a real pain in the butt. John was certainly no academic slouch, but passing Arthur, academically, was not in the cards, although he did score higher on the intermediate algebra Regents exam than Arthur.

Both were really good kids and always very kind to me. I never envied them, but I admired the way they dressed and comported themselves.

My first outside of school contact with John or Arthur occurred when we were in the third grade and John saw me going into the library, which was directly across the street from their house. John invited me to come over and play, and I did.

Arthur joined us, and we were playing when something happened that I can't really recall, but I think it was an argument with Arthur. Without warning, John came up behind me and socked me in the left eye as hard as he could. Arthur was as surprised as I was, and I can't remember anything coming of that incident, but I do remember that I never went back to play with them again.

Judge and Mrs. Tasker, their parents, were good people, and in talking with Judge Tasker, it was pretty apparent from whence came their smarts. Judge Tasker was one very sharp man as well as being a very nice guy.

In high school, John was the best dancer in the class as well as the best-dressed, and I saw him as my arbiter of the social graces. He and Arthur were charter members of the Porch Gang, and I had many great conversations with both of them.

During our senior trip to Washington, John and Arthur took JoAnne Sturm and Diane to the Shoreham Hotel, where Dick Contino, a famous accordion player and, coincidentally, a draft dodger, was playing, and I thought that date was the epitome of cool. Since coming to the Washington DC area, I have attended a few functions at the Shoreham, and on those occasions I recall that event.

After graduation, my contacts with John and Arthur diminished considerably. I do remember when they came home from Cornell (Arthur) and Brown (John) in the summer of 1958. Both were wearing low-cut Converse sneakers with the little red, white, and blue tab in the back. Soon, most of the kids were wearing them. They were trendsetters.

When I got out of the army in 1967 and was home before going to Michigan State, I was going to the library when I saw John trimming the hedge in front of their house. I went over to talk with him. We had a good conversation, and that was the last time I saw John until the Class of 1957's fiftieth reunion.

John had taken Dale Corwin to the Blarney Ball that our class put on when we were freshmen. At the reunion, he brought her a replica of the corsage he had given her that night in March of 1954 and, in so doing, stole the show.

In April of 1971, I took Lee out to Greenport just before we left for Vietnam. While walking down Main Street, we ran into Mrs. Tasker. She was most gracious and also enthralled with Lee. We had a very nice visit, and I was glad to have run into her.

I reconnected with Arthur at the 1982 class reunion and have been in contact with him, and his lovely Lucia, ever since. Both have been very helpful with my books, and I enjoy their company very much.

On October 29, 2014, Young and I went up to Greenport to help John and Arthur celebrate their seventy-fifth birthday. The party was held in a local restaurant, NOAH. It was a huge success..

Don.

Compared with the other friends I have profiled in this chapter, Don Macomber is the one with whom I had the least contact. However, after I reconnected with him at our forty-fifth reunion, I found him to be a wonderful example of a self-made man, with a story worth telling.

Don was in the B group until high school, and we didn't take many of the same classes in high school. Don was not athletic, and we didn't have that interest to share. My impression was that Don never rejected the other kids, but neither did he seek any of us out; he was just someone who didn't want to let us in on who he was.

What I found most unusual about Don is that I don't remember him hanging around with anyone in the class or having a best friend. If someone had asked me, "Who was Don's best friend? I would have answered, "I don't know." However, if I were asked, "Who are his enemies?" I would answer, "I am pretty sure he doesn't have any." Don was always respectful to teachers and friendly when approached by the other kids, but he just didn't seem to want to take our approaches to the next level.

In our high school days, Don was always working. I can't remember a time when he didn't have some kind of a job. He was the doorman and usher in the local movie house, sacked and loaded potatoes, stocked groceries, delivered propane gas tanks, and cleaned up the drive-in after the movies. If Don had applied the energy in the classroom that he applied to his outside jobs, he would have been one of the best students in the class, and in the class of 1957, that would have been an accomplishment.

In recalling Don, I remember how articulate he was and that I never heard him cuss. He also impressed me as being very self-contained without being antisocial.

Academics were not Don's forte. He would say, "I was in the top 40 in the class," not mentioning that there were 46 the class. The draft was in effect when he graduated in 1957, and Don, not seeing himself as the "dog face soldier type," enlisted in the air force.

With the exception of basic training at Lackland Air Force Base in San Antonio, Texas, Don spent his entire enlistment at Loring Air Force Base in Northern Maine. After completing his enlistment, Don moved to Boston to pursue fame and fortune.

Don's quest for fame and fortune began, when he picked up a discarded newspaper and read a help wanted ad sponsored by the National Cash Register seeking those with mechanical aptitude for an apprentice program. Don was accepted for the program, which ultimately led to his being selected for computer training.

The use of computers in the business arena was just catching on at this time, and Don got in on the ground floor. As a computer field engineer, Don did the repair and maintenance on the computers at the Federal Reserve Bank in Boston.

In 1964, Don took a job with Honeywell and transitioned from hardware engineering to software engineering. In the following years, he worked for Digital Equipment Corporation in New England and, after moving to Florida, for Gould Computers and Modular Computers.

While working for Honeywell in 1969, he met and married his lovely Mary. After Mary got her law degree, they moved to Kittery, Maine, where she opened a family law practice and Don began working for Digital Equipment Corporation. In 1970, their son Keith was born, and in 1971 their daughter Fran was born. By 1981, they had tired of Maine winters and decided to move to Florida, where they both worked at Gould Computer Systems, Don as a diagnostic engineer and Mary as a contracts officer.

In 1995, Don fulfilled what he told me had been a lifelong dream by getting a degree in communications from Florida Atlantic University. With a college degree, Don was now qualified to apply for jobs that paid a third of what he was making as a computer engineer. Rather than work for someone else, Don and his daughter Fran, who had a degree in gerontology, bought a Home Instead Care franchise while Mary stayed at Gould (which became Encore Computer) as their corporate attorney. Home Care Instead provided caregivers to senior citizens who wanted to stay in their own homes. Don and Fran sold the franchise in 2002, and Don officially retired, as did Mary from Encore.

After we reconnected, Don and Mary were in the DC area, and we got together for dinner. We had a great time, and Don mentioned that his hobby was collecting books about US presidents. Don has become a voracious reader, and his current collection is of first editions, of which he has over six hundred. This was just one of the many aspects of the "new" Don Macomber that I found so interesting.

A very big part of Don's and Mary's life in retirement is travel. They have traveled to China, Europe, Australia, and New Zealand as well as much of the United States and have twelve trips scheduled for this year.

Neither Don nor I were great achievers back in Greenport. In discussing our youth, I have found that we both share a lot of love for Greenport as well as the experience of turning our lives around after leaving Greenport, albeit with one major difference,. Don did it on his own, while I had a lot of help. In attaining success, Don has earned my utmost respect and admiration as well as a friendship that I wish we had back in high school.

Chapter 9

SCHOOL

Greenport Grade and High School (GG&HS) was built during the Depression, as one of Roosevelt's Works Progress Administration projects. From my first day of school in September 1944 until I graduated in June 1957, I attended school in the same building. This was my home away from home, and a very good home it was. The teachers were good as well as kind, the classrooms were warm, and many of the friendships I made there are still going strong.

Although I didn't realize it at the time, being a member of the class of 1957 made me a part of something very special. That class graduated with a record of unsurpassed academic accomplishment and set standards of excellence for all who followed. My experiences in each class and with each teacher affected me in different ways: some good and some bad, but all memorable.

Miss Loper, Kindergarten

Corporal punishment was alive and well when I started kindergarten, and I experienced it firsthand from the hand of Miss Loper, the kindergarten teacher. On my very first day of school, when Mom left me at the classroom door, I didn't want to stay. When I started to run after her, Miss Loper yelled at me to sit down. When I didn't comply quickly enough, she grabbed me, hit me on the left arm, and sat me down.

The most difficult aspect of kindergarten was that I was only in school for half a day and was home by noon. Mrs. Heaney wasn't taking care of us anymore, Mom was at work, and the house was empty. "Latchkey kid" was an unknown term at that time, and even though our door was never locked, I was a de facto latchkey kid—and a very lonely one.

With the money I had left over after buying my breakfast candy bar, I would stop at Santacroce's store on the way home and buy a candy bar or a Mrs. Wagner's apple pie and bottle of soda. That was lunch.

One day, Chris Montgomery, who lived near me, took me home with him. On the way, we walked along the railroad tracks that ran by his house. I tripped and hit my forehead, just over my left eye. Blood gushed out, my face was covered with blood, and I started to cry. Chris also started crying.

I didn't know what to do, so I ran to Mrs. Heaney. Mrs. Heaney didn't get excited at all. She cleaned the blood off my face and hands, gave me a cloth to hold over the gash in my eyebrow, and took me to Dr. Kaplan's office, which was across the street.

Most of my post-kindergarten afternoons were much less eventful. I didn't have any friends with whom I could go and play, and there wasn't anything in our apartment to keep me busy or entertained. Some days, I would wander around town, but when it rained, I just stayed in the house waiting for Bill to come home from school.

A poignant recollection from those days was an afternoon when I just sat in front of the house, going through magazines that had been left out for a paper drive. I remember looking at the *LIFE* magazines and the war pictures, which I liked. When the sun went behind the clouds, I cried, and I stopped crying when it reappeared. I can't recall anything bad ever happening to me during that time, but it was a very lonely time and not one of which I have fond memories.

There were two teachers for each of the grades, an A class and a B class. In what turned out to be a very fortuitous event for me, I was assigned to the A class.

Miss Agnes Schaumburg, First Grade

On my first day in first Grade, I went to school with Bill. He had been in Miss Schaumburg's class when he failed first grade and would now have Miss Sawyer as his teacher in 1B.

When we got to school, Bill went into Miss Sawyer's classroom. I followed him and was a little upset when Miss Sawyer made me go to Miss Schaumburg's room. This turned out to be another of the more fortuitous events in my scholastic career. The smartest kids in first grade were in 1A. Arthur Tasker was the smartest kid in every grade, with Diane Woodward a close second. Arthur's brother, John, Jonathan Sperling, Bill Lieblein (after second grade), Benita Pouvolauskas, Don Hunton, and Holten Brandi were the academic elite of the class, and by osmosis they provided me with the first academic inspiration I ever had. They were good kids who set a good example, and I couldn't help wanting to be more like them.

Miss Schaumburg was very strict and would frequently threaten to send us back to kindergarten if we didn't behave. Mom and she were church friends, and Mom liked her very much. I had mixed feelings about her, more positive than negative, but we did get along.

I don't know how it came about, but I got in an argument with Miss Schaumburg on one occasion. She corrected my pronunciation, and I said, "That's the way my mother told me to say it, and she is a really good reader" (which Mom was). Miss Schaumburg laughed and said, "John, not as good as I am." I had to say, "Oh yes she is," and Miss Schaumburg just let it go.

Miss Schaumburg started us on the *Dick and Jane* books and

was a fine reading teacher. Reading was what I did best, and I owe her (as well as Mrs. Heaney) so much for teaching me to read.

Sharon Lellman and Dale Corwin were the two stars of the B class as well as two of the cutest girls in the class of 1957. I am still in touch with both of them, and I find both of them every bit as attractive today as they were back then.

I never saw myself as being poor, compared with my classmates, but I did notice differences. Number one among these was that whereas I wore the same clothes, from the skin out, every day of the week, many of my classmates wore different clothes every day. All of the kids seemed to have some kind of mark on their upper left arm, and as I found out, it was a vaccination mark. I think I was the only one in the class who didn't have one. Kids would talk about the "Tooth Fairy" and how much money they found under their pillow. When I asked Mom about this, she didn't know what I was talking about.

My personal hygiene was minimal, and if my classmates or teachers noticed, they didn't say anything. I know that Bill and I got a bath in a big iron tub once a week when the weather was warm and a lot less often when the weather was cold. Mom would heat kettles and pots of water on the top of the stove, pour it in the tub, and give us a scrubbing. Neither Bill nor I brushed our teeth until we were in sixth grade and the PTA passed out free toothbrushes and toothpaste.

There was an incident that occurred when I was in first grade that left a very positive and permanent impression on me. Mom's payday at the movie theater was Friday, and on one of those paydays, Mom told Bill and me to meet her there after work. When we got there, she had just finished and was putting on her coat. She had left her purse on a chair in front of the ladies' room. When she went to pick it up, it was gone, and with it her week's pay of twenty-one dollars.

The police took her report, and the story made the *Suffolk Times*. This was a real crisis for mom, and she was very upset.

One of the teachers heard or read about it and, although she didn't know Mom, gave her twenty dollars. If that had been the only such kindness extended to us, it would have been significant, but the sheer number of such gestures, by so many Greenporters, became the difference between just surviving and living.

By the end of first grade, I knew that I liked school. I had yet to have any kind of academic problems, liked the kids in the class very much, liked the food in the cafeteria, and especially appreciated the warmth of the classrooms. Who could ask for more?

Miss Lillian Ging, Second Grade

In second grade, the differences between me and my classmates became more subtle. The Department of Education was having the teachers pass out nutritional surveys, in an attempt to assess how well students were eating.

The questionnaires we were asked to fill out had questions about what we ate for breakfast, and for the first time, I learned that people ate things like eggs, bacon, pancakes, waffles, fresh fruit, oatmeal, and so on for breakfast. In filling out the questionnaires, I used to lie so as not to feel different than the other kids.

I never felt as if I was starving, but I was always hungry and, as a result of the very low nutritional content of what I did eat, malnourished. When I went to other kids' houses to play, I found one of the best parts of those occasions was that their parents would give me things to eat, like homemade cake, pie, and cookies, that I never got at home. In particular, I remember going home with Ben DeJesus, who would fix us cornflakes and bananas for snacks. On these occasions, it was not uncommon for the kids' mothers to comment on how skinny I was and ask what, and sometimes if, Mom was feeding me. I didn't see this as their being nosy but being genuinely concerned, and I appreciated it, but it got to a point where I would decline offers of food. I felt that acknowledging my hunger and accepting something to eat would reflect badly on Mom.

One of the long-term effects of my childhood dietary habits

is that I eat very fast. The faster I ate, the more I ate, and eating more was my main goal when I sat down to eat. In the army, during basic training, we were given seven minutes to eat lunch, and I had no problem meeting that deadline. I was 117 pounds when I enlisted in the army and 125 pounds when I finished basic training. Putting on weight during basic training is rare.

Tuesday was "bank day" in second grade, and Miss Ging would collect money from kids who wanted to deposit money in the bank. When I asked Miss Ging how much it cost to do this, she told me it didn't cost anything, and I began depositing twenty-five cents each week. I think Stanley Kaplan and I were the only two kids who did this.

My most negative memory of second grade was that I began to have trouble with arithmetic. That problem continued on into mathematics and was the major flaw in my attempts at academic success.

Miss Ging was a friend of mom's from church and I think showed some favoritism toward me. My final report card from her was straight As, and I know I didn't deserve them. That was the last time I got straight As until I was in graduate school at Michigan State.

More important than giving me As was something else Miss Ging did for us. One Sunday morning after Mass, Mrs. Ficurelli, a former landlady to whom Mom owed back rent, confronted Mom on the steps of the church. Miss Ging was nearby and heard the conversation. The next day, after school, Miss Ging gave me an envelope and said, "John, please take this to Mrs. Ficurelli." It was the back rent. Miss Ging took a very personal interest in me, and in so doing she gave me a positive perspective on teachers that negated the impact of some of the bad teachers.

Mrs. Young, Third Grade

My most humiliating experience in grade school was an incident that occurred in third grade. We had seven or eight teachers that year after our teacher, Mrs. Young, and her husband, the Lutheran minister, left Greenport.

One Friday afternoon, Mrs. Young announced that on the following Monday she was going to check our hair and scalps to make sure they were clean. As promised, she did, and when she got to me, she announced to the class, "John's hair doesn't look as though it has been washed." I was embarrassed and thought that for Mrs. Young to publicly humiliate me in that way was at best insensitive and at worst cruel and unconscionable.

Miss Sinsebaugh, Fourth Grade

Miss Sinsebaugh was the stereotypical irascible, old maid teacher and had no problem meting out corporal punishment. Many of the kids were pretty much intimidated by her, and I was actually afraid of her.

Each morning and afternoon, she would take the boys to the restroom on the other side of the building. On one of those occasions, I saw a GHS alumnus, Jimmy Fitzpatrick, who was in the army, in the hall. I knew him and said, "Hi, Jimmy." The words were no sooner out of my mouth than Miss Sinsebaugh gave me a haymaker slap in the face and said, "There's no talking in line." My eyes teared up, and I just kept walking.

As noted in my chapter on the Heaneys, I had a real problem learning long division. I think that my inability to learn long division, at least the way she taught it, colored her overall perception of me, and she saw me as one of her failures.

Long division may have been a problem for me, but I did okay in the other subjects. The history we studied was Greek mythology. I loved the stories about the Greek gods, the Trojan horse, and the battles between Athens and Sparta. It was in this class that my lifelong love of history began.

As mean and nasty as I may have seen Miss Sinsebaugh to be, she spent an inordinate amount of time after school trying to help me. I can't imagine a teacher doing that today. As much as I feared and even disliked Miss Sinsebaugh, I also had an abiding respect and admiration for her dedication.

Mrs. Avis Norton, Music Teacher

In fourth grade, we began taking music classes. Mrs. Norton would have us sing, and it was a fun class. I didn't have a good voice, but I very much enjoyed the class.

During one of the classes, Mrs. Norton was explaining the notes of the scale and announced an after-school class during which she would teach some basics of reading music. All we would need was a harmonica.

I didn't go to the first class because I didn't have a harmonica, but I got one before the second class. When I went to the class, it had already started, and I knocked on the door. She opened the door, and I told her that I had just gotten my harmonica and would like to take the class.

"The class is full" was all she said to me before she closed the door. There was no "I'm sorry, John, you're too late," and I was crushed. The harmonica had cost only $2.50, and I talked Mom into getting it for me so that I could learn to read music. Mom was very much in favor of that, and now I was going to have to tell her that she had wasted her money.

Mrs. Mabel Tillinghast, Fifth Grade

Mrs. Tillinghast was the best teacher I had during grade school and the first teacher to ever tell me that I was smart. My best subject throughout my school years was history. This was due in a very large part to the fact that I was a voracious reader and had a very good memory.

On one occasion, I got a 100 on a twenty-question history test, and Arthur Tasker must have had a brain fart, because he got a ninety-five. Beating Arthur on any kind of test was the athletic equivalent of running a hundred yards for a touchdown with a broken leg and evoked in me a sense of academic pride that I had never before experienced.

At dismissal that day, Mrs. Tillinghast asked me to stay for a minute. She told me that she thought I was a lot smarter than I thought I was and that if I would just believe in and apply myself, I could be a very good student. That was another first for me.

Beyond the class room, Mrs. Tillinghast also extended herself. On several occasions, Mrs. Tillinghast paid Mom to clean her house, and on a few of those occasions, according to Mom, the house didn't need cleaning. This was just another example of the innate generosity that the people of Greenport extended to us.

In addition to Mrs. Tillinghast's interest in me and what she did for Mom, what I remember most about that year was that Dick Breese became one of our classmates. Dick was a member of the Breese athletic dynasty and, in my opinion, the best athlete in the family. From the early 1940s when the oldest brother, Earl, starred on all of Greenport's athletic teams until Harry, the youngest boy, graduated in 1960, a Breese was the star on all of the school's athletic teams.

I am sure it was because Dick was in our class that Dorrie Jackson, the football and baseball coach, began taking the boys in our class out for PT. Whenever we would choose up sides for softball, Dick would pick me to be on his team, as he knew he could more than make up for my shortcomings. When Dick came over to The Lot to play in our pickup games, we would make him hit left-handed. It didn't make much difference, as he could hit the ball out of the lot from either side of the plate.

In high school, we were on the same football, basketball, baseball, and track teams, and Dick was not only the best player on each of those teams but also the best all-around athlete with whom I have ever been associated.

I knew all the Breese brothers, and I played on the same football teams with Tom, Dick, and Harry, the youngest boy in the family. Playing on the same teams as Tom, Dick, and Harry Breese had a ring to it and was one of my more pleasant memories.

While I was assigned to Ft. Holabird, Maryland, I ran into

Earl, the oldest of the Breese brothers, who was a Master Sergeant in the Military Intelligence Corps. We reminisced, and when I see him now, we talk about mutual MI acquaintances.

All of the boys, Earl, Curtis, John, Tom, Dick, and Harry, were first-class gentlemen, and I never heard any of them utter a word of profanity, flaunt their talent, or belittle those less gifted than they. I am still in regular touch with Dick, and he is the banana on my Cheerios.

One of the academic insights I took away from fifth grade was that I respond better to positive reinforcement than negative criticism. When Miss Sinsebaugh was screaming at me in fourth grade while trying to teach me long division, I assumed that this was the way all teachers reacted to slow students. Mrs. Tillinghast showed me a new and better way, which I have applied to my own teaching.

Mr. Carl Calvin, Sixth Grade

Mr. Calvin, my sixth-grade teacher, was my first experience with a male teacher, and I liked it. He was from Maine, had a very distinct Maniac accent, was an ardent Boston Braves fan, and loved to talk baseball.

The one incident I remember from that year came about as a result of my obsession with reading. The desks we had at that time had tops that we had to lift to get our books or whatever else was stored therein.

One day, Mr. Calvin told us to take out our geography books. I lifted the desk top and was about to grab my geography book when I saw, and started reading, a paperback book about baseball's very first All-Star game. I became engrossed and didn't tune in to the geography class until Mr. Calvin slammed the desk top down on my head. I was a bit stunned and spent the rest of the day with a headache.

He got my attention but was lucky that he didn't hurt me worse than he did. He also confiscated the book, and I had to plead with him to get it back because I had borrowed it from Jim Heaney.

For some reason or other, I didn't have any problem with arithmetic that year, which made sixth grade a better year than most, and by the end of the year, I was looking forward to junior high school.

"Nice kid, mediocre student, doesn't try very hard, but has potential to improve" is how I would have described myself as I entered seventh grade. The class academic hierarchy had been established, and I was not among the leaders. If I were going to be among them, I would have to, as Jonathan Sperling said, "start to get serious about school."

During the summer prior to entering seventh grade, I had worked almost every night in the bowling alley. In the fall there would be league bowling Mondays through Thursdays, and a couple of Sundays every month, there would be matches with teams from Riverhead, the county seat. I would be working at least five of those nights, and getting serious about school was a challenge that would be difficult to meet.

It would be easy to say that work kept me from being a good student, but in my heart, at least at that time, I knew this wasn't true. Lack of motivation was the problem. The money I was making was more important than getting good grades. Until that mindset changed, my grades wouldn't, and unfortunately, that was okay with me. I knew my grades would never be bad enough to keep from getting promoted to the next grade.

Mr. Fred Gibbs

Mr. Fred Gibbs was our homeroom teacher as well as the history teacher. He had been around for a very long time, and his lesson plans were yellow with age, but he imparted more factual information than any teacher, including my college professors, I ever had. His course prepared me very well for the New York State history course I took in college, in which I did well.

Most of Mr. Gibbs's classes started with an empty blackboard, and by the time the class ended, it was filled with trivia. I remember one class when we were talking about the settling of the West. Mr. Gibbs noted that the Winchester '73 played a significant role in that part of American history and asked, "What was so special about the Winchester '73?"

No one answered until I said, "There were only a thousand of them made, and each was numbered." I had learned that from a Jimmy Stewart movie, and Mr. Gibbs wrote "One in a thousand" on the board. I am a "fact" kind of person, and I just soaked up the information Mr. Gibbs passed on.

Mr. Gibbs was a disciplinarian, and I remember one occasion when one of the boys in the class, George Vallely, mouthed off to him. Mr. Gibbs walked slowly down the aisle, without saying a word, and almost knocked George out of his seat with a slap.

During the Christmas vacation of my freshman year in college, I ran into a member of the Board of Education. After exchanging pleasantries, he said, "John, we finally got rid of Fred Gibbs." I was very disappointed.

Ms. Vera Ketcham

Ms. Vera Ketcham was our seventh-grade mathematics and English teacher, and she was very good at both. Just as I had done to Ms. Sinsebaugh in fourth grade, I drove Ms. Ketcham to distraction as she tried to teach me arithmetic. Rarely did a week pass when I didn't have to stay after school at least two times to do the homework I hadn't turned in or get help with arithmetic. Ms. Ketcham was much more patient than Ms. Sinsebaugh had been and managed to help me get a C+ in arithmetic, which for me was pretty good.

I have to say that in Mrs. Ketcham's English class, I shined. I liked grammar and reading, and as a result of Mrs. Heaney's teaching me how to do crossword puzzles, I had a good vocabulary. I think I actually impressed Ms. Ketcham, and that was a very positive experience for me.

Mr. Henry Thorne

Henry Thorne was our science teacher, and I disliked him more than any teacher I ever had. Mom knew him from her days as a chambermaid at the Wyandanch, where he lived, and raved about him, but I never saw anything positive about him. I remember him telling the class that he wished we were all robots. When I asked him, "Then why do you teach?" his answer was, "Because I can." I really didn't think he could. The fact that I got the lowest grade I ever received in school (49) in his class may have influenced my opinion.

One of the legendary stories about Mr. Thorne was that on one occasion, he confronted Roy Tuthill. Roy was the older brother of Reg Tuthill, one of my high school heroes, and a good friend. During that confrontation, Roy picked up Mr. Thorne and dumped him headfirst into the wastebasket.

When I asked Reg to confirm or refute this story, he told me that it was true. Roy had been expelled from school as well as offered the choice of going in the military or reform school. Roy went into the air force.

I knew Roy after he got out of the air force and found him to be a very nice and easy-going guy. It occurred to me that to have done what he did to Mr. Thorne, Roy would have to have been seriously provoked. And knowing Mr. Thorne, I am sure that he was.

In 1955, Mr. Thorne left GHS, and the rumor was that he had made a pass at one of his female students. Four years later, I was in summer school at Albany State and having lunch with a high school teacher with whom I was taking a class. Suddenly, Mr. Thorne was standing in front of me and effusively greeting me. "John, how are you? What are you doing here?"

He also greeted my lunch companion, Maurice Goyette, who was the librarian in the same school where Mr. Thorne was teaching. Mr. Thorne was clearly uneasy during our conversation, and I am pretty sure he was concerned about me blowing the whistle on him. I didn't.

When I was doing interviews for this book, I spoke with Sandra "Sandy" Appelt, a classmate and one of Diane Woodward's best friends. She was a very cute little girl and a bit impish. We shared a disdain for Mr. Thorne, and in discussing him, Sandy said, "One day, Mr. Thorne told me I would have to stay after school the next day but didn't tell me why. When I told my mother, she said, 'You tell Mr. Thorne that I will be coming to school to pick you up.' When I told Mr. Thorne that my mom was going to pick me up, he told me I wouldn't have to stay after school."

Sandy went on to say that among the mothers, there were rumors about Mr. Thorne being a real creep. The negative impression I had of Mr. Thorne was something I took with me when I became a teacher, and I used it as a reminder of what not to do.

Of the many events that took place while I was in seventh grade, the one I remember most is one in which I didn't participate. In 1951, just after school started, the PTA sponsored a ballroom dancing class. The class would take place on Monday nights, and because I worked then, I couldn't take the class. For more than sixty years, I have regretted not taking that class. One of the long-term effects of my not taking dancing lessons was to make sure that both of my sons did, and I am encouraging both of my grandchildren to do the same.

Mrs. Maureen Van Popering

Eighth grade was pretty much the same as seventh grade, with one major exception. Mrs. Maureen Connolly Van Popering, or Mrs. Van, was our eighth-grade English teacher, and she was an excellent teacher. She influenced me more than any other teacher I ever had in GG&HS or college.

Mrs. Van was big on reading, and one of her mantras was, "Good readers are good writers, good speakers, and good students." She was very strict, and the word on her among the junior high kids was that Mrs. Van was not one with whom you screwed around.

Once Mrs. Van was walking up a flight of stairs, and one of

two boys standing in front of a window across from the stairs whistled at her. Mrs. Van turned around, walked down the stairs, and slapped the boy she thought had whistled at her in the face, breaking his glasses. In a conversation I had with Mrs. Van a few years ago, she told me that she had been afraid she might lose her job over this, but apparently neither the boy nor his mother ever complained.

Occasionally, Mrs. Van would read to us, and she read beautifully. One of the stories she read to us was Daphne DuMaurier's "The Birds," and I was captivated. Afterward, I talked to her about the story, and my interest seemed to strike a chord with her. Shortly thereafter, she suggested that I read Nicholas Monserrat's *The Cruel Sea,* which turned out to be one of my all-time favorite books. That conversation marked the beginning of a change in our relationship from the teacher-student to mentor-student, and I could not have had a better mentor.

One of the questions I have always had about my education was, "How did I come to be signed up for the college prep courses in high school?" I know I never was given a choice as to which courses I wanted to take and was pleasantly surprised when I saw that I would be taking Latin but a bit anxious about taking algebra.

In interviews with former classmates, I asked them how they ended up taking college prep classes, and they told me, "they were just assigned to us." As it turned out, that wasn't the way it was for me. Recently, I contacted Mrs. Van to ask her for a photograph that I could use in the book. In the course of our conversation, I asked Mrs. Van how it came to pass that I took college prep courses.

She told me that in the spring of 1953, Mrs. Diller came to her to discuss the classes rising eighth graders should take. When she came to my name, Mrs. Diller told Mrs. Van, "He has no money, won't be going to college, and won't do well in college prep courses."

According to Mrs. Van, she told Mrs. Diller, "John isn't his brother, Bill. He is a bright and very good kid who deserves a break." Ultimately, Mrs. Van prevailed, and Mrs. Diller very reluctantly signed me up for the college prep courses. Mrs. Van was not only a great advocate but also very prescient and apparently saw something in me that no one else saw. In retrospect, that was one of the most significant factors in my educational development, and it was one in which I had no input.

Eighth-grade English was the only course I ever took with Mrs. Van as a teacher, but she became our ninth- and tenth-grade homeroom teacher, and in that capacity, her maternal interest continued. On the first day of school, she noticed my football shoes behind my desk, picked them up, and said, "What are these for?"

When I said, "I'm playing football," she said, "You won't be if your grades slip."

When I wanted to drop algebra, she talked me out of it. On another occasion, she feigned horror and said, "John, how can you see with those glasses? Give them to me!" Seeing through them was difficult, as they were coated with dandruff and dust and complemented my ragamuffin appearance.

Mrs. Van's very personal interest in me continued after she stopped teaching. As much support and encouragement as Mrs. Van gave while she was teaching, she went above and beyond after her teaching days were over. One of Mrs. Van's best friends was Terry Lindsay, the secretary and administrative assistant to Norman Klipp, the town supervisor. Mr. Klipp had to authorize all welfare payments to all Greenport's welfare recipients, and because I was eighteen and out of high school, Mom's welfare check was in jeopardy.

I don't know exactly what transpired between Mrs. Van and Terry, but I know for certain that Terry made sure Mom continued to get her check while I was in college. Had she not done that, I would have joined the military or gotten a job to support her. Mrs. Van looked long and hard to find something in me that she felt was worth saving, and when she found it, she made sure I made the most of whatever talents or gifts I had.

I had no knowledge of the Mrs. Van/Terry Lindsay save John Sullivan alliance at the time it was occurring and only learned of it about several years ago. I had called an old friend, Larry Tuthill, who was a good friend of Mrs. Van's, and he mentioned it to me. I don't know what I would have done had I known, but I have a sense that I would not have gone to college, at least not at that point in my life.

Just before school started in 1953, I had quit working at Santacroce's bowling alley so that I could play football. When I told Mike that I was quitting, he was not pleased and scoffed at the idea. I hadn't asked Mom if I could quit working in the bowling alley, and. although I knew she wouldn't try to change my mind, she wouldn't be happy about it. I wasn't making a lot of money, but I would play the punch board and win cigarettes that I would bring home to her. Mom would miss the cigarettes more than the money.

There was another aspect to my not working. Up until then, I could, but didn't, attribute my less-than-stellar academic performance to the fact that I was working nights and couldn't study. Without that excuse, the only conclusion to which I could come was that I wasn't a good student, and I had to take most of the responsibility for any lack of academic achievement. However, there were other factors.

One of those factors was that our house was not a good venue for studying or doing homework. The kitchen was the only place where I could study. However, there was a dim light over the kitchen table that would keep Mom awake if I worked there. Also, it was often very cold in the kitchen, and the chair I sat in was very uncomfortable. I know Abe Lincoln studied by candlelight and managed to do well, but I just wasn't as hearty a soul as Abe.

As dreary as our kitchen was, there was one very good memory that I associate with that kitchen. On many occasions, I would come home late after working in the bowling alley or attending a school function. Mom would be asleep, as would Bill, upstairs, and I would sit at the kitchen table, eating toast, as I read. Since Lee passed away, I find myself repeating that particular experience, but in a much more comfortable kitchen.

Having signed up for the college prep courses, I was taking algebra and Latin as well as English, history, science, and art. I did well in history and English, not bad in Latin and art, and less well in science, but I did fail algebra. I actually studied, but just couldn't get algebra, or any of the other math courses I would take. That failing, in conjunction with a lack of motivation, were the difference between being a mediocre and good student.

In high school, I was exposed to a greater variety of teachers than I had been in elementary school, most of whom were very good. All of my teachers had an impact on me, but because I was older when I underwent my high school experiences, I think they had a more lasting effect on me. High school was a very defining experience for me, and I still look back on those days with overwhelmingly fond memories. Here are the high school teachers who helped create those memories.

Dorrie Jackson

Coach Jackson, or CJ, was not a teacher in the pure sense of the word, but he was the member of the GHS faculty with whom I spent the most time. For three hours a day, five days a week, and twenty-nine games over four football seasons, CJ was a significant presence in my life. He may not have influenced me in the way Mrs. Van did, but I know I learned more about life from him than I did from any other member of the GHS faculty.

The first time I met CJ was when Jack Heaney took me to one of his football practices in September of 1950. Greenport had won the championship in 1949, and Jack was back to play as a post-graduate (PG). CJ was the assistant coach to John Ryder, and they were a great coaching team.

On that occasion, I was out on the field, waiting for the players to come out of the locker room, when CJ noticed me. He came over to me and said, "Hey, little guy. What's your name? Do you have a brother on the team?" I told him my name and said that Jack Heaney's mother took care of me and that Jack had brought me to practice. CJ then asked me if I wanted to have a catch with him. I said yes. That was the first time I had ever had a catch with a football, or really been exposed to the game, and I loved it. During the course of that season, I attended a lot of practices. When CJ had the time, he would throw the ball around with me, and I came to like him very much.

I started fifth grade that year, and as I have previously stated, CJ began taking the boys in the fifth grade out for a gym class. We played touch football, softball, and basketball. Those classes were my first exposure to playing sports. Prior to those classes, I had never so much as had a catch with anyone. CJ continued to take us out for gym classes through sixth grade, and in junior high, physical education was an integral part of our curriculum.

In junior high, CJ and Mrs. Donohue, the girls' gym teacher, would monitor our study halls, and I got to know CJ better. He would often read us stories about athletic heroes such as Jim Thorpe and Babe Ruth, discuss GHS's football and baseball teams, and encourage some of the kids to go out for the teams. He never suggested that I go out for the team.

During one of those study halls, Jimmy LaBad passed me a salacious magazine featuring pictures of bare breasted women. CJ saw the transaction and said, "John, what have you got there? Bring it here." He confiscated the magazine, without comment, and never returned it. Jimmy got pretty mad at me and punctuated his displeasure by pounding on me.

After lunch, when the weather was bad, kids would go to the gym to wait for the afternoon classes to begin. CJ and Mrs.

Donohue would be the monitors, and what I remember most about those times was that they would sit in the top row of the bleachers watching the kids and arguing vehemently. I never knew exactly what their arguments were about, but the angrier Mrs. Donohue got, the more CJ smiled, and he just seemed to be having a lot of fun.

It was during these lunch hours that I became aware of just how competitive CJ was. He would challenge anyone who wanted to test him to a free-throw shooting contest, with a candy bar or ice cream bar as the prize. Whoever made the most baskets out of five free throws won. I never saw CJ lose. CJ would balance four quarters on the back of his hand, jerk his hand back, and catch the quarters, one by one, before any of them hit the ground. No one could compete with him.

The only sports I ever saw CJ play were softball and basketball. There was a very good local softball team in Greenport, and CJ played shortstop on the team. He was an awesome hitter, and I saw him hit one of the longest home runs I have ever seen in a softball game. In a tournament game against a semi-pro team, CJ's leadoff, bunt single was the only hit the team got.

When I was a senior, I organized a basketball team to challenge the GHS faculty. When I broached the idea to CJ, he said, "We'll play, but with one stipulation: You can't press us, and you have to use a zone defense." He, and the faculty, ran us off the floor.

On occasions, CJ would pick up Harry Bubb and me when we were hitchhiking to Southold Town Beach. On one of those occasions, Dorrie Jr. (DJ) was in the car, and CJ was telling him how one of the professional quarterbacks would practice taking snaps from the center until his hand bled. "That's what it takes, if you want to be good," he told DJ. DJ's answer: "Football is his life, but it sure isn't mine." CJ was not pleased.

When I moved to Reston in 1975, I ran into DJ, who was the manager of a Long and Foster Real Estate company. He recognized me but didn't remember my name. The last time I spoke with DJ was in November 1978. I had read in the *Suffolk Times* that CJ would be coaching his last game on November 4, and I wanted to get his phone number so that I could call to congratulate him. I got the number and did call. Mrs. Jackson answered the phone and put CJ on. He was gracious and cordial as well as very grateful for my call. I also attended CJ's retirement party, and I don't remember DJ being there.

Once I began playing football for CJ, I began to understand what a really good coach he was. One of his greatest talents was his ability to relate to the players. Each player was different, and CJ treated him as such. I had seen CJ "go off" on players, but I think this was more for show than anything else. He intuitively knew which buttons to push to get the most out of each player. In none of the diatribes did he ever use profanity, and when I hear today's high school coaches profanely berate their players, I long for those halcyon days of yore.

There were players to whom he never had to say a word, and they would give one hundred percent on every play. Henry Myslborski and John Montgomery were two of these guys. If whatever tactic CJ used didn't work and the player didn't give a maximum effort, that player didn't play.

During lunch hours, weather permitting, CJ would "hold court" at the rear of the school, in front of the tennis courts. CJ was a master storyteller, and he would discuss hunting, cars, whatever sports headlines were in the papers, and the sport of the season. I remember him telling Henry Myslborski that hunting with a shotgun wasn't much of a challenge and that he would rather hunt ducks or rabbits with a .22-caliber rifle.

On another occasion, CJ told Fred Gagen, one of our super subs, "Fred, if you can run four laps around the track (one mile), in less than ten minutes, I will start you in the next game." Everyone laughed, but I said to CJ, "Coach, I'll run twenty laps if you'll start me." CJ said, "John, a liability on the field is an ass set on the bench, and you are one of the team's greatest assets."

One of the things I did to curry favor with CJ was to pose questions about baseball to him. I had a book called *Knotty Baseball Problems*, and I would give CJ a new problem every day, none of which he could solve. He finally bought the book from me.

CJ showered with the team, kidded with us, and, away from the football field, was a fun guy to be around. When he would see me in the shower, without fail, he would always ask me when I was going to put some flesh on my bones. CJ, as good a coach as he was, was at his best when he was interacting on a personal level with his players.

The strongest profanity I ever heard CJ use was "Gosh darn it!" On one occasion when I was manager of the baseball team, we were playing Southold on a very cold spring day. Tom Breese was pitching a shutout, and all was going well.

At one point, Tom was on second base, and CJ gave the steal signal, that being both hands in his jacket pockets. Tom couldn't believe that CJ was having his pitcher try to steal, but he followed the signal and stole third.

At the end of the inning, CJ went off a bit on Tom. "Gosh darn it, Tom, why did you steal?" he asked in a very accusatory tone.

"Coach, you gave the steal signal" was Tom's answer.

CJ paused and said, "My hands were cold."

CJ coached clean and honest games, with no dirty playing or even bending of the rules. He didn't run up the scores, as evidenced by his putting me in a game. Except for Dick Morrissey, Herb Goldsmith's predecessor at South Hampton, CJ had a great relationship with all the opposing coaches as well as some of the opposing players, for whom he wrote college letters of recommendation.

One of the things that CJ did as a coach that puzzled me

was play Harry Bubb ahead of Phil Proferes at first base. Phil was taller by about four inches and was a left-handed hitter and fielder, as were most first basemen. From what I saw, Phil was also a much better hitter than Harry. As competitive as CJ was, this didn't make sense to me, until I factored in CJ's dislike of Phil's father, Tommy. Mr. Proferes was a rabid baseball fan, and his son George was a terrific pitcher. George played football one year, and I remember being at a practice that year when Stan Skrezec put a very hard, but clean tackle on George. Mr. Proferes started yelling at Stan, accusing him of playing dirty, and CJ got very angry. From that point on, CJ never had much to say to Mr. Proferes or Mr. Proferes to him. I am convinced that is why Harry played ahead of Phil, and I was a little disappointed in CJ.

CJ also had an incredible grandmother. Every time a player screwed up, CJ would tell any and all who would listen that his grandmother could do better.

If you were a friend of CJ's and had a weakness to exploit, you were also vulnerable to one of CJ's practical jokes. One of my jobs as manager of the basketball team was to call in the results and box scores of each game to *Newsday*. Halfway through the season, CJ asked me if I was getting my check. He told me that I was supposed to get five dollars for each game I called in. I knew he was kidding and never checked it out with *Newsday*, but I didn't think that this was one of his better jokes.

CJ was a bit of a micromanager, and Tom Breese told me that when Jimmy Atwell was our quarterback, CJ called most of the plays. Herb Goldsmith, the South Hampton coach, used to call Jimmy Atwell "Dorrie Atwell." Dick Breese also told me that when he was the quarterback, "CJ liked to control the game and called most of the plays. At the high school level, that wasn't all that common, and I think CJ was a pioneer in doing this."

I remember getting in a discussion with CJ about this in a study hall. His rationale for calling the plays was that it would take a lot of the pressure off the quarterback. He also mentioned that he had a better view of the whole field than the quarterback, which put him in a better position to call the plays. CJ's coup de grâce comment was that Otto Graham, the great Cleveland Browns quarterback, had his coach, the legendary Paul Brown, call the plays.

CJ's reasoning made sense, but I felt that he made the calls because he knew that he was smarter than any high school kid, and the chances of the team winning were better if he called the plays.

One aspect of CJ's coaching about which I had some reservations was that if you played on one of his teams, you were a football player first and a student second. He would get very upset when a player had to stay after school for academic reasons. I remember one practice when one of the starters had to stay after school for some help with Latin. "Ten years from now, he won't remember one word of Latin" was CJ's comment when he found out the player would be late. He seemed to forget that only one in ten thousand kids who play high school football ever play after high school, and no one on the team would ever have to remember any of the plays we ran.

Ed Skrezec was one of the best players CJ ever coached, but that didn't prevent CJ from disciplining him. During one of our practices, CJ was explaining a variation on one of our standard plays. Ed, Cliff Utz, and Ralph Cervone weren't paying attention, and CJ went off on them. "Get out on the track, and don't come back until I blow the whistle!" he screamed.

Cliff and Ralph came back in after two or three laps. Ed never came back to that practice. He ran twenty-nine laps before practice ended. In a way, CJ had cut off his nose to spite his face. We really couldn't run the first team offensive plays without Ed, and we didn't have a good practice.

CJ's advice on smoking was, "I know some of you smoke. Just don't let me catch you, and for your own health, keep it to a minimum." At another practice, it began raining very hard, and

CJ had us go back into the locker room, get out of our uniforms, and meet in the gym, where he went over the plays and blocking assignments on the blackboard. At some point during that chalk talk, someone wasn't paying attention. CJ went into one of his tirades and ordered us back into our uniforms and onto the field. We practiced for another two hours in the pouring rain.

We didn't have any kind of dryers to dry our uniforms and had to drape them on the steam pipes in the basement in the hope that they would dry before the next practice. We practiced in damp, clammy, and smelly uniforms for the next three days.

Before CJ sent us out for our pre-practice laps around the track, we would gather around him for a pep talk. For me, this was one of the best parts of the practices. One night, during his pep talk, CJ said, "If I kick you off the team, don't consider it final until the next day. Don't turn in your uniform until I see you the next day and make it final." He never kicked anyone off any team that I was on.

Another of CJ's "things" was that if you came out for the team, you stayed until the end of the season. As he put it, "Quitting is quitting, and quitting is never good."

On a few occasions, when CJ felt as if he hadn't got his practice plan completed, he would turn on the field lights to extend our practice time.

The championship in 1953 had drawn a lot of new players to the team, and a very successful team in 1954, in conjunction with the loss of nine seniors, drew a lot more kids to the 1955 team, some of whom had never played football before. One of those who had never played before and who turned out to be a real contributor to the team was Bill Lieblein. During one of the lunch hours when CJ was holding court, he asked me, "John, what do you think about Bill Lieblein playing linebacker?"

"His strength is being a down lineman, and I don't think he is fast enough to cover ends out in the flat or backs out of the backfield" was my answer. CJ seemed to take my advice, to the team's benefit and my self-satisfaction.

On occasion CJ would let most of the varsity players leave practice early so that he could work with the newer players, and on Saturdays, before the season started, he would do the same. This was great for developing some of these new players, but more importantly, at least for me, it meant that I got to play in the back field in some of these practices. I actually scored a touchdown in one of the scrimmages, and those scrimmages were the most fun I had while on the team.

As good as he was, CJ wasn't perfect. During a scrimmage, it seemed to me that Bill Pell was really hurting. I stood up before the ball was snapped and said to CJ, "Coach, I think Bill is hurt."

CJ didn't like it and very sarcastically said, "Are you hurting? Do you feel his pain? If he's hurt, he'll tell me. Worry about yourself." CJ was definitely one of the "tough it out, play through injuries" coaches.

In the West Hampton game during my senior year, John Moore, our center, really got his bell rung. We were on defense, and John had made a bone-jarring tackle that left him dazed. He came off the field, and it was clear to me that he was out of it. When we got the ball back, John was a little reluctant to go back in, and I remember CJ goading him by saying, "Do you want to play this game? If so, get out there." John was still out of it, and I don't think CJ should have sent him back in.

Be the aforementioned as it was, CJ had a 151–48–5 record at the time he retired, and he must have been doing something right. He was the second most winning football coach in Suffolk County history and was a legend.

After leaving Greenport, I was stationed in Ft. Bliss, Texas, and ran into a soldier who had played football for CJ at Lyons High School in upstate New York. He raved about CJ.

In my travels with the agency, I would occasionally send him postcards from the countries in which I was working, and on a couple of occasions, I called him. There were two occasions, since leaving Greenport, when I met and had a talk with CJ. The first of these was after I came back from Vietnam in 1975. I was working in New York City and took a day off to go out to Greenport. I checked in at the school's front office and took the familiar walk back to his office next to the gym.

CJ was in, and the warmth of his greeting outdid any expectations I had. We talked for more than half an hour and relived some great moments. The only team picture he had on his wall was one of the 1953 team. We went over The Play in the 1953 East Hampton game as well as the play that beat us in the 1954 Northport game. We also caught up on old friends, and I can't think of many conversations I enjoyed more than that one.

His parting comment was, "John, you really seem to have done well, and you deserve every good thing that has come your way. Keep the good things coming." Although I saw CJ again at his retirement party, his parting comment after I saw him in his office is a memory I won't forget.

During the background investigation done on me in conjunction with my application for a job with the CIA, the investigator interviewed CJ, whom I had listed as one of my references. Before I retired, I read my personnel file and read CJ's comment: "Pound for pound, he was one of the toughest players I ever coached." I appreciated his kind words, but I, as well as the guys with whom I played, would have recognized this as one of CJ's bigger whoppers.

CJ retired in 1978, and Jack Skrezec sent me an invitation to the retirement party. I didn't get to spend much time with CJ, but he did acknowledge my drive from Virginia during his speech, and we did talk for a few minutes. I think Mrs. Breese, and all the Breeses who had played for CJ, were there that night. Bill Lieblein and I sat at their table, and it was a great farewell to CJ.

When I reflect on CJ's influence on me, my first thought is that his allowing me to try out for the football team was one of the best things that ever happened to me and a major part of my upbringing in the village that raised me.

Mr. William (Bill) Carruthers

Mr. Carruthers was one of the history teachers, and I remember him well, not because he was such a good teacher but because he was so different from the other teachers. During my time in GHS, there was a little ditty dedicated to Mr. Carruthers and sung to the tune of the Cornell alma mater, to wit:

To the west of Greenport Village
With its bars of steel
Is Greenport High School
Ruled by Willie the Wheel

Mr. Carruthers was a good teacher and a force with which to be reckoned. From day one, in his freshmen history class, he taught with an intensity that I had never seen in the classroom. He was all business and, at least to me, intimidating.

If I were to use an adjective to describe Mr. Carruthers, it would be "unapproachable." With almost all of my high school teachers, I could engage in small talk, but with Mr. Carruthers, it didn't seem appropriate. One of my conclusions was that he was basically a shy person and not comfortable loosening up with the students. No teacher that I know of put more energy into teaching than Mr. Carruthers, and I admired him for that. But I also felt he would have been a better teacher, and lasted longer, if he had loosened up a bit.

I don't know how much Spanish Mr. Carruthers had taken in college, but he would frequently lapse into very poor Spanish. He would pronounce Chile as "Sheeeelay" and in saying good-bye would parrot the very popular Les Paul and Mary Ford song, "Vaya Con Dios," with his own version, "Vaya Con Deeeeeos."

Mr. Carruthers walked with a very pronounced limp, which was often imitated by the students. But in what I saw as a case of overcompensation, he was also a very good dancer. I can remember one occasion when he announced that he was a better dancer than any of the dancers he saw at our school dances. I did see him dance on one occasion and would have sold my soul to dance as well as he did.

Irish Catholic that he was, Mr. Carruthers was a member of St. Agnes's parish, and I would regularly see him at Mass but never at any of the parish social events. When I introduced him to my mother, he seemed very uncomfortable, and I remember Mom saying, "John, Mr. Carruthers seems a bit sad."

He was very partial to the class of 1957, and in what I thought was a less-than-nice thing to do, he volunteered to take Mr. Bombardier's place as our class adviser. I thought Mr. Bombardier was doing a great job and didn't know why Mr. Carruthers was doing this. In any event, Mr. Bombardier had the class vote on Mr. Carruthers's offer. A vote was taken, and Mr. Carruthers's offer was soundly rejected.

There was an incident when two seniors put a spindle on Mr. Carruthers's desk chair and he sat on it. He had to get a tetanus shot, and the two boys were expelled. Two days after the incident, Mr. Carruthers was back on the job, with business as usual. One of the miscreants was, in my opinion, a good guy and ultimately became the chief of police in Riverhead, the county seat. The other miscreant beat me up in the boys' room when I was in fifth grade and was suspended from school.

If Mr. Carruthers had a social life, it wasn't in Greenport, and he didn't seem to socialize with any of the faculty. His verbal and nonverbal behaviors made him a difficult person to approach, which seemed to be the way he wanted it.

While I was in Albany, Mr. Carruthers up and left Greenport, apparently without giving notice. When I came home for the Christmas break, Mr. Bubb told me that Mr. Carruthers had stopped to get gas on the way out of Greenport and told him, "I just can't take it anymore." Mr. Bubb said that Mr. Carruthers looked totally worn out and was a little teary-eyed. He also told me that he had wanted to ask Mr. Carruthers to park his car and talk for a while but just couldn't do it.

If Mr. Bubb's interpretation of Mr. Carruthers's condition was accurate, I can only conclude that this was a very sad end to the career of a man whose biggest mistake was that, although he masked his care for his students very well, he cared too much.

I never found out what happened to Mr. Carruthers, but his twin brother, Bob, was a member of my parish in Albany. I introduced myself to him, but finding him to be as aloof and standoffish as his brother, I never tried to engage him in conversation again. The two life lessons I learned from Mr. Carruthers were that there has to be more in your life than your work and that his way of teaching may have worked for him, but the cost was very dear.

Miss Helen Kurachuk

Miss Helen Kurachuk was the math teacher, and I took algebra from her. She had a bit of a Russian or Ukrainian accent that would get more pronounced as she got impatient or excited. The only one-on-one contact I had with Miss Kurachuk was an occasion when I went to her to get some help with math. She told me it was too late for me, and it was. I failed algebra.

Like most fourteen-year-old boys, I had my Walter Mitty pipe dreams of heroic deeds, but I knew these were just that—pipe dreams. However, although I saw the idea of my becoming a doctor as unrealistic, I did think that there was a one in a million chance that this dream might come true.

I had read Morton Thompson's *Not as a Stranger* and decided that an MD/GP was what I wanted to be. I would join the military, become a medic, and take it from there. "There" was college on the GI Bill and then medical school.

Failing algebra changed all that. I had always had a problem with arithmetic, but as hard as I studied, I just couldn't get algebra. Not doing well in algebra did not bode well for me trying to pass chemistry and physics, and even if by some miracle I could have passed these courses, my grades would not have been good enough to get me into a pre-med program, let alone medical school. My dream of being another Dr. Kildare was over.

Miss Lois Walsh

Miss Walsh was the Latin and world history teacher; she was soft-spoken, petite, and kind of cute. She drove a huge Buick and could barely see over the steering wheel. I loved both of her classes. One day, after a world history class, she took me aside and said, "John, I know it is not my place, but you really should get that tooth fixed. In this world, appearance counts." I was flattered by her concern but in no position to follow her suggestion.

As mild-mannered, petite, and soft-spoken as she was, Miss Walsh had no trouble controlling her classes. She knew her course materials and how to teach, and the kids liked her too much to get out of line.

Mr. Roland G. Levy

Mr. Levy was the biology, chemistry, and physics teacher and also a bit of a character. He was big, jocular, and severely asthmatic. He was also noted for handing out punishment with a meter stick. I saw him break a meter stick on Eugene King's upper arm, and on one occasion, he used it on me. On that occasion, Mr. Levy came into the class, announced he was in a bad mood, and said he didn't want to hear a sound. I turned and said to JoAnne Sturm, "This is going to be a long class." Mr. Levy heard, me, picked up the meter stick, walked around the room, and, when he got to my seat, hit me very hard. He was a big guy, and it hurt. I thought he had gone over the line, and I lost some respect for him. It was an overreaction to a very minor transgression.

It would be an overstatement to say that Mr. Levy was prone to violence, but his immediate response to any breach of conduct was to grab the meter stick. I do recall one incident when he completely lost it with a student, without using the meter stick, and it was the scariest event I ever saw in a classroom.

At the time of the incident, squirt guns were in vogue, and teachers were ordered to confiscate all squirt guns. I was a junior in high school, and Mrs. Tillinghast, my fifth-grade teacher, saw one sticking out of my pocket and confiscated it.

Mr. Levy came in to the classroom one day, with a squirt gun in his hand, and jokingly squirted the boy sitting in front of me in the face. Unfortunately, Mr. Levy's target responded by going along with what he thought was a joke and squirting him back. Mr. Levy went ballistic.

He grabbed the kid by the neck with his left hand, forced his head back on the lab table while he squirted him in the face, and screamed, "Who do you think you are?" Mr. Levy's face was purple with rage, and I thought he might really hurt the kid, who by that time was crying. The moment passed, and the room was still.

Mr. Levy was visibly shaken, and I got the impression that he knew he had gone too far. As much as I liked Mr. Levy, I think he should have been fired, and if he had done that to one of my sons, I know that he and I would have had a very serious problem.

If Mr. Levy's victim had told his parents what had occurred, I am sure Mr. Levy would have been fired. However, in those days, if you got in trouble in school, the last thing you would do was tell your parents.

There was an aspect to that class that was different from any other class. Jimmy Atwell, the quarterback on the football team, was in the class and a very good guy. He would come in every day, put his head down on the desk, and take a nap. He took no part in the class at all, and Mr. Levy never called on him. I think Mr. Levy and Coach Jackson might have had some kind of agreement whereby if Jimmy showed up for class and didn't cause any problems, he would get a passing grade.

Mr. Levy was also one of the teachers I knew outside the classroom, as he bowled on one of the teams in Santacroce's bowling alley and used to come in and pass the time with Mike

Santacroce, the owner. He was a real baseball fan, and that was probably the only commonality we shared. I enjoyed talking baseball with him.

He refereed basketball games and worked in Veteran's cigar store, where he clerked, shined shoes, and drove a taxi. I remember watching one of my classmates getting a shoeshine from Mr. Levy and thinking, *There is no way I would ever ask one of my teachers to shine my shoes, and if I were the teacher, there is no way I would shine one of my student's shoes.*

When Mr. Levy was granted a fellowship to do some advanced studying at the University of Alabama and the Board of Education refused to let him go, he resigned. The last I heard of Mr. Levy was that he was teaching science in Rio di Janeiro at the school run by the US State Department.

Mr. Douglas Tompkins

Mr. Douglas Tompkins, our English teacher, reminded me of Mr. Chips, James Hilton's schoolteacher character in his novel *Goodbye, Mr. Chips*, and I thought he was great. He was tall, bespectacled, gray-haired, and rather distinguished-looking. I remember that at one point he would lecture from a rather high stool and reach out with a long, bamboo snapper pole to get students' attention.

He was one of our class advisers, along with Mrs. Van, and I remember an incident in particular when we were preparing to put on our class dance, the Blarney Ball. Mr. Tompkins said that he was going to make a replica harp to hang from the ceiling as a decoration for the dance and would appreciate some help. I volunteered.

On the following Saturday, Mr. Tompkins and I spent almost eight hours in the school's shop making that harp. Mr. Tompkins was no amateur, and he created a very good replica of a harp. I had never worked on an arts-and-crafts project before that day, and I found it to be educational as well as a lot of fun.

Mr. Tompkins had a classical education, and knew something

about everything. I can remember him helping me with my Latin during a study hall which he supervised, and interjecting a law of physics in a Shakespearean quote. He was almost courtly in his demeanor and always tipped his hat when he said hello to mom. He rode a racing bike to stay in shape, and on one occasion, I remember him cutting the very high grass on an overgrown lot with a scythe. Some saw these things as being eccentric. Not me.

Mr. Tompkins was a very scholarly man but a bit naïve in dealing with the then-current brand of student. He made a serious mistake when he confronted one of the kids in his class. The kid, James Minyard, beat him up badly, and neither he nor Mr. Tompkins ever returned to class. I missed Mr. Tompkins and felt bad for James because he was one very nice kid.

Several years later, when I was a senior in college, one of my fraternity brothers, Jay Curtis, approached me and asked if I knew a teacher named Doug Tompkins. I told him I did, and Jay told me that Mr. Tompkins was the English teacher in the school where he was doing his practice teaching and that Mr. Tompkins had asked for me.

I saw Mr. Tompkins as a great example of how a teacher should teach and conduct himself. In the classrooms in which I have taught, I have tried to follow his example.

Mr. Herbert (Herb) Egert

Starting with my junior year in 1955, Mr. Egert became the math teacher at GHS, and a great one he turned out to be. Unfortunately for me, as good as he was, he couldn't do much for me. I do remember one geometry class when we were going over the homework. Mr. Egert put one of the problems on the board and started going through the process of solving it. At one point, he stopped and said, "I can't do this one." In the one and only time this ever happened, I raised my hand and said, "Mr. Egert, I think I have the answer."

He looked at me and said, "Go to it, John." I did, and I got the right answer. As a teacher, on the occasions when I couldn't answer a student's question, that incident came to mind.

Mr. Egert was from West Hampton, where he had played football, and was also an alumnus of Albany State. When I was accepted to Albany State, I asked Mr. Egert about the university, and he regaled me with tales of wine, women, song, sports, fraternity life, and, lastly, academics. By the time I left for Albany, I was more eager than anxious about going to college.

My most memorable Mr. Egert moment came about as a result of an incident Mrs. Egert, who was a special education teacher, had with one of her students who had apparently threatened her. I was in the study hall when Mr. Egert came storming in. The kid who had allegedly threatened Mrs. Egert was in the study hall, and when Mr. Egert got to his desk, he grabbed him and really went off on him. Mr. Egert was livid, shaking with anger, and I thought he was going to beat the kid to a pulp.

Mr. Bombardier, who was supervising the study hall, just watched, and I don't know what else he could have done. When Mr. Egert finished his tirade, he turned and started to walk out. Just before he got to the door, he turned back and said, "This is the only time you will get a warning." He then left.

There was a deadly silence in the room, and I saw the kid take a knife out of his pocket, open the blade, and put it up his sleeve.

After things settled down, I went up to Mr. Bombardier's desk and told him what I had seen. His answer was, "What do you want me to do about it?"

I said, "I don't know, but 'nothing' is not the right answer."

I then went over to where Bill Lieblein was sitting and told him what I had seen. I said to him that if Mr. Egert came back in the room, we should be ready to take on the kid. Bill was all for it. Mr. Egert didn't come back, and I often wonder what would have happened if he had.

On my trips back to Greenport, I usually see Mr. Egert, and I always enjoy talking with him. At the most recent all-class reunion, I did see him, and I was saddened by the current state of his health. He is walking with a cane and does not look, or sound, well. He had a profound and very positive impact on GHS and is another of my good memories of those halcyon days of yore.

Mr. Gerard Bombardier

Mr. Bombardier came to GHS as a business education teacher, but when Mrs. Diller became the school's guidance counselor, Mr. Bombardier became the French teacher. In comparison with the other teachers in GHS, I would rank him first.

He also became the faculty adviser for our class and my instructor in St. Agnes's Confraternity of Christian Doctrine Class (CCD), which we attended on Wednesday nights. He was a very good CCD instructor and very popular with the kids.

My most memorable Mr. Bombardier incident occurred after I asked Carlotta Wilsen to go to a dance with me. I needed a ride to get her there and asked Mr. Bombardier to help me out. He was chaperoning the dance and said he would be glad to help. We were to meet in the gym, and he would take me to Carlotta's house to pick her up. I got to the gym, but Mr. Bombardier didn't. It was getting late, and Reg Tuthill, one of my teammates, noticed my concern and asked me, "John, what's wrong?"

I told him, and he said, "Let's go. I'll take you." When we got back to the dance, Mr. Bombardier was there and very contrite.

On another occasion, we were talking about discipline in the classroom. I don't know how the conversation started, but the subject of corporal punishment came up, and Mr. Bombardier said, "John, when a teacher has to resort to corporal punishment, it is because he or she has lost control of the situation." It is something I have never forgotten and have applied in my own teaching experiences.

Before I left for Albany, Mr. Bombardier gave me a beautiful, wool topcoat that I wore throughout my college years. Mr. Bombardier left Greenport during my freshman year in college to take a position in Pleasantville, New York. I stopped in to see him on my way back to Albany one day and ran into him in the school's main hall.

He was surprised and glad to see me, and we had a nice conversation before he had to rush off to a class. Later that year, he died of a heart attack.

Miss Evelyn Orr

Miss Orr was the school librarian and the only teacher in GG&HS with whom I ever had a serious run-in. She was overweight, had a slight speech impediment, and was the object of a lot of student derision. Kids would rattle the tables and chairs when Miss Orr walked around the library. She was referred to as "Heavy Evvie," and the refrain "Farmer's chore, move Miss Orr" was often heard. Kids, me included, could and would be mean.

The library was located on the third floor of the school, adjacent to the study hall, with a connecting door. I remember one occasion when Marge Kiski walked into the library without closing the door and Miss Orr yelled, "Close the door! Were you born in a barn?"

Marge answered, "No, in a cow pasture, and we couldn't afford furniture." Ms. Orr did not laugh, but I did, as I found Marge's answer witty and to the point.

I have always admired people who could come up with witty answers, à la President Kennedy. When Helen Thomas, the doyen of the White House Press Corps, asked, "President Kennedy, when are we going to send a man to the moon?" President Kennedy, without a pause, answered, "As soon as Senator Goldwater wants to go."

My problem with Ms. Orr occurred at the end of my sophomore year. I was in the cafeteria line and got out of line to use the restroom across from the cafeteria. When I returned to the line, I tried to get back in the place where I had been when I left. Miss Orr was the line monitor that day. She saw me, accused me of cutting in line, and told me to go to the end of the line.

I told her what had happened, and she said, "I don't want to hear it! Get to the end of the line!" I just walked away and didn't eat lunch that day.

That afternoon, I walked from the study hall into the library. When Miss Orr saw me, she said, "John Sullivan, you owe me an apology, and until I get it, you will not be allowed to come into the library!"

Up until that point, I didn't think I had said anything to Miss Orr for which I had to apologize. But in response to her denying me access to the library, I said, "Please, hold your breath waiting for an apology." I went back into the study hall and never went back to the library again until I was doing some research for this book, sixty years later.

Apparently, Miss Orr reported this incident to Mr. Banker, the principal, who in turn asked Coach Jackson to speak with me. Coach Jackson actually pulled me out of a class that afternoon to talk with me. "John, I don't know what you said to Miss Orr, but she is really upset, and I think you should apologize to her."

I told him my side of the story, and his final word was, "John, I know you, and I know you are a good kid. It may not be the right thing to do, but apologizing would be the smart thing to do."

Of course, I didn't do the smart thing, I don't recall even speaking with Miss Orr over the next two years, let alone going into the library, but I know that she voted for me when I applied for the Ging scholarship and sincerely congratulated me when I got it.

Mrs. Kathleen (Kitty) Diller

My academic accomplishments in high school paralleled my performance in junior high school: not very good but not bad. I can't blame it on the lack of guidance, but prior to the end of my sophomore year, I had never had a guidance or counseling session. At the end of my sophomore year, Mrs. Diller became the guidance counselor.

On my first and, as far as I can recall, only meeting with Mrs. Diller, she asked me what my aspirations were. When I told her, "Probably joining the military when I finish school," Mrs. Diller said, "I don't know, John. You might not be able to pass the physical, and with your grades you might want to think about working in the A&P."

She may have been right, but I found her attitude to be dismissive. That, in conjunction with her treatment of Jonathan Sperling, led me to have less-than-warm feelings about her.

As I entered my senior year, I still had no thought of going to college. Early in the fall, Mrs. Diller came into an English class and asked, "Who wants to take the regents scholarship exam?" As was the case when Coach Jackson asked me about trying out for the football team, I did something very impulsive that turned out well.

I had no idea of what the regents scholarship was, but I asked Mrs. Diller, "How much does it cost?" Mrs. Diller answered by saying, "It doesn't cost anything, but I think your grades are too low."

Normally, I would have accepted this, and I don't know why I didn't, but I said, "Would you please go and check?" I was very surprised when she spun on her heel and left the room. I think her intention was to show me and the class that she knew what she was doing.

When she returned, she said, "You qualify, but by .26 of a point." I said, "Thank you. I'll take the test." That turned out to be one of the best, if not the very best, decisions I ever made.

I was working in Bubb's gas station when Mrs. Van drove up and told me I had been awarded a scholarship. From that moment on, everything changed. College suddenly became a realistic possibility. Later, that same day, Mrs. Diller also came by. Her first words to me were, "You didn't know how smart you were, and I am very happy for you." She also commented that I had finished ahead of Diane Woodward in the grading of the exam. That surprised me more than the winning of the scholarship.

Mom really didn't understand what all this meant, but because I was happy, so was she. I still wasn't convinced that I would actually be going to college, but I thought I had better apply to a school, just in case. I applied to one college, Albany State Teacher's College. I wanted to major in history and minor in English, but Mrs. Diller convinced me to major in business education and minor in history, and that is what I put in my application.

I am sure Mrs. Diller meant well. She thought business education was the easiest major at Albany State and a path of least resistance for me. She was wrong on both counts. BE was a difficult major, and the three semesters of accounting I took were hard and wasted time.

A vivid memory from that particular time was of coming home from confession one Saturday afternoon and suddenly thinking, "I really want to go college." Up until that point, it was more a case of other people wanting me to go to college, rather than me wanting to go; not because I didn't want to go but because I didn't want to get my hopes up.

A military career had always seemed a viable option to me, and I even thought of trying to get into the naval academy. When I looked into it and found out that any vision weaknesses had to be correctable to 20/20, that dream went out the window. I had astigmatism, and my vision was only correctable to 20/25. That left the option of being an enlisted man.

I had recently read Leon Uris's *Battle Cry*, and enlisting in the Marine Corps was what I planned to do. The scholarship changed all that. Being awarded a scholarship opened the door to college for me, but I still had to be accepted for admission by Albany State. When I was accepted, I made a promise to myself that I would be a much better student in college than I had been in high school. As it turned out, I found Albany State less academically challenging than high school had been.

After I was accepted by Albany State, Mrs. Diller's interest in me picked up, and she couldn't have been nicer. That Christmas, she gave me two new, and very warm, blankets. She also had me take some kind of competitive test for admission to Catholic colleges. Apparently, I did well, because two weeks later she told me that she could get me a partial scholarship to Notre Dame. Being a rabid Notre Dame fan, I would have walked to South Bend, but because I could only apply my regents scholarship to a New York State school and the Notre Dame scholarship was not nearly enough, I had to decline.

I still had to go to Albany for an interview and was scheduled for an interview in late February of 1957. Up until then, I had never taken a trip outside of Greenport on my own, other than hitchhiking to Riverhead, which was twenty-five miles away. I was anxious about the trip but was also concerned about my missing front tooth and was wondering what kind of impression I would make.

I had to go alone because we couldn't afford the train fare for both Mom and me to go. I think that was the first time Mom realized that I would be leaving home, and she didn't like it.

I borrowed a suitcase from Mrs. Bubb and, on a very cold Friday, left school early to catch the three o'clock train to New York City. Fortunately for me, Sue Park and her mother were on the train.

Sue was a freshman at GHS and a very attractive young lady. She was a friend and had a poise and grace that I found remarkable in one so young. One of my most embarrassing moments in GHS was when I let the F-word slip in her presence. She didn't admonish me but looked at me with a sense of disappointment that shamed me.

Sue introduced me to her mother, Mrs. Muir, and when I told them where I was going, Mrs. Muir said, "John, you are going to have to get over to Grand Central Station from Penn Station. You will come in our cab, and we will drop you off."

That might not seem like such a big deal to most people, but it was for me. I knew I was going to have to get to Grand Central but had absolutely no idea as to how. I had never ridden in a taxi or been in Penn Station, and I was anxious. What Mrs. Muir did saved me money, time, and, more importantly, stress. It was a big deal.

I arrived in Albany at about nine o'clock, found a hotel (not a very good one), got up at six o'clock the next morning, and took a bus out to the campus. The interview was anticlimactic, and I was on my way back home by noon. What I most remember is that Mr. Jones, the director of admissions, asked me, "You still like girls better than boys, don't you?"

Mr. Jones and my student escort seemed a bit turned off by my missing tooth, and I knew that I was going to have to get the tooth fixed before I started college. Shortly after our return from the senior trip, in April, I went to the dentist to see what could be done about my missing front tooth. He recommended pulling the good upper front tooth and replacing the two missing teeth with something called a "flip," a very inexpensive plastic bridge. He charged me eighty-five dollars. With my flip, I felt a little less anxious about going off to college, but I still had some fears to overcome. I wasn't the brightest light on the Christmas tree, and flunking out was a big concern.

Academically, Albany State was the most difficult of the state schools in which to gain admittance, and I never understood how I managed to do it. regents scholarship or not, my GPA just wasn't good enough. At the most recent all-class GHS reunion, I think I found out how that came to pass.

Dr. Robert Neidich, the assistant principal at the time I graduated, was at the most recent all class reunion. After we exchanged greetings, he took me aside and said, "John, one day, after you got your regents scholarship, Katie Diller came into the office and told me and Mr. Banker that we had to do whatever it took to make sure John Sullivan got into college." I think whatever it took included interceding for me with the admissions people at Albany State, and I am sure that is what they did. I cannot imagine that kind of help happening at a bigger, much more impersonal school.

Graduation went well. Of course, Mom cried buckets, but what was most memorable for me occurred when I walked across the stage to get my diploma from Mr. Banker. The applause was thunderous and seemed to go on forever. I saw it as a great farewell. Greenport Grade and High School. The faculty had served me very well, and I look back on my school days with a great sense of satisfaction and gratitude.

Several years ago, one of my classmates, Bob Adams, passed away. The funeral was held in Annapolis, and I attended it with Sharon and Rich Brooks. Bob's parents were there, and after the service, I approached them to offer my condolences. Mrs. Adams had substituted in GHS on several occasions, and I didn't know if she would remember me. I had never met Mr. Adams.

"Mrs. Adams, I don't know if you remember me, but I am John Sullivan."

"John, of course I remember you. You were my favorite student, and I am so proud of you." That came as a complete and very moving surprise to me, and a very pleasant one it was.

Not long ago, I had a conversation with Mrs. Van, and I brought up the ovation I got at graduation. In response, she said, "But John, you were Greenport's favorite son. What did you expect?"

The author, at 18 months.

Lee

The author's older son John.

The Author's younger son, Jimmy

The Author's grand children,
Katie and Andrew

The author, with neighbors,
and wonderful friends, Don
and Julia Aanstead,

The author with Bernie and Maria Heaney, two of the people
who made Greenport a wonderful place to grow up.

Greenport High School's 1953 championship football team. The author is in the front row, lower left-hand corner.

Greenport High School, Class of 1957. The author is in the second row, 3rd from the right, next to Diane Woodward.

Mrs. VanPopering (Mrs. Van), Author's teacher, mentor, friend, and wonderful benefactor.

Aerial View of Greenport

Chapter 10

THE DARK SIDE

As great a place as Greenport was, there was a dark side of life in town. Racism, sexual deviance, and some bad actors were a less visible aspect of life in Greenport, but they were present nonetheless.

Racism in Greenport was omnipresent, and you didn't have to look far to find it. In the Sullivan house, I never heard the N-word, nor can I ever remember using it. My awareness of racism began in high school, when it occurred to me that there were no blacks in my Latin or French classes. In my four years in high school, Bobby Howard was the only black I ever saw in a math class. I don't recall any blacks in the chemistry or physics classes. More mystifying to me was that I can't recall seeing a black at any of the high school dances.

Jimmy Atwell was the quarterback on our 1953 championship team and the only black on the team. He was also a starting guard on the basketball team and the catcher on the baseball team. I never saw him at any of the postgame parties. One black kid, Eli Shoates, had come out for the football team in 1953, but he broke his wrist in the second game and was out for the season.

When I overheard the president of the Board of Education

say, "He's a nigger, and you can't teach a nigger anything," I thought that might have had something to with the paucity of blacks in the college prep courses.

Schiavoni's pool hall and bowling alley openly discriminated against anyone who wasn't white. I remember a young Filipino-American in his U.S. Air Force uniform coming in to play pool and Mr. Schiavoni telling him, "Go and play with your own kind."

One of the gas stations where I worked was Gladding's Esso Station. On the door to the men's restroom was a sign that read "Out of Order," yellow with age. The restroom was only back in service to whites.

There were no blacks in the fire department, and in 1951, Carlos "Dusty" Dejesus became the first black on the police department. There were no black salespeople in any of the stores in Greenport or black waitresses in any of the restaurants.

On Sunday mornings after Mass, I would go down to Ging's to buy the paper and then to Corwin's Drugstore to get a dish of ice cream. On one of those occasions, a black crewman off one of the bunker boats asked Mr. Taplin, the owner and pharmacist, for a glass of water. Mr. Taplin gave him the glass of water. When the man finished and put the glass on the counter, Mr. Taplin took the glass and smashed it in the sink.

On another occasion, one of Greenport's finest was directing traffic in front of the movie theater as it emptied. A car with a black driver apparently didn't stop quickly enough when the officer signaled for a stop. Our finest went up to the driver's window and said to the driver, "Boy, you better keep those black eyes of yours open when you drive through here."

The most brutal incident of racism I witnessed occurred one summer afternoon when I was eleven. I had just come out of the arcade and was walking by the bus stop when the bus from Riverhead pulled in.

Herb Kaelin, the bus driver, got off the bus and yelled to one of Greenport's finest, who was standing on the corner, "Some guy fell asleep, and I can't wake him up." Our local gendarme woke the man up by screaming, "Wake up, nigger," and beating him with a nightstick. He continued to club him as he dragged him off the bus and marched him off to jail.

The only racial incident I ever saw in school was when I was a freshman. A white kid called Ken Mosby the N-word. Ken hit him in the jaw, lifting him off his feet and over a desk. The kid Ken hit was one of the bad guys, and Ken one of the great guys. I was very pleased by what Ken had done.

Given the incidents I have cited, I am finding it hard to believe that at the time they occurred I didn't see them for what they were and saw them as "just the way things are." I know that my indifference was benign but find little consolation in that.

Since my days in Greenport, the racial climate has changed— and, from what I have seen, for the better. There were also some *Peyton Place* aspects of life in Greenport that I only recognized in retrospect.

In August 1954, I had just finished mowing the lawn at the Clark house on Long Island Sound and was hitchhiking home when a little old man in a mint-green 1951 Plymouth picked me up. He wore a baseball hat, glasses, a white T-shirt, and khaki pants. He looked almost frail and seemed pleasant enough as he asked me my name and where I went to school. The ride didn't last fifteen minutes, and as he let me out on the corner of Fifth Street he said, "Do you want to go up to the woods this afternoon and fool around?"

Without pausing, I said no and walked away. At that point in my life, I knew of one "queer" in Greenport and had very strong suspicions about two others, but I certainly had no homosexual, or for that matter heterosexual, experience. As uninformed as I was in sexual matters, I knew what the man was asking of me and wanted no part of it. Telling Mom, or anyone else, didn't occur to me.

The following Saturday, I was mowing the lawn and trimming the shrubs at the Bartlett House, on the corner where the man in the green Plymouth had let me off, when Martha Raynor, who lived on the opposite side of the street, approached me.

"John, do you know that guy across the street?" she asked, pointing to the little old man, sitting in his green Plymouth. "He's been watching you for the last two hours."

Note: In my chapter on Greenport, I commented that life in Greenport was a fishbowl existence but afforded kids some protection. This incident makes that point very well. I told Mrs. Raynor that I recognized him, finished the yard work, and walked down to the police station. Bud Goldsmith, Dusty DeJesus, and Joe Rhodes were there.

Bud Goldsmith always called me Dick Tracy, and his first words to me were, "What can we do for you, Dick?" I told him what had happened and gave him the license plate of the car.

Joe Rhodes ran the plate, and when the name of the owner of the vehicle came back over the radio, I learned the name of my stalker, Harry M.

Bud said, "Dick, here's what we want you to do. You let this guy pick you up. We will follow him and arrest him." I had no fear of my new friend, but I also didn't have much faith in Greenport's finest. I declined Bud's suggestion and left without another word. There was no, "If he keeps showing up where you are, or if he contacts you, just let us know," and that surprised me.

School started, as did football practice, and Mr M parked on the edge of the practice field and watched. When I went home for lunch, he would be parked on the corner. After two days of passing him on my way home for lunch, I told my brother and one of my classmates, Fred Randall. Bill and Fred accompanied me home for lunch the next day.

As expected, he was there. I ran to the car, with Bill and Fred behind me, and said, "You tried to pick me up this summer and

I told you, 'no thanks.' This is the third day you've been here on this corner, and you've been watching me at football practice."

"I've never seen you before, and I don't know who you are" was his reply.

I then called him by his name, Harry M. and told him that I had reported him to the police. Fred Randall then grabbed him and pulled him halfway out of the car window, saying as he did it, "It would be a very good idea if you never showed up around here again."

That was the end of my problem with Mr. M. But the next summer, while coming back from mowing the Clarks' lawn, I saw Mr. M. coming down the North Road in the same Plymouth. He didn't offer me a ride, and I never saw him again, but there was a follow-up.

On my first summer home from college, I worked in Porky's restaurant. One day, during a conversation with one of the waitresses, Joyce G., she mentioned that she had a neighbor who was wonderful to her kids. The neighbor was Mr. M.

I have no idea as to whether or not Mr. M. had stalked any other kids, but based on my knowledge of pedophiles, I think he had. If that were the case, I think Greenport's finest may have dropped the ball on Mr. M.

Greenport was a very conservative town in which homosexuals were in the closet and did not advertise their sexual persuasions. Three of my classmates turned out to be gay, and I thought there was one who stayed in the closet. Two of the male teachers in GHS turned out to be gay, and two female faculty members were fired for being gay. I knew four female students who turned out to be gay, one of whom I liked very much and had contemplated asking out.

One of the teachers, whom I liked, was a married man, and it was rumored that he had been having an affair with one of his students. He was fired for making a pass at one of the loveliest of my classmates. His taste was superb but his morals abominable.

I was in study hall when the girl to whom he had made the pass came back from wherever she had been, in tears. Mrs. Van, who was running the study hall, took her aside, spoke with her, and got a look on her face that I wouldn't want to see directed at me. She then took her down to the principal's office. The teacher was summarily fired.

Two Greenporters whom I knew pretty well turned out to be pedophiles. One of them is now dead, and the other is in a mental institution.

Another incident that was a reminder of Greenpot's dark side was the suicide of a friend and classmate, Bill Mallett. Bill and I had been classmates since first grade and were friends, but not close. We were altar boys, and in 1954, he had come out for the football team just before his suicide.

The day before his suicide, a hurricane had hit Greenport, and there were a lot of trees down, some power outages, and beach erosion. The day after the hurricane, I was working in the Colonial Pharmacy when Bill came in. He was carrying a camera and told me he was going out to take some pictures and needed film. As I was giving him his change, he said, "John, can you serve Mass for me tomorrow morning?" I told him that I couldn't, and he left.

In retrospect, maybe I should have said yes. Instead I live with the thought that had I done so, what followed might not have happened. It also occurred to me that Bill knew that he wouldn't be around the next day and had been planning his suicide. I may have been the last person with whom he spoke.

That was on a Tuesday, and every Tuesday, there was a Novena at St. Agnes's, for which I was always the only altar boy. I was in the sacristy waiting for Father Holland when Mom came in. She was working in the rectory that week.

"John, Father Holland is over at Bill Mallett's. He just committed suicide."

The Novena was a little late in starting, and Father Holland made no mention of what had happened. On the way home, Mom insisted on going by the Mallett house. I thought this was not the right thing to do, but I couldn't dissuade her, and off she went without me.

When Mom came home, she told me that Bill had hanged himself and went on to say that Bill had some real problems in that he "liked boys better than girls." She told me that Bill's parents had consulted with Father Holland, who referred them to a psychologist in South Hampton. For some reason, I was very proud of Mom for not telling me that while Bill was still alive.

My brother, Bill Lieblein, Ace Cottrell, and I were the pallbearers for Bill's funeral. As an altar boy, I had attended several funerals, but none was as sad as Bill's. One of the saddest aspects of Bill's suicide was that it took such a tragedy for Bill to draw attention to himself. He was a very nice kid whom no one disliked, but he was also someone who never hung around with the other kids and whom the other kids didn't get to know.

Most of the class, and several teachers, turned out for the funeral. At the graveside, Mr. Mallett completely broke down. At that time, homophobia was alive and well in Greenport, and "coming out" had not been an option for Bill. Had it been, maybe Bill wouldn't have had to take his own, very personal and tragic way out.

Another memory I have of Bill's suicide was that the Greenport cop who investigated the suicide would show the rope Bill used to hang himself to the neighbors, asking, "Does anyone want to see what a rope that someone used to hang himself looks like?"

There were some "bad actors" in Greenport when I was growing up there but no such thing as a criminal element. There were a few well-known wife beaters in town, but that was not seen as a crime. Drugs and gang activity were unknown, and most parents felt that if their children graduated from high school they had done their job. That has changed.

On my first trip to Greenport after coming back from Vietnam in 1975, I was walking with my suitcase to the motel where I would be staying and fell in behind two teenaged girls. I couldn't help overhearing them and was stunned by their profanity. They dropped the F-bomb and MF-bomb with impunity, nonstop. It got to the point where I tapped one of them on the shoulder and asked, "Where did you kids learn to speak? I can't believe how filthy your language is."

One of them replied, "Who the f—k do you think you are?" She then said, "Kiss my ass?"

I told her, "Move your nose and I will consider it."

I mentioned this incident to Bernie and Maria Heaney, and Maria told me that Greenport had really changed. She went on to say that the Third Street park was an open drug market and kids could get drugs as easily as alcohol. That was not the Greenport I remembered.

In considering who the bad actors were, the first name that comes to mind is Bobby Waterhouse's. In February of 1966, Bobby beat, raped, and strangled a seventy-seven-year-old woman, Mrs. Nell Carter. He claimed that he had been "stoned" when he killed Mrs. Carter and was sentenced to twenty years to life.

Bobby was released on parole after serving nine years and ten months of his sentence. He subsequently moved to Florida, where he beat, raped, and murdered another woman. Last year, Bobby was executed after spending thirty-five years on death row in Stark, Florida.

Bobby was a few years younger than I, and I knew him on a first-name basis but knew his two older brothers, Roger and Chet, better. There was also a sister, Bev, who, from what I knew of her, was a very nice girl.

Although Bobby was Greenport's most infamous former resident, I found his cousin, Ron Quarty, to be more threatening. Based on my contacts with Ron and psychology courses I took, my conclusion is that Ron bordered on being psychopathic. From his first day in school until he was finally expelled, Ron was always in trouble, in school and with the police. Two incidents come to mind.

My first memory of Ron is at a basketball game when I was in sixth grade. There were three fans from the other school sitting in front of me, and Ron was sitting behind one of them. The guy Ron was sitting behind was wearing a very nice leather jacket. Ron was chewing gum, and he would take a few chews, remove the gum from his mouth, and stick it on the back of the leather jacket. He had put five pieces of gum on the jacket before one of his friends noticed it. When that happened, Ron ran.

Dr. Lamb, the principal, was at the game, and the guy with the gum on his jacket took it to Dr. Lamb. Ron's family had to pay to have the coat cleaned.

On another occasion, during the lunch hour, Ron set fire to the grass on an empty lot near the school. He was suspended from school for this.

At heart, Ron was a mean kid. One incident I can cite to make that point is when Ron threw Bobby Heaney's new bike off the Fifth Street dock. When Bobby's father, Jim, came home from work and Bobby told him what had happened, Jim and Bobby went looking for Ron.

When Jim saw Ron in front of Rouse's, he got out of the car, grabbed Ron, and put him in the car. They went down to the dock where Jim threw Ron overboard and told him not to come back without the bike. Ron brought the bike to shore.

CJ thought Ron was someone worth saving and, more importantly, someone who could be a good football player. Ron had taken up weightlifting and definitely had the physical tools to play football, but he had no understanding of how to run a play. He only lasted on the team for a couple of weeks, but during a scrimmage, I tried to tackle him. Ron balled up his fist and straight-armed me in the Adam's apple. I went down as if I had been shot. I couldn't breathe and was writhing on the ground. CJ ran over to where I was on the ground and said, "I guess that'll teach you not to tackle high."

One day, during lunch hour, Ron shoved Sal Vindigni, one of the teachers. Mr. Vindigni picked Ron up by the throat and slammed him into the tennis court fence.

Later that year, Ron shoved Dr. Neidich, the assistant principal. Dr. Neidich expelled him on the spot, and Ron never came back to school. He enlisted in the army but didn't make it through basic training. The last news I had about Ron was that he had apparently been shoved off a building on which he was working and died as a result of the fall.

On a visit back to Greenport, a couple of years ago, I was in Rich Fiedler's studio, shopping for a couple of paintings, when Rich said to me, "John, you'll never guess who was just in here." He then told me that Billy Quarty and Roger Waterhouse had just stopped in and that Billy had bought a painting. Billy was Ron's uncle, and for much of his life he had a serious drinking problem.

Rich then went on to tell me that Billy had dried out, carried on the family trade of stone masonry, and done quite well. "He has bought several paintings, and even though his hand shook when he signed the checks, but none of them has bounced."

During that visit, Roger told Rich of a visit he made to his brother Bobby on death row, in Florida. During the visit, Bobby had introduced him to a fellow inmate who he said was a nice guy. The inmate was Ted Bundy, the notorious serial killer.

Alcoholism was a serious problem in Greenport, and there were several members of the "Greenport Town Drunk Society." Some were like Otis, the friendly town drunk in *Mayberry RFD,* and some were of an entirely different stripe—that is, mean and violent. Hookey Whaley was very definitely a member of the latter group. I never knew his first name, but he was almost a fixture in Greenport's landscape. He had lost the use of his legs at a very young age. Below the waist, everything had atrophied, but he had the chest and shoulders of a gorilla. Hookey was an alcoholic and could always be seen sitting in the doorway of the building in which he lived with a beer nearby. He knew Bill and me by our first names, and on a few occasions, he asked me to go to the store and buy beer for him, which I did.

It was almost common knowledge in Greenport that Hookey had killed two of his drinking buddies but that the police couldn't prove it. Jerry Heaney was the first person to tell me that, and I heard Mike Santacroce say that Bud Goldsmith had told him that Hookey had killed two men.

On a more personal level, I had a nemesis while growing up who rained on many of my parades: Dick C. Dick was a year older than I, lived down the street from me, and, for reasons still unknown to me, made my life much more difficult than it already was. One aspect of the relationship was that the only times he picked on me were when other kids were around. When there were no other kids around, we seemed to get along well.

Dick joined the football team in the same year as I, and he was one very tough player. Though too small to be really good, he was a lot better than I ever was. In 1954, we were playing Northport, whose starting end was Dan Lotz. Lotz was six foot five and weighed 240 lbs., and I remember him swatting Dick off like a pesky mosquito as Dick tried to block him. Dick kept coming back for more. There was no quit in him.

My two worst memories of Dick are of his feeding my baseball glove to a dog and of his trying to step on my Achilles tendon during a baseball game. The first incident took place out in front of my house.

I had been having a catch with Nathan Goldin and Don Hunton when I stopped to go into the house to take a leak and left my glove on the curb. The glove was very old and worn, and t had been given to me by Joe Buckin, one of the town team's baseball players.

When I came back outside, Dick was there feeding the glove to a dog and chasing the dog. I caught the dog and got the glove back before much damage was done. The sheer meanness of what he had done was lost on him, and he was laughing. That was the first time in my life that I ever wanted to kill someone, and I am ashamed of the fact that I was too frightened to fight him over what he had done.

On the second occasion, I was playing first base in a pick-up game. Dick hit a grounder to the second baseman, and he made the easy throw to me. Dick wasn't even close to being safe, and I had stretched out with my left foot on the bag to take the throw. My toe was on the bag, with my ankle up, and instead of trying to touch the bag, Dick leaped in the air, aimed his right foot for my left ankle, and tried to stomp it. I turned to see where he was on the base path and saw what he was doing. I yanked my foot off the bag just before his foot came down. Had I not done so, I am sure that he would have torn my Achilles tendon. If he had run into me to get me to drop the ball, I would have seen that as part of the game. But he was already out, and what he had tried to do was done to hurt me.

After Dick dropped out of school, I would frequently see him in Rouse's sweet shop, at high school dances, and basketball games, and on those occasions, we got along fine. Since my Greenport days, I have had two contacts with Dick. The first of these was in October of 1993, after I met his daughter, Beth, at the Naval Academy. She was there to pick up her boyfriend and I to pick up my older son, John. John and her boyfriend were in the same class. She had recently graduated from Tulane and told me she was planning on moving to the DC area the following fall.

I subsequently called Dick, and we had a great conversation. I suggested that if Beth was looking for a job, I might be able to help her get a job with the CIA. Dick thought that was a great idea, and I set up an appointment for Beth with a personnel officer. Things didn't work out with Beth and her boyfriend, and the interview was canceled. I had been looking forward to seeing Dick again and am sorry things didn't work out.

My last contact with Dick was when I was in Greenport for a mini-reunion with the class of 1957. I ran into Dick and Stan Droskoski at the Islands End golf club, and he couldn't have been nicer. Dark side notwithstanding, there was a lot more sunlight in Greenport than clouds, and I left there as an optimist.

Chapter 11

CHAMPIONS

My freshman year in high school was the best of the four years I spent in GHS. It started with the 1953 football season, during which we went undefeated and untied. We were the first undefeated, untied team in the history of GHS. Being even a very small part of that team was one of the best things that ever happened to me.

When I went out for football, I had no illusions. At 105 pounds, I would have to run the hundred-yard dash in less than ten seconds to have the slightest chance of playing, let alone starting. That being said, there were moments when I had fantasies of scoring the winning touchdown or making the big defensive play. I also thought that when CJ let me try out, he thought that I wouldn't survive the preseason and would quit.

One of the reasons I survived was because, for the most part, the older and bigger guys took it easy on me. I never asked them to do it and had some mixed feelings about it, but I am glad that they did. Had they not taken it easy on me, there is no way I could have made the team.

Tom Breese and Bill Pell, the two captains, were really good about that, and I have a feeling they may have put out the word to go easy on me. This isn't very flattering, but it is true. At a larger school, I would never have been able to even get on the field with what would turn out to be a great bunch of guys. To me, that was worth the humiliation of knowing that as a player, I didn't, and probably never would, measure up.

Not measuring up didn't mean I wasn't trying, and in putting out a maximum effort, I think I earned the respect of a lot of my teammates. Their respect gave me a self- respect that I needed, which was a buffer against some of the harsher aspects of life in Greenport.

As much as CJ worried about me getting hurt, we were often short-handed at practices, and he had to play me in scrimmages. In one of the scrimmages, I got hit in the mouth and was bleeding pretty badly. I was playing across the line from Joe Barszczewski, and he stood up and said, "Coach, I think John is hurt."

CJ came over to check me out, and when he saw the blood, he said, "John, what happened?"

I told him that nothing had happened and that I wanted to stay in. CJ said, "Okay, John. I wish had had ten more just like you."

Practices were hard. After school, we would get into our uniforms as quickly as possible and get out to the field. When all the players were on the field, we would do some calisthenics, after which CJ would send us onto the track for laps. We would usually take four or five laps, but regardless of how many we took, at some point, CJ would blow his whistle. Then we would have to sprint, all out, to the practice field. That was probably the only thing I did well at practice, and Dick Breese and I used finish first and second in these sprints.

We didn't have enough players to have separate offensive and defensive teams, and all the starters played both ways. In practices, CJ emphasized offense, so I had a lot of practice playing defense against one of the best offensive teams in Suffolk County.

I never missed a practice and occasionally would make a

tackle, but the more I played, the more I realized that it takes more than wanting something very much to make it happen. My real moment of truth came one night when CJ let me play with the first team. The play we ran was T-26, with Ed Skrezec, the left halfback, running the ball between the right tackle and right end. My assignment was to block the defensive end, Gene King.

Gene wasn't very big, but he brushed me aside without much effort. The next thing I knew, he was stretched out parallel to my shoulder. Bill Dinizio, the fullback, had hit him like a runaway train, with a block I would never be able to match. The lesson I learned from all of this was that if you can't do the job, you don't, and shouldn't, get the job. If I had been good enough to start, CJ would have played me a lot more.

Of course, there are occasions on the athletic field, as well as in the classroom and elsewhere, in which favoritism plays a role. But in sports, at crunch time, it is those who can get the job done who play.

I also learned that there are players who go all out, regardless of whom they are playing against. Cliff Utz was one of those players. On one occasion, CJ was running a no-contact drill at half speed, to make sure the offense knew their blocking assignments. The defense just stood in place as the play was run. I was playing middle linebacker, and every time Cliff ran past me, he would elbow me. I didn't say anything, but John Montgomery, the starting center, saw what he was doing and told him to knock it off.

On another occasion, in a scrimmage, I intercepted a screen pass behind the line of scrimmage and was still in the air when Cliff tackled me. That was the hardest hit I ever took, and I am proud of the fact that I got up and trotted back into the defensive huddle. In a game against South Hampton, I saw Cliff execute the same tackle against Irey Etheridge, South Hampton's very fine end. It was a perfectly clean tackle and one of the hardest I had ever seen. Irey had to leave the game.

By the first game, I had survived the conditioning drills, the one-on-one tackling drills, and the scrimmages without getting hurt. I was in the best shape I had ever been in and was having a lot of fun.

Bob Wells, who had joined the faculty that summer, was CJ's assistant coach and would be coaching the basketball team. He and CJ were a good team, and Coach Wells was always great to me. All through preseason practices, we had no kicker to do either the kickoffs or extra points. Floyd Feldman, a good basketball and baseball player, had come out for the team just to do the kickoffs, but he wasn't doing very well. The week before the first game, we were practicing kickoffs when CJ told Ralph Cervone to try a couple of kickoffs. After about five kicks, CJ told him he would be doing our kickoffs. We never did get a PAT kicker.

Up until the week before our first game, we were practicing six days a week, three hours a day, and we were all eager for the season to start. Then it would be four hard days of practice and a light practice on Friday. The games were much easier than the practices, and the time went a lot faster.

Our first opponent was Smithtown, an away game. CJ had a tough time finding a uniform small enough for me, but he found one. My number was fifty-eight, and getting that first uniform was a big deal.

We kicked off to start the game and season. On the kickoff, Cliff Utz was kicked out of the game for unnecessary roughness. Joe Barsczewski, a junior who had never played football before, subbed for him, played very well, and became the team's super sub.

There was one other regular sub on the team, Fred Gagen. He, Ralph Cervone, and Joe Barsczewski were juniors playing football for the first time and were a primary factor in the team's success. Fred and Joe would spell Rich Cowan, a senior and starting guard, or Ralph Cervone, when he needed a rest, and that gave the team a depth it had never previously had.

Bill Dinizio, who, along with Dick Breese and me, was the only freshman on the team, scored on our first possession, on a screen pass. It was all downhill after that. We won 26–0.

I had no expectations of playing, and when Coach Jackson asked me if I wanted to go in, I was almost too surprised to say yes. But I did, and in I went. When I checked into the huddle, Tony Volinski, our starting halfback, greeted me with, "Don't get hurt." On the first play, the guy I was supposed to block tore my helmet off and threw it down field. I questioned his lineage, and Bryant Young, our second-string center, told me, "John, you aren't big enough or tough enough. Watch your mouth." I didn't screw up or get hurt, and the ride home was great.

A part of the pregame ritual was going to the movies on Friday night. There were several Friday nights when I couldn't come up with the money to go, and that was more painful than not having enough to eat.

Our second game was another away game, this one at South Huntington. One of the things I remember most about that trip was that at Friday night's practice, CJ told us, "The kids up there are into marijuana. Be careful."

We arrived in plenty of time for the game, put our uniforms in the visiting team's locker room, and were walking around the school when Ralph Cervone found a Coke machine. He got a Coke and was just putting the cup to his lips when CJ came on the scene.

"Ralph, what are you doing?" he screamed, and then he told us to get in the locker room. Once we were all seated, he read Ralph the riot act. "It is ninety degrees out there!" and "I'd like to make a living playing against you" (which didn't make sense to me), were parts of his rant, and I thought he was doing this more for effect than because he was really angry.

Ralph was a big, good-natured guy who turned out to be a real mainstay on the team. He played tackle and kicked off for us.

Cliff Utz had nicknamed him "Animal" after the POW portrayed by Robert Strauss in the movie *Stalag 17.*

At one point during his tirade, CJ threw a clipboard against a row of lockers. The clipboard hit Dick Breese and fell at my feet. Whatever CJ's reasons were for going off on Ralph, they apparently worked. We went out on the field and won 33–0, and once again, I played. CJ put me in as a defensive back. As behind as South Huntington was, I knew they would be passing. I also knew that once the QB saw me, he would be throwing in my direction, and he did.

On the second play, as soon as the ball was snapped, I saw the right end, Nick Algerio, head right for me. The QB overthrew the ball, and I intercepted it, at least until Algerio hit me. He didn't even try for the ball but just waited for me to touch it. His helmet hit my right elbow, and his shoulder caught me right in the ribs. When I hit the ground, I lost the ball. On our next possession, we punted. I am sure that I recovered the ball, but the referee disagreed. That was the most time I would ever play in a game.

After this game, people began to take notice of us. More spectators were showing up at practice, and *Newsday*, the biggest paper on Long Island, was picking us as a real challenger to East Hampton, who had won the previous year's championship.

Northport was our opponent in game three. John Ryder, Northport's coach, and Coach Jackson had both come to Greenport in 1949, Coach Ryder as the head coach and Coach Jackson as his assistant. Greenporters had nothing but good memories of Coach Ryder, and everyone was looking forward to the game, which would be our third consecutive away game.

Jimmy Atwell, our QB, scored two TDs on runs around the left and right ends. We also managed to score an extra point and won 13–0. After the game, there was a lot of camaraderie between the two teams, and Coach Ryder came into our locker room to renew old acquaintances and congratulate us. The week before our game with Northport, East Hampton had beaten them 40–0, and the Northport players were giving us dire warnings about East Hampton. "They are big, tough, and mean; good luck."

East Hampton was our next opponent. We would be going into that game unbeaten and hadn't been scored on. *Newsday* picked East Hampton to win, and CJ used that to motivate the team.

The thing I remember most about the East Hampton game was that CJ put in a special play for the game. We were a T-formation team, and CJ put in a pass play from a single wing formation, a hook and ladder pass. On that play, Jimmy Atwell would throw a pass to Tom Breese, in the flat, and Tom would lateral the ball back to Reg Tuthill, our fullback, trailing out of the backfield.

East Hampton's "Player" was a huge tackle named John Tilley. His nickname was "The Monster" and he was worthy of the title. He played on both sides of the ball and was equally effective on both sides. Bill Pell and Ralph Cervone shared the responsibility of trying to control him.

The practices the week before the game went well, and I thought CJ did a great job of preparing the team. My impression was that the guys who would be playing the game were confident that they were going to win.

Saturday, October 17, 1953 was overcast and cool. I was certain that I wouldn't be playing but knew this was going to be a good game and was eager for it to start. As it turned out, it was the best game of my four years on the team and the turning point in Greenport's football fortunes. We scored first, in the first quarter, on a quarterback sneak by Jimmy Atwell from the five-yard line that had been set up by a good punt return by Tony Volinski.

Ed Skrezec was arguably the best running back in the county, and East Hampton focused on him. CJ crossed them up by running Tony Volinski more than usual. East Hampton scored a TD and extra point in the second quarter, and we went in at halftime down 7–6. During halftime, CJ was very calm and said, "We are going to score twice next half, and they'll score once." He turned out to be right.

In the third quarter, Tony Volinski scored the TD that put us ahead to stay as we held East Hampton scoreless. In the fourth quarter, Tom Breese scored on the play that CJ had put in just for this game, but with a game-winning improvisation by Reg Tuthill. Tom caught the pass from Jimmy Atwell and lateraled it to Reg, who, seeing that the East Hampton tackle in Tom's lane had fallen down, lateraled the ball back to Tom. Tom may have been a little surprised, but he ran the ball 54 yards for a touchdown.

The crowd went wild. The way our defense was playing, there was no way East Hampton would come back. They did score one more TD, but when we got the ball back, we ran out the clock, with Ed Skrezec running the last play into the line and stopping. CJ had coached a terrific game, and it had been a real team effort. Three different players scored, and the offensive and defensive lines were outstanding. Everyone played well, but if I were to give the game ball to anyone, it would have been Henry Myslborski, one of our guards. He constantly pressured Bobby Yardley, the EH quarterback, disrupted EH's running plays, and opened holes for Volinski and Skrezec. No one came off that field more beat up than Henry, and he had obviously "left it all on the field."

Only thirteen of us had played in the game, and all were exhausted when they came off the field. CJ's timing of substitutions was masterful and a significant factor in our win. I would have been a serious liability had CJ put me in the game, and I probably would have been hurt. Even so, to have played even one down in that game would have been something about which I would still be bragging.

When the final whistle blew, it was as if we had won the Super Bowl. The crowd ran out on the field, and it was chaos. East Hampton hadn't lost a game in almost two years, and some of their players didn't take the snapping of that streak very well.

As we were going through the gate to get to the locker room, Mr. Jimmy Pirillo, one of our fans and a really nice man, tried to congratulate Bob Yardley, the East Hampton quarterback. Yardley was in tears, and when he went after Mr. Pirillo, two East Hampton players had to hold him back.

In our locker room, there was pandemonium, and Bill Pell came up with idea of having a parade through town. That was the icing on the cake and the end to one of the most memorable days I had in high school.

We were 4–0 after that game and had three games to go: LaSalle, West Hampton, and Seton Hall. None of these was a strong team, and unless someone got hurt, it would be all down-hill to the championship.

LaSalle was a private military school. We would be playing them at home, at night, and this game would provide me with the occasion of my most negative football experience. In the first quarter, I was standing along the sideline with my helmet in my hands when Tony Volinski broke away for an eighty-four-yard TD run. As he crossed the line, I threw my hands up in the air, with my helmet still in my hands. Unfortunately for me, it was at that instant that CJ chose to walk in front of me. My helmet caught him right in the mouth, chipping one of his front teeth.

CJ got a bit upset. Coach Wells, who had seen what had happened, came over to me and said, "John, you'd better go sit on the bench."

I was the only player who didn't get into that game, which we won 38–19. CJ's anger at me for breaking his tooth is under-standable, but I also thought his not putting me in the game was small, petty, and mean.

After that game, there was a party at Cliff Utz's house, and for whatever reason, I wasn't invited. As bad as I felt over not playing in the game, I felt worse about not being invited to the party;as that let me know that I wasn't an accepted member of the team.

I was shooting pool in Schiavoni's when my brother came in and said, "Reg Tuthill just came to the house to invite you to the party. He said, 'John is a member of the team, and he should be there.'"

Reg's gesture was another one of those "Little Things That Mean a Lot,"events and I believe he didn't give it a second thought. This was the first co-ed party I ever attended, and I loved it. The party also turned out to be somewhat of an educational experience for me. Up until that party, I thought only unattractive girls "did it." The girls at Cliff's parties were some of the most popular and attractive girls in the school, and the thought of them "doing it" had never entered my mind. But one of the lovely young ladies at the party did "do it" and ruined my illusion.

As far as I could see, there was no other sex going on at the party. Some of the guys brought their girlfriends, but there were no public displays of affection. There was no drinking at the party, and it was a lot of fun. Mr. and Mrs. Utz left the house in Cliff's hands, and no one got out of hand.

There was a lot of food in the kitchen, prepared by Mrs. Utz, and Mrs. Pell, Bill's mom, had made a cake for the party. Several people were standing around the kitchen table, eating and talking, when Fred Gagen picked up the cake and held it in his right hand. He wasn't drunk, and I don't know what made him do it, but he started hefting the cake in his hand and looking at one of the cheerleaders, who was Bill Pell's girlfriend. She looked at Fred and said, "You wouldn't dare." Fred did dare, and he hit her in the face with the cake. That was as out of hand as the party got.

Our next game was against West Hampton, and I got to play. We beat them 31–6, and the championship was ours. On the bus going home, it was strangely quiet, and as if the guys who really won the game just wanted to quietly enjoy being champions. Whatever their reason, I enjoyed what was happening.

The final game would be a home game against Seton Hall on November 7. On November 6, there was a small hurricane, with torrential rains, and the game had to be postponed until Veterans Day, November 11. A team banquet celebrating our season had been organized by Cliff Utz's father for that day, and I thought it would make for a great way to end the season.

We won the game 31–13, and there are three things I remember about the game. The first is that on the last play of the game, the Seton Hall quarterback threw a pass right to me. I was set to catch it when Bryant Young, a senior and our second-string center, yelled, "John, I've got it." I remember thinking, *This is Bryant's last game. Why not?* Bryant made the interception and was immediately tackled.

I never had another opportunity to make an interception, and at times I regret not having tried for it. I also think that what I did was a nice thing to have done and perhaps one of the many reasons why I wasn't as good a player as the other guys. Good players *always* go for the ball.

On a more serious note, Reg Tuthill was seriously injured in that game. He was in a pileup and got kicked in the head by one of our players. He came off the field and was completely out of it. I sat next to him on the bench, and when I tried to go over his plays with him, he was completely lost.

He knew my name, but not some of the other guys, and it became obvious to me that Reg needed to get to a hospital. I remember his younger sister coming over to see how he was doing, and she got a bit alarmed.

Reg was ultimately taken to Columbia Presbyterian Hospital in New York for extensive treatment which thankfully resulted in a complete recovery. This incident put a real damper on the joy of going undefeated.

After high school, Reg went to Ithaca college, subsequent to which he became the first intern at Air Freight International, where he really blossomed. When I was teaching school at Cohoes

High School, I met an Ithaca student who was interviewing for a teaching position, and I asked him if he knew a guy named Reg Tuthill. His immediate answer was, "Doesn't everyone?" He went on to tell me that he had worked for Reg, driving a bus at Ithaca, and that Reg had been a good boss. He also commented that someday Reg would be a millionaire. Currently, Reg and his lovely wife, Ruth, are retired and living in Orient, a beautiful village on the very tip of Long Island's North Shore. They thrive on their children, grandchildren, and philanthropy.

The banquet that night was great. It was held in in Mitchell's restaurant, the best restaurant in Greenport. I had never eaten there before, and the meal was one of the best I ever had. CJ said a lot of nice things about me, and although I knew a lot of what he said was harmless hype, it felt good. I was sorry that the season was over, but I went to basketball tryouts the very next day and moved on.

Coach Wells ran the tryouts, and I know I was better than some of the guys who made the team, but I got cut. The same day he posted the list of guys who made the team, Coach Wells recruited me to be the manager of the basketball team.

A few weeks after the football season ended, CJ called a meeting of the team to tell us that if we wanted, he would order jackets to celebrate our championship. He said the jackets would cost twenty-two dollars, and as soon as he collected the money, he would order the jackets. When I didn't give him my money, he took me aside and asked me why. I told him that I had quit a job to play, and asking my mother for the money was just out of the question. He said no more.

When the jackets came in, he called a meeting. The team had all chipped in to get me a jacket. As grateful as I was, I was also very embarrassed, but that was a very nice way to end the football season.

Basketball season morphed into spring, and more good things

happened. I had my first date and first kiss, and I thought life couldn't be any better.

An incident that occurred in April 1954 that would have a significant effect on me was the loss of the cap on my upper, left front tooth. I was walking down the aisle in the study hall when it just fell out. I had no social life at that time and didn't think of how this would affect any future social life. It also occurred to me that I would be playing football for the next three years and would probably lose the cap again. That, in combination with mom's unwillingness to get it replaced, made athletics more important to me than they might otherwise have been.

In March, CJ asked me to be the manager of the baseball team, and of course I said yes. CJ was an outstanding baseball coach, and the team was very good. My best memory of that season was Tom Breese's no-hitter against West Hampton. He walked the first batter and then set down the next twenty-one. The most interesting aspect of the game was that his brother, Dick, was his catcher.

That June, I decided to attend the class of 1954's graduation ceremony. I had never attended a graduation before and was curious. During the awards phase of the ceremony, I wasn't paying much attention when I heard, "The prize for the greatest growth and development in athletics, John Sullivan." I was caught completely by surprise, and I could not have scripted a better ending for what had been a great year.

That summer, I was eagerly looking forward to the upcoming football season. East Hampton had lost most of its starters, and Northport was the only other team to have given us a close game the year before. It looked as though we were going to establish ourselves as a force in Suffolk County football.

My contribution to the team had been minimal, but I was a member of a championship team, and for the first time in my life, I felt as if I were a part of something very good. I got some recognition for being the smallest kid on the team, and I reveled in that attention.

I have coached three of my older son's soccer teams to undefeated, championship seasons and one of his basketball teams to a championship. I have also been present when he led his high school tennis team to a state championship. None of the emotional highs I experienced on those occasions equals what I felt when we won the 1953 championship.

Earlier this year, I attended my granddaughter Katie's cross-country meet for the Anne Arundel County (MD) Championship. Katie was the only freshman on the varsity, but unlike me, she was a real point getter for her team. She placed in the meet, and her team won the county championship.

Recently, I went to Katie's cross-country team banquet. She was given her varsity letter and a trophy for being the most improved runner on the team. Katie was on cloud nine, and I couldn't help recalling my feelings at the football team banquet I attended after our 1953 championship season.

I am not as involved in my grandkids' athletic pursuits as I was with John's and Jimmy's, but Katie's accomplishments have really given me another reason to just keep going. Kristen, Katie's mother, is a marathon runner and ran the Boston Marathon that ended with a terrorist attack. She works with Katie and does a much better job than I ever could. I have been on two championship teams but never had any kind of individual championship. Before she finishes running, I am sure Katie will experience both, and I can only hope to be around when she does.

Chapter 12

TEAMS AND
TEAMMATES

By the time I started my sophomore year, my involvement in sports defined me. I was an average student and nice guy, but more importantly, at least to me, I was also a member of the football, basketball, and baseball teams.

Over the summer, I saw a repeat of the 1953 football season as very possible; it would not be a cake walk, but we did have a lot going for us. CJ switched Henry Myslborski from guard to running back, and he and Ed Skrezec were our running backs. Ed was among the top three running backs in Suffolk County, and Henry turned out to be very good. Bill Dinizio had proven himself as a fullback, both as a blocker and runner, during the 1953 season. He had put on some weight over the winter, and I was expecting him to have a great season.

During one of the practices before our opening game, I had a clear shot at tackling Bill. I hit him at the belt buckle with my shoulder, wrapped my arms around his waist, and was feeling satisfied when his legs drove into my chest, my arms flew open, and he literally ran over me.

Cliff Utz and Ralph Cervone were All-County tackles, and John Montgomery was the best center in the county. Tom Breese would be tough to replace, but Bill Claudio was a fine athlete and could handle the position, as could Harry Bubb, who would be replacing Bill Pell. Jim Atwell had been a good quarterback and would be tough to replace, but he was five feet seven inches tall, and didn't weigh 150 pounds. CJ had been grooming Dick Breese to replace Jimmy, and he was ready. Dick was six foot four, weighed two hundred pounds, could throw the ball on a clothesline over sixty yards, and was as hard a man to tackle as I have ever tried to bring down.

Dan Lillis was a bigger and faster than Dick Cowan, the guard he replaced, and Dick Corazzini would be the other starting guard. Joe Barsczewski and Fred Gagen would continue to be super subs, and the starting team was pretty much set.

When practice started in September, you could sense the confidence in the team. Although CJ cautioned against getting overconfident, I did hear him say to Coach Wells, "You know, Bob, I think we have something special here, and we could do it again."

Captains were not appointed by CJ but were elected by the team and had to be seniors. There were no nominations, just a vote, and the two top vote getters were co-captains. The election was one I wouldn't forget. Ed Skrezec, Cliff Utz, Ralph Cervone, Harry Bubb, Henry Myslborski, John Montgomery, Joe Barczewski, and Fred Gagen were the seniors. CJ was pushing for Cliff to be captain. He would have him lead the calisthenics drills, and I remember him saying, "Most of the other guys have a chance to be captain of another team, but football is Cliff's only chance." He also pointed out that being the captain on a team sport looked good on a college application, and Cliff would be going to college. Ed Skrezec went to Hofstra on a football scholarship, and Cliff played football at St. Lawrence. They were the only two seniors on the team who went to college.

We voted on the Monday night before our first game. After counting the votes, CJ called us together just inside the locker room and announced, "Your captains are Ed Skrezec and Henry *Millboski*." CJ could never pronounce Henry Myslborski's name correctly.

I was very pleased that Henry was one of the captains. He was one of the shyest guys on the team and very unassuming. But I also saw him as one of the toughest as well as smartest players on the team, and it pleased me that a lot of the other guys felt the same way.

For me, things did not look promising in terms of getting more playing time. Winning a championship gave the football team a real boost in status and attracted a lot of recruits for the 1954 team. All of them were bigger than I and had a lot more potential. Like it or not, CJ had to play them ahead of me to give them game experience.

I also think that the fact that I, a small and less-than-talented player, had actually played in four games inspired some guys who otherwise would not have come out for the team to do so. In any event, the 1954 team was almost twice as big as the 1953 team, and expectations were high.

Bill Mallet was one of those who tried out, and his suicide was a distraction. But hardly any of the guys knew him, and we had a practice the night of the funeral. CJ never mentioned it at any of the practices, and I thought that a bit strange.

Another of the guys who came out for the team was Richard "Richie" Sledjeski, and with him came his father, Walter "Porky" Sledjeski, the owner of Porky's restaurant, one of Greenport's best restaurants. Mr. Sledjeski became a real benefactor to the team. Before our away games, Mr. Sledjeski would give CJ some money to buy snacks for us on the way home, and at the end of the season, he would put on a banquet for us in the restaurant.

One incident I won't forget took place during the Easthampton game. We were beating them like a drum, and CJ was subbing liberally, but he didn't play me. I started bugging him, and he sent me to the bench. Mr. Sledjeski saw what had happened and convinced CJ to put me in the game.

The season started out well. We beat LaSalle 18–0, and Coach Wells had tried to get CJ to put me in the game, but I guess an eighteen-point lead was not enough. Our next game was South Huntington, and we beat them 32–13. I got to play and thought we were confident going into the Northport game. Northport turned out to be the toughest game of the year and was a great game. It was a home game, and we were both undefeated when we met.

The thing I remember most about that game was that, just as he had done in preparing for the East Hampton game the year before, CJ came up with something new for the Northport game. During Monday's practice, CJ made some changes in the defense. He pointed out that when Northport went into an unbalanced line to the left, leaving just an end and tackle to the right of the center, they would occasionally run a reverse to the weak side, with Walt Gerner carrying the ball.

To defend against this, CJ told our left tackle that when Northport went into its unbalanced line, he was to hold his position and contain instead of going with the flow of the play to the strong side. Northport ran the play. Our left tackle crashed inside and was blocked as Gerner ran around him for seventy-three yards and a touchdown. We lost, 12–7. That was the only game we lost that year. After Northport, we ran the table, beating Smithtown 27–0, South Hampton 21–7, East Hampton 33–7, West Hampton 20–0, and East Islip 26–12.

The most memorable of that season's games was the South Hampton game. The South Hampton coach, Dick Morrissey, was a bit of a wild man and was raging up and down the sidelines the whole game. When one of his players was hurt, he ran out on the field, threw him over his shoulder, and carried him off the field. We went in at halftime up 14–7.

Once we got into the locker room, we could hear Coach Morrissey raging in the visitors' locker room. CJ just said, "Listen to him. We've got this one." CJ didn't say another word until we went back out on the field and won, easily.

Expectations had been high, but there was no weeping or wailing at the end of the season. The team had played very well and lived up to most expectations. One play had been the deciding factor in our only loss, and no one was walking around with his head down. The saddest part of that season was that we would be losing eight seniors and would have to do some serious rebuilding for the 1955 season.

The 1953–1954 basketball team, led by Dick Breese, was good and finished 11–7. Dick made the Suffolk County All-Star team, and prospects were good for a better 1954–1955 season Frank Swann was a welcome surprise and the team's best rebounder. He was also the strongest kid in the school. Ken Mosby, one of my classmates, was the best pure shooter on the team, and Jimmy LaBad, another classmate, was our weak-side forward. We suffered from a lack of depth and good guards.

During that season, Dick Breese and I became even better friends, and I got to know Frank Swann very well. He was a mass of muscle, shy, and very soft-spoken. I don't know why he liked me, but he did. A benefit of that friendship was that during a basketball game in gym class, I got in a nasty argument with one of the players on the other team. When the game was over, I went into the locker room to use the restroom.

Unbeknownst to me, the kid with whom I had the argument followed me, and when I came out of the restroom, he was waiting for me. He started hassling me, and I don't know what would have happened if Frank hadn't suddenly appeared. Frank had witnessed the argument and seen my antagonist follow me.

"John is my friend. You aren't. Leave him alone and get your ass out of here" was all Frank said, and the confrontation was over.

One of the things I liked best about being on the basketball team was that over the Thanksgiving and Christmas vacations, Coach Wells would have practices during which former players on vacation from college would come and play pick-up games.

Track was my best sport, but I wasn't horrible in basketball and got to play in some of the pick-up games. The gym was a good place to be when I didn't have any place to go. Playing basketball in a warm gym with a lot of good guys beat the hell out of spending time in a cold, dreary house.

As high as expectations were for the 1954–1955 basketball season were, the chances of winning the championship were still pretty slim. Mattituck was the team to beat, and they were very good. We got off to a very good start and were 7–0 when we played Mattituck on their court. In what turned out to be a great game, we won 62–61. When the final buzzer sounded, I went a little more nuts than any of the players. I had a game program and had all the players sign it. I still have it.

When Coach Wells saw me doing that, he said, "Let's not get ahead of ourselves. We have a long way to go." He was prescient.

Bob Burns, the *Times Review* reporter, had picked Mattituck to win. In his write-up of the game, he maintained that Mattituck would win the league championship.

We were in the driver's seat, and the league title was ours to lose, which is what we did. The key game was South Hampton. Elton Etheridge was South Hampton's leading scorer, and Coach Wells assigned Dick Breese to guard him. Dick held him to five points, but Walt King scored eighteen. In the second half, Coach Wells put Dick on King. Dick shut him down, but Etheridge scored twenty points. More importantly, South Hampton double- and triple-teamed Dick, leaving a lot of our guys with open shots, but no one would take them.

Another factor may have been that one of our guards was less than ready for the game. During halftime of the JV game, I went out to the bus to get the scorebook I had left there. On the way back to the gym, I saw the guard and some Greenport fans drinking beer. That guard had a bad game.

During the bus ride home, Coach Wells said to me, "If there was ever any doubt about our being a one man team, there isn't anymore."

The season ended with us in a tie with Mattituck for first place in our division. We played them in Riverhead, and they beat us 72–54. Coach Wells' comment on the bus ride after this game was, "If we had won the championship, I would have felt as though we backed into it. Mattituck is a better team."

I wasn't the baseball team manager this year and had only the 1955 football season on my horizon. With the loss of seven starters, and two other experienced linemen from the 1954 team, it was going to be an uphill battle to be competitive. Dan Lillis, one of the captains, would be the only lineman who had ever started a game. One end, Ed Ewell, and the two starting tackles, Bob Biggs and Ed Rowe, had never played organized football. Dick Breese, Dick Corazzini, Bill Dinizio, and Jack Skrezec had the potential to be a great backfield, but they didn't have much of a supporting cast.

We started the season against South Huntington and lost. A week later, it was discovered that the South Huntington quarterback, Amato, had been ineligible to play. They had to forfeit the game, and we were declared the winner. We then lost to Northport. Bob Biggs, our left tackle, was hurt and lost for the season. Bill Lieblein took his place.

Smithtown was next, and we won 12–7. Our next opponent was South Hampton. They had a new coach, Herb Goldsmith, a Greenporter who was the younger brother of Bud Goldsmith, Greenport's best-known cop. He and CJ were Ithaca alumni and good friends.

In my four years of playing football, that was the only game in which I didn't want to play. It was freezing cold, just above zero. My feet were like blocks of ice, and I would have had to thaw out before going into the game. One of the spectators came over to the bench and offered me a blanket, which I declined.

During the first half, the wheels came off the bus. We couldn't do anything right, and at the end of the second quarter we were behind 18–0. When we went into the locker room, CJ didn't come with us, and Coach Wells told us that CJ was too mad to even talk to us.

When we got the second half kickoff and drove the ball down the field for a touchdown, CJ came back to the bench. We kicked off, and Elton Ethridge ran the ball back for a touchdown. They beat us 37–6, and their first team was on the field until the last play. The bus ride back to Greenport was very somber, but we bounced back the next week, beating East Hampton 31–13.

We then lost to West Hampton, 19–12. It was a very hard-fought game, and the fans on both sides got a bit out of hand. After the game, in the locker room, CJ said, "We didn't lose; we just ran out of time."

Our last game was against East Islip. We were 3–3 going into the game and needed a win to salvage a winning season. And then Dick Breese got sick. On the bus, he became nauseated, and CJ had to take him off the bus, where he threw up. He had a very bad case of the flu, and CJ used him only on offense.

At one point during the game, Dick really got his bell rung, and CJ took him out for a few plays. He had Jim LaBad take over at quarterback until he could get Dick back in. Jim had no experience at quarterback and had never so much as taken a snap before this game.

Dick was our best offensive and defensive player, and his absence from the field was critical. Dick Corazzini was playing in Dick's spot on defense, and Walt Shaefer, the East Islip quarterback, seeing a five foot five defensive back, threw a touchdown pass over Dick's head to put East Islip ahead for good. Dick broke away on a seventy-three-yard run in the fourth quarter but got caught, and we couldn't push the ball in. Walt Shaefer, the EI quarterback, and I became fraternity brothers in college, and I remember discussing that game. He told me that at the half, his coach had told him to start throwing at "that little kid playing corner back."

The bus ride home was grim, and I had never seen CJ so down. We had lost to Northport, South Hampton, and West Hampton, but this game was different. The fates had conspired against us, and CJ knew we were the better team. After going 14–1 over the previous two seasons, a losing season, was hard to take, and ending the season with a loss made it more so.

Our expectations for the 1956–1957 basketball team were high, but once again, Mattituck beat us out for the league championship. We actually had a better record that year than we had the year before, 15–3, but Mattituck went undefeated and beat us twice.

One of the more memorable moments of that season occurred in our game with Bridgehampton. We were playing them at home, and with four seconds to go in the second quarter we were down by four points. Bridge Hampton took the ball out under our basket. Carl Yastrzemski, the future Hall of Fame baseball player, stood on our foul line to take the in-bounds pass. Coach Wells was yelling for someone to cover him, but it was too late. Yaz took the in-bounds pass, turned, and took a set shot that went in.

Another memorable moment occurred after our game at West Hampton. As noted, the Greenport/West Hampton football game that year had ended in a near riot and some hard feelings between both teams To get things back on track, the Westhampton basketball team hosted a social hour with us after our game. It was a very nice event and, to my way of thinking, the kind of thing that high school sports should be all about.

Over the winter, a decision had been made to start a track team, with Coach Wells as the coach. I was ecstatic. Running was something I knew I could do, and size was not a factor. I also looked forward to actually earning a letter based on my performance. My event would be the mile run.

I was the team's second-best miler, with Dick Breese (who else?) being number one. My best performance was in the league championships at West Hampton. I finished fourth, behind Santos Abrils (West Hampton), Fred Simes (Shelter Island), and Dick Breese.

After the track season, Coach Wells organized an interclass track meet in which I beat Dick Breese in the mile run, not because I was a better runner but because I kept training after the track season, while Dick was playing baseball.

Winning that race was a great way to end the school year. I had a great summer working at the gas station and was looking forward to the football season. With Dick Breese, Jack Skezec, and Bill Dinizio in the backfield, and a much more experienced line, there was reason to be optimistic.

During the 1956 season, we played Riverhead for the first time in years. Riverhead had been Greenport's archrival for many years, and we hadn't played them since 1951 or 1952, when they beat us 56–0.

CJ and Mike McKillop, the Riverhead coach, were very good friends, and Coach McKillop came to our pep rally the night before the game to give us a talk. After Coach McKillop's talk, CJ asked some of the team members to say a few words, and surprisingly introduced me by saying, "Here is a player who probably won't be playing tomorrow." My few words were to guarantee a victory. The team made good on my promise and beat Riverhead 20–0.

Ed Ewell was our starting left end, and on the day of the game, he had attended a wedding reception for his sister before coming to the game. When he showed up for the game, he was a little less than sober. During the game, he tackled the Riverhead quarterback in the end zone for a safety. Those were the only points he would score all that season.

Our toughest game that year was our next to last game against West Hampton. We had mended fences since the 1955 game, but they were pumped for the game. Jimmy LaBad made a great fourth-quarter catch in the end zone of a pass from Dick Breese to win the game. He had dropped a pass earlier in the game, and one of the Greenport fans, who may have been a little drunk, screamed, "Catch the ball, you black SOB." At Monday's practice, the following week, CJ told us that the man who had hurled the racial slur had apologized to him and asked him to apologize to Jimmy.

During the week before the game, I sustained my first real football injury. In a scrimmage, I was playing linebacker, right behind Art Nichols, the biggest kid on our team. On a running play through his hole, Art stood up, and I couldn't see who had the ball. I was back on my heels, looking for the ball carrier, when Jack Skrezec, the lead blocker, hit me. His shoulder hit my locked left knee, and I went down.

My knee swelled up, and there was a lot of pain, but I could walk on it. For a couple of days, it was very tender. But the injury was not bad enough to keep me out of our last game, which was a home game against East Islip.

Before we went out on the field for the game, CJ asked, "How many of you have been on the team for four years?" Dick Breese, Bill Dinizio, and I were the only ones, and CJ appointed us captains for the game. That was a great gesture on CJ's part. That gesture didn't extend to having me start the game, which was understandable, but I still wish that it had.

I got to play in the game, and we won pretty easily. That win gave us the league championship and another undefeated, untied season. Our seven wins were the beginning of a twenty-nine-game winning streak. This was the last time I would play football on any kind of organized team, and I couldn't have written a better scenario for ending my football career, such as it was.

After the last football game, there was a party at Bill Dinizio's house at which I got drunk for the first time in my life. I left the party and went to the movies, where, during the cartoon (*Bugs Bunny*), I stood up, pointed my finger at the screen, and yelled, "Pow! Got ya, Bugs!" Carl Utz and Micah Kaplan, two of my teammates, took me home.

The next day, I had a terrible hangover but went to Mass, where I took a bit of teasing. That afternoon, while I was working at the gas station, kids would drive by beeping their horns and yelling, "Got you, Bugs."

Jerry King, the owner of the Coronet restaurant, stopped in for gas and said in a more serious way, "John, you are a good kid. Last night may have been fun, but don't make it a habit." Jerry King was another Greenporter who cared, and I took his advice seriously There would be another reprrecussion..

Intermediate algebra was my first class on Monday morning. When I showed up in class, Mr. Egert was writing on the blackboard. He waited until he was sure all of the class was seated, turned around, pointed his finger at me, and said, "Pow. Got ya, Bugs!" There was one more occasion, nine years later while I was in the army, when I got drunk. That was not only the last time I got drunk but also the last time I took a drink.

Shortly after the end of the season, while playing basketball in the gym, I jumped for a rebound and felt something pop in my left knee. When I came down, my knee buckled, and I felt more pain than I had ever experienced..

There were no orthopedic surgeons in Greenport, but Dr. Kaplan told me that I had torn all of the ligaments in my knee and broken the synovial capsule. He put me on crutches until I could walk without pain. The pain eventually went away, but it took another two months before I could straighten my leg. Since then, I have had two operations on the knee, and it still gives me problems

The 1956–1957 basketball season was almost a carbon copy of the previous season. Mattituck and Bridgehampton were the only teams to beat us, and we once again finished behind Mattituck with a 15–3 record. Dick Breese finished his basketball career, having scored over a thousand points, and once again made the Suffolk County first team all-stars.

By the time track season started, my knee was feeling a lot better, and I went out for track. Just before our senior trip to Washington, I was lifting a large, fallen branch at the rear of the gas station, and my knee buckled. That ended my track season.

Fifty-eight years after graduating from GHS, I still remember the teams I was on and the teammates I had as my best memories of high school. I am still in contact with Dick Breese, Harry Bubb, Reg Tuthill, Bill Lieblein, Bill Dinizio, Ken Mosby, Jack Skrezec, Bill Pell, and Tom Breese, all of whom help me keep those memories alive. I am convinced that I would not have been able to accumulate those memories in any other place than Greenport.

Chapter 13

ON MY OWN

By the time I graduated from high school, I was pretty much on my own. I more or less came and went as I pleased, and after I began working in the gas station during my junior year, I never took another cent from mom. She gave me all the emotional support that any kid could ask for, fed me, and washed my clothes, but in terms of decision making as well as financial support, I was on my own.

When I got off the train in Albany in September of 1957, I wasn't afraid, but I was anxious. Except for my senior class trip to Washington and my interview trip to Albany, I had never spent a night away from home. College was a whole new world for me, and I had a lot of questions.

Bill was the only roommate I had ever had, and having a nonfamily roommate would take some getting used to. What were the protocols involved? Would we get along? Was there a laundry in the dorm? How would the food be? Would I fit in with the other kids? Where was a Catholic church? What happened if I got sick? Where would I keep my money?

Mom had never had a checking account, nor had I, and I arrived in Albany with a little over three hundred dollars in my wallet. I used the money from the Ging scholarship to pay my dorm fees and used some of the money I had brought with me for books. Buying my own books was a new and expensive experience.

I kept my money in my suitcase and was very frugal. Breakfast and dinner were provided, and I didn't eat lunch very often. I wanted to keep my money on hand in case of an emergency, until my regents scholarship money came in, and I managed it pretty well. The scholarship was for $175 a semester, and I remember that the first thing I bought with that money was a winter coat.

I had opted not to attend the orientation for freshmen and showed up at my dormitory, Sayles Hall, a day before all the freshmen returned to campus. Once the freshmen returned, I met my roommate and a lot of other good guys. The room I would be sharing was a lot better than my room at home, and my roommate was great from the get-go. My first thought was, *I think I am going to like it here.*

The living conditions in Sayles Hall were better than those I had in Greenport, and many of the friendships I made there are still going strong. One of the friends I made in Sayles Hall, Jim Kelly, remains the best friend I ever had, and my younger son is named after him.

For me, one of the real pluses of living in Sayles Hall was that there was a pool table in the game room. While working in Schiavoni's bowling alley and pool room, I had learned to play pool. Although not very good in comparison with the local competition, I could more than hold my own with the Sayles Hall players. Mark Twain is quoted as saying, "Proficiency at billiards is a sign of a misspent youth." I never misspent any of my youth and found the money I spent playing pool was well spent.

On my first Sunday in Albany, I awoke to the sound of hundreds of high heels clicking on the pavement as the girls in Brubacher Hall, the girls' dormitory, went to Mass at St. Vincent DePaul RCC, which was two blocks from Sayles Hall. It did occur to me that the chances of finding a nice Irish Catholic, or at least Catholic, girl might be pretty good.

Another thought that occurred to me on that day was that there was no one to wake me up. Mom had always done that, and we never had an alarm clock, Often, especially after I had worked late at night, Mom would have to harangue me to get up and serve Mass. Who was going to do that now? That was my first awareness of being on my own.

On Monday and Tuesday of that first week, I registered for my classes, bought my books, and found my way around the campus. Until I got my class schedule it never occurred to me that I would be spending only eighteen hours a week in the classroom, leaving me with a lot of free time. On Fridays, I had only one class, a three o'clock history class. I was used to being in class all day, every day, and this new regimen would take some getting used to.

As I was to find out, a lot of kids cut classes. I didn't cut a class until my third semester, and cut less than five classes during my years at Albany State.

Albany State didn't have a football team, but touch football was big. Sayles Hall had a team, and I played one game. I was playing halfback and pass blocking when a classmate, Ken Taylor, who was rushing the passer, hit me. He had locked his hands in front of him and hit me with both of his forearms. I did a complete somersault in the air, and when I landed, the wind was knocked out of me. That was the last time I played in any kind of organized football game.

One of the more pleasant adjustments was to the fact that for the first time since I began comparing myself with my friends and classmates, I didn't see myself as being much different than any of them. We were not necessarily equal, but I was also not less than they in any noticeable way.

We all pretty much dressed alike, and there were some who, by choice, dressed worse than I did. Back in Greenport, I didn't acknowledge or deny my economic status. It was obvious. At Albany State, there was a presumption of economic equality among all of the students, and I loved that presumption and the anonymity it gave me.

I had survived being less well off than my contemporaries in Greenport through the generosity and good will of their families. And in so doing, had incurred a debt that I hoped I would, someday, be able to repay. At Albany State, I didn't have any such worry, and was relieved.

During the first couple of months, I studied harder than I ever had in high school, even though it wasn't necessary. The courses I was taking weren't that difficult, and I wasn't having any trouble keeping up, but I was so afraid of flunking out that I overdid it on the studying.

Fear of flunking out wasn't the only damper on my social life. My inability to dance was much more of a factor. Fifties music was the best dance music ever, and not being able to dance to that music was a real downer that inhibited my social life.

Prior to attending Albany State, I had never heard of the Neumann Club. When my roommate told me it was a social club for Catholic students and suggested we attend a meeting, we both went. Father Donald Stark was the club's chaplain, and my initial impression of him wasn't good. His parish in Albany was St. Patrick's, and he mentioned at the meeting that he usually said the nine o'clock Mass.

The Sunday after the meeting, I went over to St. Patrick's to hear Father Stark preach. The subject of his sermon was teenage romance. During the sermon he was so derisive and sarcastic in referring to young people who thought they were in love that he completely turned me off. I never went to another Neumann Club meeting.

Getting jobs in Greenport had been a problem, but it was not in Albany. With the amount of free time I had, I began working, first in the kitchen of the largest dormitory, Brubacher

Hall, and then in the snack bar of the student union. There was also a bulletin board in one of the academic buildings where job offers were listed. From that bulletin board, I got a lot of yard maintenance jobs.

The money I was making wasn't huge, but it was more than enough to take care of my modest wants. Once I started working, I always had some money. I could go to the movies, eat a lunch, and buy an occasional shirt or other article of clothing. Among the first of those that I bought was a pair of shoes, and so for the first time in my life, I had two pairs of shoes.

I was very much an extrovert, didn't have any trouble making friends, and was enjoying college very much. With a student body that had four girls for every boy, one might think getting dates was easy. Probably it was, but not for me. There were a lot of girls who were friends, many of them were very pretty, and even a few who I thought might be interested in going out with me. But I never asked them out or hit on them.

There was one very pretty girl, another freshman, who actually asked me to take her out, and another who told me she would go out with me, but I never followed up on their offers. I just didn't have any frame of reference for dating and was afraid of making a fool of myself.

In early November, I attended a meeting of the student council, became enthusiastic about what was going on, and shortly thereafter ran for freshman class senator. I was elected, and school got to be more fun.

As had been the case back in Greenport, there were those at Albany State who, for whatever reason, took a protective interest in me. The most memorable of these was a guy named Jerry Cerne. He was six foot eight and weighed almost three hundred pounds.

There were also those who, like some in Greenport, saw me as too mouthy and didn't care for me. The most memorable of these was a classmate who also lived in Sayles Hall. He was a fat, flabby, and obnoxious ass with whom, from the first time I met him, I couldn't get along.

One day in PE class, we were playing touch football when I dove for a fumble. I recovered it, and as I rolled over with the ball and looked up, Jerry blotted out the sun. He dove for the ball and landed on top of me. I think he thought he had hurt me, and he immediately got up, saying, "Jesus, John, I'm so sorry. Are you okay?" From that moment on, we were friends.

Later on during that game, a play was over when my fat, flabby, and obnoxious classmate hit me from behind and knocked me down. Jerry picked him up and dumped him headfirst into a huge trash barrel.

By the end of October, I was working between thirty and forty hours a week. Working in the cafeteria and the student union snack bar guaranteed that I always had enough to eat, and life was good. The big problem I had with working was that I couldn't say no to people who wanted me to do jobs for them. People for whom I worked referred me to other people, and it got to be too much.

Another aspect of college life about which I was unaware was the fraternities and sororities. There were only four fraternities, Alpha Pi Alpha, Kappa Beta, Potter Club, and Sigma Lambda Sigma. Each has its own fraternity house and distinctively colored jacket, but I had no idea how to join.

One night, when I was working in the student union, I was whistling "Gaudeamus" from Sigmund Romberg's *Student Prince,* when one of the Kappa Beta brothers, whom I didn't know, asked me, "Are you trying to tell me something?"

"What do you mean?" I answered.

"Do you know the name of the song you were whistling?" he asked.

"Yes. It is 'Gaudeamus' from Sigmund Romberg's the *Student Prince,*" I answered.

He looked at me a bit oddly and told me that it was the melody for the Kappa Beta hymn.

In November, the fraternities began having open houses. At that point, I had no great interest in joining a fraternity, but my roommate and a few of our friends did, so I went to some of the open houses.

After the open houses, the fraternities started inviting those they wanted to pledge their fraternity to dinner. I got one of these invitations and went. My roommate got invitations from all four of the fraternities. Eventually, he, I, and several of our friends decided to pledge APA, and I found the fraternity experience to be a great part of college life.

I hadn't given much thought to being homesick, but I was, and I eagerly awaited the Thanksgiving vacation. Just before Thanksgiving, there was a small flu epidemic on campus, and it was decided to start the Thanksgiving break the Friday before Thanksgiving instead of the Wednesday before. The extra vacation days were great and went too quickly. Homesickness notwithstanding, I was beginning to like college. From Christmas break onward, I couldn't wait to get back to Albany.

My grades for the first semester were two As, two Bs, and two Cs. Any fear of flunking out was gone, and I knew I could compete, academically. With that in mind, I began to think about a social life. I had not gone on a single date during the first semester.

At the start of the second semester, one of the psychology professors asked for volunteers to participate in a dance class while his students would observe the group dynamics. "Dance class" were the words that got my attention, and I signed up for the class. One of the other volunteers was a very cute little girl from Hadley, New York. Her name was Loris, but she went by Lori. I remember telling her that I had read an article in the *Saturday Evening Post* in which the wife of the subject of the article was named Loris. I don't know why I remembered that name, but I did. Lori said, "I doubt that very much,"

When it came to girls, I was completely guileless, and I was offended that Lori would suggest that I was lying to her. Regardless, I was very attracted to her. The fact that she was taking a dance class led me to think she might not be a great dancer, and that was a plus for me.

Unfortunately, the only dance that was taught was the Paso Doble, but it was fun. It took me about a month to work up the courage to ask her out. My choice for a first date was to invite her to go with me to the annual musical production put on by the arts and drama group. That year they were putting on *The Boyfriend*. I thought it would be a good first date, and it was.

That was the sixth date in my life and the first date that wasn't a dance. I didn't have to worry about stepping on Lori's feet or sitting out dances that I couldn't do, and I had a great time. It was so good that when I took Lori back to her dorm, I asked her out again, to go to a movie, and I was stunned when she said yes. Thus began my first relationship with a girl.

On our way to the movie, we had to pass St. Vincent's. As was my habit, I made the sign of the cross. Lori said, "You're a Catholic?"

When I told her I was, she said, "I'd better watch what I say."

On the way back to her dorm, after the movie, I told her, "This is the first time I have ever taken a girl to the movies."

"I don't believe you" was Lori's answer. Again, Lori's bluntness surprised and disappointed me; but not enough to blunt my attraction to her.

After our next date, we kissed for the first and last time, but we continued to go out until the middle of the first semester of my sophomore year. I realized that my love was unrequited and that Lori hated hurting my feelings. To ease her pain, I just stopped asking her out. We remained good friends, and I didn't have another date for almost a year.

The rest of the year went very well. I missed the dean's list by a tenth of a point, had made a lot of friends, and was eager to start my sophomore year. The small hitch in this euphoria was that during finals week, I was playing softball and reinjured my left knee. I remember hearing Dr. Kamen say as he operated on me, "There isn't much I can do for this kid. It's like broken eggshell in here." He put me in a hip to ankle cast and told me to see an orthopedic surgeon in six more weeks after the cast came off.

During the spring break, I had asked Mr. Sledjeski (Porky) for a job in the restaurant that summer, and he hired me. I needed that job badly and worried that going home with a cast on my leg might negate that offer.

My trip home for the summer break was one of the more interesting parts of my first year in college. With my leg in a cast, I took a bus to NYC and hobbled from the Port Authority to Penn Station. I had missed the last train to Greenport and thought I could wait in there until the next morning. When a cop told me I couldn't stay in the station, I took the train to Port Jefferson, which was about fifty miles from Greenport. There was an all-night diner across from the railroad station, and I asked the man on duty if I could stay there until sunup. He told me that I could but also told me that the truck that delivered the *NY Daily News* to Eastern Long Island would be coming through at four o'clock and that I could probably catch a ride with him. That I did, and it was one of the scariest rides I have ever had.

We drove through the thickest fog I had ever encountered, and I had to stick my head out the passenger side window to direct the driver. We drove at about twenty miles per hour, and I thought the trip would never end. At about seven o'clock he dropped off at the same corner where my stalker had dropped me off in 1954.

Mr. Sledjeski told me that as long as I could stand and walk around, I could start work, and I did the very next day. I washed the dishes, cleaned shrimp and vegetables, and thought I had a pretty good job.

David Whipple, the chef, was a local, but I had never met him and knew nothing about him. I was still on crutches when I began working, and on a few occasions, Dave had to give me a ride home. I had the feeling that he didn't like doing this, but I got along with him and, at least initially, didn't have any problems with him. The waitresses were great and treated me very well, and except for when we really got busy, the job was fun. If there was a fly in the ointment it was our Saturday night meal, short ribs of beef. It got to the point where I just couldn't eat them, but the rest of the meals were very good.

There was a freezer in the barn behind the restaurant, and every night before closing, Dave would go out to the freezer and bring in the meat we would need for the next day to thaw out in the sink. In order to turn on the light in the walk-in freezer, Dave had to put his hand through a hole in the wall and flip on the switch.

One night, Richie, Mr. Sledjeski's son, sneaked out and waited behind the wall. When Dave, with a tray filled with meat in his arms, reached through the hole to turn off the light, Richie clamped his hand over Dave's. Dave threw the tray of meat up in the air and came screaming back into the kitchen.

Over the Fourth of July weekend, Mr. Sledjeski took me into the dining room and introduced me to a very nice couple, a Mr. and Mrs. Rath. I still had my cast on, and Mr. Sledjeski told me they would be giving me a ride home. The next day, Mr. Sledjeski told me that Mr. Rath was going to pay my way through school. I thought that was great and didn't give it much thought.

Wednesdays were Mr. and Mrs. Sledjeski's day off, and they would usually go up island with friends for a day out and a good dinner. On one of those Wednesdays, I had a very serious run-in with Dave. My cast had come off the day before, and I worked that afternoon without any problem.

As soon as I came in the next day, Dave started in on me. "Your days on Easy Street are over" was his opening shot, and it got worse as the day went on. Dave's attack came as a complete surprise to me. We had not had any problems up until that day, and I didn't know how to handle what was going on. It came to a head later that afternoon when Dave and I had to unload a delivery truck. We were almost done when Dave handed me a push broom and said, "Clean this up. I will be checking, and it better be clean."

I had had it and said, "Dave, I don't know what your problem is. You have been on me all day, and if you don't knock it off, I am going to shove this broom so far up your ass that it will puncture your lung." We didn't speak for the rest of the day.

That night, when Mr. and Mrs. Sledjeski got home, Dave and Mr. Sledjeski had a conference. Mr. Sledjeski then came back in the kitchen and tore me a new ass. The language he used in excoriating me was pretty raw, and he didn't mince words, but he didn't fire me. I wanted very much to tell him what he could do with his job, but for once, I held my tongue. I wasn't thinking about Mr. Rath's paying for my education, just that I couldn't afford to quit that job.

I understood that Mr. Sledjeski had to ream me out. He needed Dave a lot more than he needed me and had to placate him, even if it was at my expense. I didn't expect an apology, but I had always held Mr. Sledjeski in very high regard, and he had disappointed me. There was another side to the story of what had happened, and I wish that he had at least asked me for my perspective.

The next day, Betty Conklin, the head waitress, jumped on Mr. Sledjeski for what he had done, but no more was said. Over the next few weeks, I don't think I exchanged more than ten words with Dave, but I lasted out the summer.

Shortly after Labor Day weekend, Mr. Sledjeski and Mr. Rath gave me a check for the year's room and board at Albany

State. I took the check and gave it some serious thought before giving it back. I owed Greenport too much already for all they had done for me and didn't want to increase the debt.

Mr. Sledjeski didn't take my refusal very well, and I was sorry about that. His heart was in the right place, but I was the wrong target for his benevolence. The people of Greenport had gotten me to college, and the least I could do is go the rest of the way on my own.

Three days later, I went to get a haircut before returning to Albany. Mr. Mazzo, the barber, told me, "John, Porky was in here yesterday telling us what an ungrateful little bastard you are. I don't know why you did what you did, but you did the right thing." That summer would be the last I ever spent in Greenport.

On the same day that I gave the check back to Mr. Sledjeski, I turned down a similar offer. One of mom's friends, Teresa Scott, had a good friend whom I knew only as Mr. Moyer. He was also a customer at the gas station, and he always tipped me when I gassed up his car. Before I left for college the previous September, he handed me a hundred dollars told me that if I ever needed anything I should just let him know. I didn't take the money or take him up on his offer.

On this day, he saw me walking home and offered to give me a ride. During the ride, he asked me how college was going. When I told him, "Very well," he said, "Here is something that might help make it even better" and handed me some money. I didn't count it, but it looked like five twenty-dollar bills.

I said, "Mr. Moyer, if I needed the money, I would take it, and I thank you very much. But I don't need it, and I don't think it would be right to take it."

He said, "Okay, John. It's here if you need it. You're an honorable young man."

I didn't see Mr. Sledjeski again until I got back from Vietnam in 1975 and started making visits to Greenport. On each of my trips, I would stop in for dinner at Porky's, and on these occasions Mr. Sledjeski always greeted me warmly.

Mr. Sledjeski had a massive heart attack at his grandson Walter's graduation party in June of 1983, a day before his sixty-eighth birthday, and passed away. He was one of the real movers and shakers in Greenport, and his loss was felt. Greenport had been more because of his having been there and is less without him. One slight bump along the road of our friendship was not enough to vitiate all the good he had done for me and Greenport.

My sophomore year in college was okay, but the accounting classes got the best of me, and I changed my major to history. School became fun again after that, and I got a little bit involved with the basketball team, being the scorekeeper at home games and making some of the trips as an assistant manager. Dr. Richard "Doc" Sauers, the basketball coach, became a friend, and basketball was a substitute for dating.

At the end of the spring semester of my junior year, Dick Fink, the head of food services at Albany State, came into the cafeteria where I was working and asked, "Is there anyone in here who knows where Fishers Island is?" I told him I used to live there. Dick then told me that a friend of his was the manager of the country club there and needed some people to work in the snack bar on the beach. I told him that I was interested. That summer turned out to be one of the best. I made a lot of money, enjoyed the work, and met my first girlfriend.

The members of the country club were some of the wealthiest people in the United States. In a conversation between F. Scott Fitzgerald and Ernest Hemingway, F. Scott supposedly said, "The rich are different than you and me," to which Ernest supposedly replied, "Yes, they have more money." The rich may have had more money, but there were similarities that we and they shared. Some were very gracious and others boorish; some were generous and some cheap, just like us less fortunate folk. I can't recall ever envying any of the club members or even fantasizing about being rich, but did see my summer on Fishers Island, living among the rich, as an educational experience.

There was no socializing between the country club employees and members, but there were two contacts I had that stand out. The first occurred on a Saturday night, when I had taken a five-mile walk into the village to eat at someplace other than the club. I was walking back when one of the younger club members picked me up in his convertible. He was dressed in a tuxedo and going to the Saturday night dance at the club.

"This is so boring," he said to me. "Every Saturday night, it is the same thing—same band, same music, same girls. There has got to be more to life than this." I told him that my heart went out to him, and I think he detected the note of sarcasm in my voice.

The second incident occurred when I was shooting pool by myself in the employees lounge. The teenage son of one of the members and his friend came into the lounge.

"We want to play pool" were his first words to me.

"So do I" was my answer.

"How long are you going to play?" was his next comment, and I invited them to play with me. Both were terrible, and neither was faking his lack of ability.

At one point, he said to me, "I'll play you for a hundred dollars."

There was no doubt in my mind that I could make an easy hundred dollars, but the building engineer, Walt, was there, and he caught my eye with the shake of his head. I told my challenger that I had to get down to the beach house and let him and his friend have the table.

That evening, Walt told me, "John, you would have won the money but been out of here the next day."

The niece of the country club manager was one of my coworkers. Her name was Elaine, and she was a very lovely girl. Elaine was, for me, Tennyson's "Elaine, the good, Elaine the Fair, Elaine the Lily Maid of Astelot" from *Idylls of the King*, and I became totally infatuated. Elaine was very bright, as well as cute, and would be starting nursing school in the fall. She was my first girlfriend, and she made that summer the best summer I had ever had.

Another benefit of the job was that I met some people who had known my father, and one of them helped me locate my father's grave. When I returned to Fisher's Island with Young, my daughter-in-law, and my two grandchildren in 2013, the headstone was gone, and we couldn't find the grave. We had a great time on that visit, and the island was more beautiful than I remembered. Hopefully, we will be able to get back there.

At the end of the summer, Elaine and I parted with vows of undying love. We kept in constant contact, and I did get up to Boston to visit her.

My senior year went well, especially my student teaching in the Milne School. My supervisor was great. I liked teaching and was planning to teach for a year after graduation and then go into the military.

During my student teaching, I became good friends with the family of one of my students. During my visit to Albany to see my brother, just before going to Vietnam, I gave my former student a call and told him I would like to stop in and see his family.

"John, that might not be such a good idea. Louis was killed in Vietnam earlier this year, and mom is still taking it very hard." I remembered Louis, his younger brother, very well and didn't make the visit.

That year, I made the dean's list and subsequently took a job teaching at Cohoes High School, where I taught history and also coached the track team. The star of the track team was a very fine young man named Gordon Leversee. He was a great student, a fine athlete, and an all-around good kid. I recently found out that he is currently one of the deans at Keene College, in New Hampshire. We subsequently reconnected, and I take great pleasure in the fact that Gordon lived up to the great expectations I had for him.

CHS was a tough school, and the unemployment rate in Cohoes was very high. I remember Madge Hicks, the principal, telling me, "John, we don't have a truancy problem here. Life here is so much better than what they have at home that they want to be here." I saw myself in many of the kids and related to them very well.

On one occasion, just after lunch, one of my homeroom students, Donald Spain, came running into the room, holding his right hand over his eye, and said to me, "Prof, that old bitch s just hit me in the eye." Don was referring to Ms. Hicks.

His eye was red and swollen. I sent him to the school nurse, who told him, "That's an insect bite." Not many insects were out in about in February, and I found a slight bit of humor in the diagnosis.

On a more humorous note, Mary Jane Wilkolaski was one of my better students and a very nice girl. After an absence, she didn't bring in a written excuse, and when I asked her why, she told me, "My mother won't give me one." I wrote a note to her mother and told her I needed a written excuse for Mary Jane. She replied: "Mr. Sullivan, Mary Jane had diarrhea, and I didn't think it looked good on paper."

One of my favorite students, Barney Stopera, raised his hand in class one day. When I called on him, he said, "Mr. Sullivan, Tony just farted."

"Barney, what do you want me to do about it?" I asked.

"Could you please open the windows?" Barney asked.

It was February, and I declined his request.

The best part of that year was coaching the track team. We didn't have a real track on which to practice, and that was a challenge, but the kids were great. One of my more memorable experiences of that year occurred at a track practice. I was standing on the athletic field with a clipboard in my hand when a Lincoln town car pulled up next to me.

A very short man, impeccably dressed and wearing a Chesterfield overcoat (à la Edward G. Robinson, in the movie *Little Caesar*) got out of the car, approached me, and said, "Who are you.?" I told him who I was, and he said, "My name is Dawson. I'm just looking around." Without another word, Mr. Dawson got in his car and left.

As he pulled away, Dolph Spadoni, one of the kids on the team, came up to me and said, "Prof, every day in school, you guys try to teach us that honesty is the best policy. Every brick in that guy's house came from the bricks they used to build the annex. Don't tell me crime doesn't pay. He seems to be doing pretty good."

As much as I enjoyed the teaching experience, it didn't live up to my expectations, and I had trouble dealing with the apathy of the students. In July, in keeping with my agenda, I enlisted in the army.

Chapter 14

GI JOHN

As I have stated, joining the military had, for as long as I can remember, been on my agenda. After I finished my year of teaching and coaching at Cohoes High School, I went to the recruiting office in Albany to talk to a recruiter. I told that I wanted to go the Army Language School in Monterey, CA. He told me that during basic training I would be given a language aptitude test, and if I got a high enough score, I could then apply. That sounded good to me. A week later, I took my physical, and a few hours later I was on my way to Ft. Dix, New Jersey, for basic training with about fifty other recruits.

We arrived at about eleven at night and were taken to a barracks, where we were given sheets and pillow cases to make up our bunks. At five o'clock we were awakened, taken to breakfast, and then issued uniforms. By that night, we had been assigned to Company O, Third Training Regiment.

At our very first formation, the next morning, SFC John Wolfe greeted us with what I thought was a rather crude, but humorous comment. "Now, I know you dickheads are all worried about the girls you left back home. I can assure you that you have nothing to worry about. When you get back home, you will find them just like you left them, freshly f—ed."

Those first few days were pretty confusing, but things settled down pretty quickly, and the eight weeks went by in a blur of constant activity. There were three drill instructors assigned to Company O, Sergeants Cooke, Nelson, and Turner. Sgt. Turner was the scariest of the three, and he yelled a lot. But I liked him, and we got along well. One night, after spending the day on kitchen police (KP), I was told that I would have to spend the night on fire watch in the mess hall and to go to the barracks and get my mattress.

When I got to the barracks, Sgt. Turner was conducting a surprise inspection. All the recruits' foot lockers were open, and when Sgt. Turner found something out of place or not folded properly, he would upend the foot locker, spilling the contents on the floor. No foot locker escaped Sgt. Turner's dumping. When I arrived, Sgt. Turner was two foot lockers away from mine. I opened it and stood at attention waiting for him.

He had seen me come running in, and when he got to me, he said, "What's your story, Professor?" I told him I had been on KP and had to get my mattress and get back to the mess hall for fire watch duty..

"Okay, Professor. You are one f—ed up cat, but you is okay. Get the hell out of here." He didn't dump my foot locker.

There was a competition among the three barracks in our company to see which of the three barracks would score highest on the daily inspection. For the first nine days, the barracks I was in scored highest. When we came in second on the tenth inspection, Sgt. Turner called us out for a formation in front of the barracks and read us the riot act. "You dumb-ass recruits have gone from sugar to shit," he screamed. "One more time and I'll send all of you back to start all over again."

I knew that even if he wanted to do that he couldn't, but some took him at his word. That night, we covered the windows with blankets and scoured the barracks. The next day, we were back in first place.

During BT, going to Mass was not only a religious experience for me but an opportunity to get away from the barracks for an hour or so. The first time I went to a Sunday Mass, the chaplain, a Captain Capitani, came out of the sacristy and asked if there was anyone who could serve Mass. I volunteered and served Mass every Sunday while in BT.

Every Sunday, the church was packed with GIs just getting away from the barracks for an hour. Father Capitani's topic for his sermons, for the entire eight weeks, was the Ecumenical movement. Five minutes into his sermon, 99 percent of the recruits had nodded off. Father Capitani was well aware of what was happening, and it surprised me that he didn't change the topic of his sermons.

The best part of BT was the food. I ate like a refugee from a concentration camp and couldn't get enough food. Sundays were a challenge. Because I served Mass every Sunday, I had to rush to get back for breakfast before the mess hall closed. I never missed a breakfast and managed to put on nine pounds during BT.

There were no problems with the physical aspects of BT, and on our twenty-mile march, I and four other recruits finished more than an hour ahead of the rest of the company. I went through basic in the summer of 1962, a very hot summer, and I saw many guys pass out from heat exhaustion. I got so thirsty on one of the marches that I drank water from a rain barrel.

I hadn't forgotten about language school and had taken the aptitude test, but I couldn't get any help from the three DIs as to how to go about applying. Just before finishing BT, I was moving some furniture in the company commander's office when he asked me, "Sullivan, what do you see yourself doing in the army?" I told him that I wanted to go to the Army Language School but didn't know how to apply. He went to his filing cabinet, pulled out a book, and after reading a page or two, wrote something down on a sheet of paper and handed it to me. "This is the regulation that covers applying for language training. When you get to your next assignment, pull this reg., and you will be on your way."

The one thing I didn't like about BT was that I didn't get to go home after completing training, as was the usual case. From Ft. Dix, I could have taken the bus to NYC, taken the subway out to Long Island, and hitch hiked the rest of the way. That would have cost less than twelve dollars. My first assignment was to Ft. Bliss, in El Paso, Texas. Getting home from there would be a lot more expensive.

I finished BT the week before the Cuban Missile Crisis. One night, during that last week, we stayed on the rifle range until three in the morning firing off excess ammunition. The next day, there wasn't a rifle round to be found.

Ft. Bliss was a good assignment. The barracks were new, and the squad bays were divided into two-man sleeping cubicles. One of the mess halls had been awarded the title of best mess in the entire army, and eating there was as good as eating in a very good restaurant. I put on some more weight in the short time I was there.

My assignment was to Headquarter Battalion, Special Troops, and it turned out to be a great one. Most of the guys in the battalion had some college, and many had degrees. I had to interview with the battalion sergeant major to get a specific assignment. The interview went well, and I became the company clerk for Company C, Special Troops Battalion. It was a cushy job, and I loved it.

I arrived at Ft. Bliss on a Thursday morning, and on Friday things began to happen. Ft. Bliss was the headquarters for the army's Air Defense Command and the place where training on the Hawk and Nike missiles was conducted.

That Friday morning, Hawk units were being alerted to pack up and start north, to Florida. On Saturday, we were notified that

President Kennedy would be addressing the nation on Monday evening.

Monday evening, the day room was packed as President Kennedy announced the Cuban blockade. At that moment, I, and most of the men in that room, felt we were going to war, and that was probably the single scariest moment I had as a GI.

When I enlisted in the army, the enemy was the Soviet Union, and Cuba was nowhere on my horizon. My fantasy, if I had one about my life as a GI, was to go to language school, learn Russian, and help stop the spread of the Red Tide of Communism.

My position as company clerk got me out of having to do KP or guard duty. Another part of the job was that I would have to make up the daily roster for guard duty. Over Christmas, we were short-handed, and on Christmas Eve, I put myself on guard duty.

My post was a huge motor pool, and I had to continuously walk the perimeter of the motor pool twice during my tour, which lasted from six in the evening until six in the morning. It was a very windy and cold night, and I was walking the perimeter, rifle on my shoulder, when the bells in the post chapel started pealing Christmas carols in preparation for Midnight Mass.

Midnight Mass was a very special event when I was a kid. Those bells brought back some good as well as bad memories, and I can't remember any time in my life when I felt lonelier than I did that night.

After I finished my second walk around the motor pool, at about five in the morning, the Jeep took me back to the guard shack. I was lying down on a bunk when the sergeant of the guard came in and said, "Sullivan, you have a call."

When I picked up the phone, Chuck Fowler was on the line. Chuck was one of my fraternity brothers from my Albany days as well as one of my best friends. He had called to wish me a Merry Christmas, and that has to be among the top three nicest things anyone has ever done for me.

The company commander, Captain Paul Hughes, who had replaced Captain Anderson, was only three years older than I, and we became friends. When I wanted to apply to go to language school, he told me I couldn't go until he got reassigned, which happened seven months later. He signed off on my request, and in May of 1963, I began a twelve-month course in course in Russian at the Army Language School in Monterey, CA.

Captan Hughes was the best Commanding Officer I had while in the army. He pretty much left me on my own, which led me to get involved in one of the more humorous incidents in my military life.

In most army units company size or larger, there are soldiers called "duty soldiers." These guys spend their days pushing brooms and mops and keeping the company areas clean. We had three duty soldiers in our company. One of them was Pfc. Jones, and he was an original. He didn't have much formal education, was raised in carnivals, and always called me Mr. Sullivan.

One day, he came into the office with a very unattractive woman and said, "Mr. Sullivan, me and my fiancée would like to see Captain Hughes." I went into Captain Hughes's office and said, "Sir, Jones is outside with his fiancée, and they want to see you." I showed them in, and they came out a few minutes later.

Captain Hughes came to his office door and said to me, "John, Jones actually wants to marry that woman. I told him to go ahead, if that is what he wants. They're getting married tomorrow."

The next day, two of the guys in the company told me that they had seen Jones's fiancée soliciting on the Alvarado in El Paso the night before. That afternoon, I saw Jones and asked him where his wife was. "The last time I saw her, she was peddling her ass down on the Alvarado. The wedding is off," he answered.

The next day was a Saturday, and I was alone in the office when the phone rang. The caller claimed to be the brother of Jones's former fiancée and said, in words as near as I can recall,

"Sir, what would you do if some experienced soldier lured an innocent young girl out here by promising to marry her and then went back on his word?"

I replied by saying, "I'd get a lawyer. We have already gotten a lawyer from our staff judge advocate's office for Private Jones. As soon as they finish their background investigation on your sister, they will be contacting you."

None of this was true, but I felt that Jones was being scammed, and I wanted them to know that Jones wasn't on his own. Jones ended up having to buy a bus ticket back to Kansas City for his ex-fiancée, and that was the end of it.

On another occasion, a soldier volunteered to Captain Hughes that he was a homosexual. He was given a less than honorable discharge. I had to escort him off the base, and during the drive he told me that he wasn't queer and said that he was just to get out of the army.

Reveille was at five every morning. One morning, as I rushed out to get in formation, I came upon a lovely young woman wearing nothing but a blue, diaphanous negligee. She told me that she had given her boyfriend a ride back to the base a few hours ago. He had disappeared into the barracks, and she was waiting for him. This lovely vision in blue didn't know her soldier friend's name but said she would know him if she saw him. The military police took her away, to the dismay of those already in formation.

Not long thereafter, I left for the Army Language School in Monterey. I had enjoyed Ft. Bliss, but I was eager to get to Monterey. I didn't know what language I would be studying but was hoping for Russian.

As soon as I checked in, I was told that I would be studying Russian in Class R12–104, which was a twelve-month class and the 104th Russian class ever taught at Monterey. This would prove to be a defining moment in my life, in that studying Russian led to me being recruited into Military Intelligence, which ultimately was a significant factor in my decision to apply for a job with the CIA.

Monterey had a lot to offer beyond the language school. It was an absolutely beautiful location, with Carmel-by-the-Sea nearby, Pebble Beach golf course adjacent to the post, and San Francisco just a couple of hours away.

Classes began a week after I arrived, and they were intensive. We started out with more than eighty students in our class and finished with forty-one. There were army, navy, and Marine Corps students in our class as well as civilians from the various government agencies (FBI, NSA, DIA, etc.). Never have I been happier about having studied Latin than when I took Russian. The two languages are similarly constructed, so I had an edge on many of the students.

The time flew, and before I knew it, I graduated and was assigned to Ft. Holabird, in Baltimore, for a six-month course in operational intelligence. I had been in touch with Elaine, and when I left Monterey, I flew directly to Boston to see her. She wanted to tell me, in person, that it was all over. After that, I spent a few days with Bill in Albany and then took a bus to Baltimore and Ft. Holabird.

The training was very good. The most interesting part of the training was doing a seaborne incursion from a submarine. The exercise took place in Long Island Sound and was run out of New London. The food on the sub was great, but it was crowded, and I slept on a torpedo.

When we surfaced for our launch, the first three rubber rafts we inflated had holes in them, and we had to patch them before launching. On the one mile row into the beach, I was a bit nervous.

My social life did improve in Baltimore. At a USO event at Ft. Holabird, in the summer of 1964, I met a lovely girl named Jean Suelau, a Baltimore resident and a student at St. Joseph's college in Emmitsburg, Maryland. I subsequently called her, and our first date was dinner at the Chesapeake Restaurant and then *My Fair Lady* at a local theater. Jean's family was lovely, and one of the best Thanksgivings I have ever had was at her house.

One of my best friends at Ft. Holabird was another Army Language School alumnus named Dan Allman. Dan was from Suitland, Maryland, and as we became closer, he took me home on some weekends. On one occasion, we went to a Colts/ Redskins preseason game. Dan and his family were salt of the earth, decent people, and visiting them was one of the best parts of my assignment at Ft. Holabird.

Wanting to press my friendship with Jean, I implored Dan to take me down to Emmitsburg, where Jean fixed Dan up with one of her friends. On weekends, we began going down to Emmitsburg every chance we got until we finished training. Emmitsburg in the fall is something to behold, and walking the Gettysburg battlefield was icing on the cake.

After training, Dan was assigned to Okinawa and I to Germany. While I was in Oberammergau, studying German, I got the proverbial "Dear John" letter. Dan got home from Okinawa before I finished my tour, and he and Jean began dating. While I was in graduate school, I got an invitation to their wedding.

The two best times I ever had in the army came about as a result of my friendship with Jean. Jean's best friend in Baltimore and at St. Joseph's was Mary Carroll Ebaugh. MC, as she was known, spent her junior year abroad in Rome, and we had stayed in touch after I was assigned to Germany. The first of these best times occurred when she and three of her friends met with me in London over their spring break. We all did a lot of sightseeing, but one night I took MC to Claridge's for dinner.

I had read that Claridge's was J. Paul Getty's favorite hotel, and I thought MC would like it. She did, and so did I. We had four waiters attending to us, and the food was not only delicious but also less expensive than I thought it would be. The only thing

that could have made that event better would have been if that
dinner had taken place in a romantic context. But a great dinner,
with a beautiful girl, in an elegant setting was, at least for me,
one of those Walter Mitty fantasies that helped make my life
more than ordinary.

The second of these very memorable times occurred when I
invited MC and her friends to come to Oberammergau for a long
weekend of skiing. Garmisch was the site of the 1936 Winter
Olympics and just down the mountain from Oberammergau. It
was also the home of the US Army recreation center.

I made reservations in the Green Arrow hotel for less than ten
dollars a day, per person. A day's skiing pass, including all clothing, skis, and a T-bar pass, was ten dollars a day. Once again,
there was no romance, but it was a wonderful time. We toured
King Ludwig's castle, skied, and went to Mass in a monastery
where a choir of monks sang a beautiful service. Shanty Irish
kids from Greenport didn't do such things, but I was no longer
a Shanty Irish kid.

Several years later, I was coaching my son's soccer team in
a tournament, ran into Dan's brother, Bernie, and subsequently
reconnected with Dan and Jean. They have five children, three
boys and two girls, and if there is a happier family, I haven't met
them. I went to their son Matt's ordination. Dan and Jean live
near my son, daughter-in-law, and grandkids, and I try to stop
in and see them on my grandfatherly visits. We share some great
memories, and they are one of my buffers against cynicism.

My assignment at Ft. Holabird was followed by an assignment with the 513th Military Intelligence Group in Obereusel,
Germany, where I worked at the Defector Reception Center.
Most of the residents of the center were from Eastern Europe and
spoke some Russian. Therefore, I used to take them out on work
details. I was also put in charge of one of the barracks. The 513th
had two field stations, one in Berlin and one in Bremerhaven, and
I had hoped to be assigned to one of these.

Initially, when I broached this to my commanding officer he said, "Sullivan, you are a little older than a lot of the guys here, and I need you to run the barracks." Two weeks later, he called me into his office and said, "After I denied your request, you didn't piss and moan. You just went out and continued to do a good job. There is a slot opening in Bremerhaven, and I am going to send you there. You have done a good job here, and I know you will there."

Bremerhaven was the highest-producing unit in the 513th, and I felt lucky to be assigned there. The weather was terrible, but the work was great. On the day I arrived, I was given an allowance for civilian clothes and began my career as a spook.

There was a mix of civilians and military personnel assigned to Bremerhaven, and it was a pretty relaxed atmosphere. One of the civilians assigned there took a liking to me and lobbied to get me sent to Oberammergau to study German.

As good as Monterey had been, Oberammergau was better. Oberammergau is located in Southern Bavaria and is a very beautiful village. It is also the site of *The Passion Play*, a world-renowned event that takes place every ten years. In Monterey, I had been in class seven hours a day speaking Russian, I had been in an English-speaking environment for the remaining seventeen hours. In Oberammergau, I was immersed in German, in and out of class, and I learned so much more. Fifty years later, I find I have retained so much more of my German than my Russian.

I did a fair amount of translating in Bremerhaven; mostly Russian military manuals and mail intercepts. It got a little boring, but one of our agents did provide the first photograph of a Soviet nuclear submarine with its rocket launcher on deck.

Neither I nor my single colleagues could use the military mess halls. Our living quarters were above the Armed Forces Network (AFN) station, where we cooked our own meals. Some of my housemates were linguists and others technicians, and in terms of education, they were a cut above the soldiers in most units.

Scrabble and poker were the two most popular diversions, and on my second night living there, I dethroned the house Scrabble champion by more than a hundred points; to the applause of the other players. That was probably my most notable accomplishment while in Bremerhaven.

My social life in Germany wasn't much better than it had been in any place except Ft. Holabird, but I did date two German girls and two American school teachers. In another small world incident, my younger son, Jimmy, when he was a student at Virginia Commonwealth University, dated the niece of one of the teachers I had dated in Bremerhaven.

While stationed in Bremerhaven, I decided to take a vacation and go to Ireland. During that trip, I had an experience that I consider one of the strangest of my life. I took a cruise ship from Bremen to London, and from London, I took a train to Dublin. My first impression of Dublin was not good. It was very rundown and depressing. This was the city of mom's birth, and I could understand why she might have wanted to leave. I took some tours outside of Dublin and found the countryside very beautiful.

Another disappointment with Dublin was that it was the only city I visited in my twenty-nine months overseas in which I encountered anti-American sentiment. I was in a taxi when the driver asked me, "Are you with the forces?"

When I told him that I was, he said, "You goddamn Americans are going to start World War III." He then went off on American imperialism. He was very articulate, and I almost enjoyed listening to him, but I was glad when we arrived at the B&B where I was staying.

At the end of my stay in Dublin, I decided to take the overnight boat from Dunn Laore to Liverpool. When I picked up my cabin assignment, the attendant told me that I would be sharing my cabin with another gentleman.

As I entered the cabin, I saw a man with his back to me,

hanging his coat up. I stuck out my hand and said, "My name is John Sullivan." The man turned around and said, "So is mine." I thought I was looking in a mirror. He was my size, wore glasses, and had a slight cast in his left eye and a gray streak in his hair, as did I.

When my father passed away, Mom had lost all contact with his family. We didn't even have a picture of him, but Mom had told me that he was from Cork. So, too, was my cabin companion. He was also a graduate student at Trinity College, in Dublin, and a pompous little prig.

Under most circumstances, I would have engaged with John Sullivan II and gotten as much information as I could from him, but I could not warm up to him. I regret not having tried to do so.

During the time I was in Bremerhaven, I was promoted twice, once from E-4 to E-5 and then from E-5 to E-6. By the time my tour was up, I was living fat and happy, making more money than I had ever made, and living better than I ever had. Leaving the army was not an easy choice. The deal maker turned out to be the GI Bill. I wanted to get my MA more than I wanted to stay in the army.

I had already applied to and been accepted for admission to Michigan State's graduate school and was looking forward to starting the next chapter in my life. The fact that I hadn't seen a football game in three years was also a factor in my looking forward to MSU.

It took me three days to process out of the 513th in Frankfurt, and then I was on my way to the States and Ft. Jay, New York, where I was discharged. I had fulfilled my obligation and, as Mom would have put it, "paid my dues."

Paying one's dues implies somehow making a sacrifice. I never saw my military service as any kind of sacrifice and sometimes feel guilty when people thank me for my service. Every year for the last decade, I have participated in a World War II Day at Rocky Run Middle School in Chantilly, Virginia, and for the last three years I have been a guest at a dinner at Chantilly High School honoring veterans. I am humbled in the presence of many of these men. They are a constant reminder that not all veterans had it as easy as I did, and for so many of them, their service was a sacrifice.

Chapter 15

SPARTAN

My decision to go to Michigan State was in large part due to the fact that one of my fraternity brothers from Albany State, Dr. Lee Upcraft, and his wife, Lil, were there. I arrived in East Lansing nine days before classes started and stayed with Lee and Lil for a few days until I found a room to rent.

One of my first shocks was the size of the campus and student body. Albany State took up one square block and had a student body of about 2,200, most of whom I would get to know on a first-name basis. The Michigan State campus was spread over more than five thousand acres, on which were more than five hundred buildings. The student population was in excess of forty-five thousand students, none of whom I knew.

During that first week, I spent a lot of time walking around the campus and getting acclimated. The Michigan State football team, The Spartans, and band were there, practicing for the upcoming football season, and I spent a lot of time watching and listening to the band.

The room I rented was two blocks from the campus and directly across from St. John's RCC, the student parish for MSU.

The priest claimed that there were more members of St. John's parish than there were students at Notre Dame.

I became an active member of the parish, and that helped me a great deal in getting settled in. One of the priests was a member of an order and wore a brown cassock and rope sash. He was a very dynamic and physically impressive priest who gave great sermons and was very popular with the MSU students. Whenever I saw him at football games, he was always with a lot of students.

Just before Christmas of 1967, his health began to deteriorate, and over the next three of four months, he seemed to fall apart. By April, he had to use two canes to walk, his voice became almost inaudible, and he was very pale. Within a month, he had passed away. The first known case of AIDS in the United States occurred in 1967, in St. Louis, and I think the priest may have been another victim.

The high school football coach at the American high school in Bremerhaven, George Pepoy, had played football at Michigan State, and when I told him I would be going there for grad school, he asked me to look up Duffy Daugherty, the football coach, and say hello for him.

Football practices were closed to the public, but one day as I walked by the stadium, I noticed people just walking into the stadium and followed them. I hadn't seen a football game in three years and couldn't pass up an opportunity to watch a top college team practice. Michigan State had played Notre Dame to a 10 – 10 tie the year before, in what was called "the game of the century," and I was looking forward to the football season.

During the practice, Coach Daugherty came over to the bleachers where I was sitting and said to me, "Hey kid, how would you like to go out there and bump heads with these guys?" "Not today, coach," was my answer.

I then said, "Coach, do you remember a player named George Pepoy?"

Coach Daugherty replied, "I sure do. He and Tommy Yewcic

(an All-American at MSU) came from the same hometown. How do you know him?" We then spent a few minutes discussing George. I found Coach Daugherty to be a funny guy. One of his more notable quotes is, "Dancing is a contact sport. Football is a collision sport."

A couple of days before I registered for classes, I saw a notice in the student union announcing that the language laboratory in Wells Hall was looking for assistants. At that time, the Wells Hall laboratory was the largest language lab in the free world. Assistants would be needed to prepare the tapes used in the classes as well as to monitor the classes and address any problems that occurred. I thought this was a job I would like, and I went for an interview with Dr. Sergei Andretz, the head of the Russian department and the director of the laboratory.

Dr. Andretz was a hard-nosed, chain-smoking Russian immigrant, and our interview lasted about an hour, after which he hired me. I started work the next day, and it turned out to be a great job. One of the best parts of the job was working with the various language teachers preparing tapes for their classes. It gave me an opportunity to maintain my German and Russian as well as practice my Spanish. I got along very well with the Spanish faculty and became friends with several of the PhD candidates in the Spanish department.

After registering for my classes, I had an interview with the chairman of the German department, Dr. William Nolan. I found him to be cool and aloof, but he also welcomed me to the department and approved my classes.

Once classes started and I got caught up in the routine, I had a small epiphany: I was at MSU to learn, and I had better get to it. I did, and got the best grades I have ever had. Even with as many hours as I worked in the lab, I had a lot of free time, and I spent 95 percent of that time studying. I got straight As for the first time since second grade and was loving life.

Football season started, and life got even better. My seat for

the football games was very good, and I went to every home game
that season. Saturday afternoons at a Michigan State football
game were events to behold. The huge tailgate parties, the halftime shows, and the excitement of the games were all new to me
and, compared with the poorly attended soccer games at Albany
State, much more fun.

Unfortunately, the Spartans had a very bad year, winning two
games and losing eight. I did get to see USC, with OJ Simpson,
beat Michigan State, and watch Woody Hayes, the legendary
Ohio State coach, pace the sidelines in his white, short-sleeved
shirt during a snowstorm.

If there was a negative aspect to my time at MSU, it was the
weather. It snowed for the first time on September 29, and snow,
ice, and subfreezing temperatures were common. On New Year's
Eve, 1967, I was alone in my room at about nine o'clock when
one of the Spanish professors, Dr. Juanita Uceda, called. She told
me that several of the Spanish faculty members were having a
party and invited me to come over.

Her apartment was on the other side of the campus, about
three miles from where I was living. It was five below zero, and
it took me over an hour to get there. The party was a lot of fun,
and Dr. Uceda gave me a ride home. That was the only party I
attended while at MSU.

There was a lot of antiwar activity on the MSU campus, and I
saw draft card burnings and a lot of antiwar posters. I remember
seeing a young Vietnam veteran getting in a confrontation with
some antiwar demonstrators, tearing their posters off the walls
and daring them to fight him.

For some reason, he asked me what I thought of the protesters. I told him that I, like he, was a veteran and didn't agree with
the protesters' antiwar sentiments, but I thought he was wrong
in doing what he was doing. In retrospect, if I had known then
what I know now, I might have joined the protesters.

My job in the language lab was going very well. I enjoyed

the work and before long was supervising the other monitors during the night shift. There was a small world incident with one of the other monitors that I enjoy recalling. One of my former army colleagues, Chief Warrant Officer Mike Callahan, was the polygraph examiner for my unit in Bremerhaven. Sue "Sam" Drayton was one of my assistants in the language lab; she was tall, willowy, and very sweet.

Sue was a member of a group of MSU students who were sending letters and cards to wounded Vietnam soldiers. She was discussing one of the soldiers to whom she was writing and mentioned that he was an older soldier named Mike Callahan who was very flirtatious in his letters.

Mike was an incorrigible flirt. He did not look the part of a ladies' man, but he was. I can remember him stopping a very pretty German girl on a street in Bremerhaven. He asked her if she could tell him what time it was. When she lifted her arm to look at her watch, Mike said, "You don't have a ring on your finger. How can a girl as pretty as you not be married.?" He asked for, but didn't get her telephone number and said to me, "John, you'd be surprised at how many numbers I do get with that line."

As it turned out, the Mike Callahan to whom Sue was writing was my former colleague. When I repeated this story to another former army colleague, he told me that when Mike came home from Vietnam, he was bedecked with medals, still recovering from his wounds, and in high spirits.

The first girl I asked out at MSU was a Chinese graduate student. Her roommate was one of the teaching assistants with whom I worked, and she introduced us. The graduate student agreed to go out with me, but two days before the date, her roommate broke the date for her.

My second venture into dating was with a dental hygienist who was taking a French course and whom I met in the language lab. Things were going very well until she was offered a job in Switzerland. We hadn't gotten to the point where I could ask her to stay, and off she went. It was great while it lasted, but at least it was not another case of unrequited love, and that was an improvement.

Not long thereafter, I met a girl at Mass whom I recognized from a Russian class I monitored. Her name was Judy Hastings. She was very cute but also very young, and she was a freshman. She may have been young chronologically, but in terms of dating experience she was a lot older than I.

Judy, for whatever reason, pursued me with great vigor. As flattering as that was, I just couldn't see myself dating a college freshman. I declined her requests to go out with her many times but ultimately succumbed to her charms, and after the Christmas break, I did start taking her out. Thus began the longest relationship (twenty-two months) I had ever had until I got married.

In October of 1967, I saw a notice in the student union advising that a CIA recruiter would be on campus the following week. I had come to MSU committed to becoming a high school German teacher and had no interest whatsoever in joining the CIA. On a whim, I decided to do an interview with the recruiter.

The recruiter turned out to be a very pleasant man, straight out of Brooks Brothers and very bland. He told me that an MA in German was not a significant factor as a qualifier for my employment, nor was my year of Russian at the Army Language School or my three years in Military Intelligence. I began to wonder, *Just what kind of candidates is the CIA looking for?*

Our interview came to end with the recruiter telling me that he would submit my application and that I would be hearing from the agency within a few weeks. One month and then two went by without a word, and I thought the CIA had had second thoughts about hiring me. Then, in April of 1968, I got a letter from the CIA inviting me to come to Washington for "further interviews."

I spent Easter with Judy and her family in Dearborn, Michigan. Mr. and Mrs. Hastings, and Judy's younger twin sisters, seemed to like me, and the weekend seemed to be going very well. However, there came a moment when Mrs. Hastings and I were alone in the living room and she made it clear that she didn't want Judy and me to get serious. I told Mrs. Hastings that I didn't know any other way and would never treat Judy casually. Mrs. Hastings didn't respond, but she seemed very pleased that I might be taking a job with the CIA.

When I went to Washington for that first interview, I thought I would be offered a job as an agent handler and case officer, as that is what I had been trained to do in the army. As a devoted Ian Fleming/James Bond fan, I began fantasizing about being another James Bond. I saw my language capability as a real plus, and but the agency had other ideas.

The man who interviewed me was sitting with his feet on the desk, smoking, and had an ashtray full of cigarette butts in front of him when his secretary brought me into his office. My interviewer was Mr. Bill Osborne, the chief of CIA's Interrogation and Research Branch (IRB), and my initial impression was not favorable. His first question was, "How would you like to be a polygraph examiner?"

That caught be by surprise, and being afraid that if I didn't accept his offer, I wouldn't be hired, I told him that I would like to give it a try. Before I left the interview, he told me that I would be called back in a couple of weeks for a polygraph test.

When I got back to East Lansing, I told Judy that I had taken the job with the CIA. Her initial reaction was to tell me that we had to find a school in the area to which she could transfer.

Three weeks later, I went back to Langley for my polygraph test. The first person I met on that visit was Mike Tirpac. He was a personnel officer for the Office of Security (OS) and told me that I would be hired as a GS-9. He wished me good luck on my polygraph test and left me in the waiting room.

My polygraph examiner was an older, white-haired curmudgeon who was very abrasive during my test. It got to the point where I was ready to get up and walk out, but once again, I held my tongue and finished the test.

It occurred to me that the examiner knew I would be coming to IRB if I passed my test, and I thought he was just pulling my chain. When he told me that I had passed my test, he also asked me if I had any comments. I told him that I didn't like the way he conducted the test and said, "Until I met you, everyone here has treated me well, and I found your style abrasive to the point of being rude."

His response was, "You can't expect everyone to be nice to you."

"The hell I can't" was my reply. "Until I am rude to you, the very least I expect is courtesy, and I found your style very disconcerting."

We didn't come to blows, and after I entered on duty, we became very good friends. The main thing I took away from my polygraph test was that I would never conduct a test the way my examiner did.

My last two months in East Lansing went by very quickly, but there were two events that I remember very well. The first of these was the death of Dr. Andretz, the man who hired me to work in the language lab. He died of throat cancer, and what I remember most was cleaning out his office. The filters in the air conditioner were coated with nicotine tar, his ashtray was filled with cigarette butts, and the smell of tobacco permeated everything in the room. I had never smoked, and after this experience, I knew I never would.

The second event was a riot that took place on campus. It drew national attention and was one of those unforgettable experiences that, almost fifty years after the fact, I remember as if it were yesterday.

On the day of the riot, I was walking across the campus to give an exam when I saw a huge crowd in front of the administration building. A group of students had linked arms and blocked the entrance to the building. There was a guy with a megaphone stirring up the crowd. The issue they were protesting was that East Lansing police had come on campus to arrest some students for selling drugs. Based on what they were saying, my impression was that the protesters were looking for a sanctuary in which they could do very much as they pleased.

I watched as the school chancellor came to the door of the admin building and told the crowd that the state police had been called and that if the protesters inside the building did not leave, they would be arrested. He was soundly booed. Speeches were being made, and there was an almost festive air to what was going on. Then two buses loaded with Michigan state police rolled up, to more boos.

An officer got off the bus and announced with a megaphone, "We are going to go into the building to arrest those occupying the building, and if you interfere, you will be arrested." A girl came out of the crowd, confronted the officer with, "You f—ing Fascist!" and spit in his face.

The police then cleared a path to the building's entrance and started putting the students they had arrested on the bus. When the bus was loaded, the police formed a spear head in front of the bus and began to pull away. Students were pushing on the side of the bus, and a large group had gotten out in front of the bus to impede its progress.

Suddenly, a Coke bottle came out of the crowd and hit a state trooper behind the right ear. He went down on the ground with blood pouring out of the wound.

The state troopers in front of the bus and those from the second bus then engaged those impeding the bus in a club-swinging, path-clearing melee.

As I left the scene, one of the protesters ran up to me and invited me to join the protest against police brutality. I told him I hadn't seen any police brutality until a Coke bottle seriously injured a state trooper. "I don't know anything about that" was his answer.

The next day, as I was helping out with a Russian final exam, one of the students, a Hungarian immigrant whom I knew, approached me and asked me if I had seen the riot the day before. When I told him I had, he said, "That was all about free speech and expression. Those cops were suppressing our rights." He then said, to my amazement, "To me, saying 'f—k you' is just like saying 'good morning.'"

I told him that was all well and good as long as he was willing to take the consequences, those being that if he said that to me, I would push his nose through the other side of his face. If he accepted that consequence for his behavior, he could feel free to say whatever he wanted to me. That was my parting memory of MSU.

My last roommate at MSU was a PhD biologist from South America. Before I left, he said, "John, unlike most Americans who invite you to visit and don't mean it, I would really like you to visit me and my family if you ever get down that way." It didn't occur to me that such an opportunity would ever take place, but it did. During one of my earlier trips with the agency, I made a stop in the city where my former roommate was a college professor. He was also the secretary of the local Communist party. I did not look him up.

Judy had already left campus and would be spending the summer in Russia, studying Russian and touring. I packed up all my possessions and left for Virginia to start another chapter in my life.

In 2011, I was invited to give a talk at MSU. On the way to East Lansing, I stopped in Flint, Michigan, to visit Sheriff Bob Pickell. Bob was my best friend in PD and our friendship is still going strong. He was also the best interrogator with whom I have ever worked. I never saw Bob do an interrogation that didn't result in an admission, and he did it without raising his voice or using any cheap tricks.

When I got to East Lansing, I revisited my old haunts and found Wells Hall and St. John's to be smaller than I remembered. I couldn't find any of the people with whom I had worked, but my hosts were great, and I had a great time.

Chapter 16

THE CIA

If there is one aspect of my life that might give some credibility to my claim of having lived an extraordinary life, it is my career with the CIA. During my career, I did things, went places, and met people that few, if any, of the people I know did, and in the process I fulfilled many of my Walter Mitty fantasies.

I neither know nor can imagine that anyone has met more spies than I. I have been shot at on five occasions, worked in forty countries, learned three languages, and met one president (George Bush Sr.) and two Medal of Honor recipients (Roger Donlon and Drew Dix). Add writing three books and I think there is a case to be made for my having led an extraordinary life. The most significant event that came about as a result of my being with the CIA was that I met and married Lee, the fairy tale princess of one of my fantasies.

After retiring, my career with the CIA continued to affect my life. My two books were based on my career. Most of my social contacts are former colleagues, and most of the jobs I have been offered were a result of my CIA experiences. Those experiences have given me some credibility with the students I have taught at a local community college and Fairfax County high schools.

When I walked through the doors at CIA headquarters on June 11, 1968, I was awed and anxious. The main lobby with its Wall of Honor and statue of William "Wild Bill" Donovan is beautiful and a bit intimidating. My anxiety was not so much about working for the CIA per se, but more about the job I was undertaking. I had learned about polygraph at Ft. Holabird and worked with Mike Callahan, a 513th MI Group polygraph examiner, but had no relevant experience with the process, and I was worried.

There were two incidents on that first day that left me wondering about my decision to work for the CIA. The first order of business was to get a badge. After that, the new security officers entering on duty that day were taken to meet Howard Osborne (no relation to Bill Osborne), the Director of the Office of Security(D/OS), for the CIA. When we arrived, his secretary told us that Mr. Osborne was busy and asked us to come back in half an hour.

Our escort took us to the cafeteria, and while there, I ran into someone with whom I had served in Bremerhaven. He was one of our communicators and the biggest screw-up I ever encountered in the army. He had a drinking problem as well as a gambling problem, and on a few occasions I had to buy him dinner because he had no money. Twice I caught him stealing money from the coffee fund, and there was an incident in which he could have been arrested if I and two other guys had not intervened. I was stunned to see him and couldn't understand how he had survived a background investigation or polygraph test.

After meeting Mr. Osborne, I checked into IRB and mentioned my concerns about my former army friend to one of the senior examiners. We pulled the polygraph report and learned that the best examiner in IRB had tested him and that the brother of the senior examiner to whom I was expressing my concerns had done the background investigation. No action was taken.

The next incident, on a personal level, had much more serious implications for my career with the CIA. Shortly after I checked in, I was given a letter welcoming me to CIA at a GS-7 pay grade. During my last visit, prior to entering on duty, Mike Tirpac had told me that I would be hired as a GS-09.

I immediately went to Mr. Osborne, the chief of IRB, to try to correct what I thought was a mistake. I told him that Mike Tirpac had told me I would be hired at the GS -9.. "Mike had no right to do that, and we can't do anything about it now" was his answer. He lied on two counts. Mike Tirpac would not have made that offer without authorization, and all Mr. Osborne would have had to do to get me the GS-9 I had been promised was ask.

My next move was to go to my training officer. He had interviewed me for almost an hour after my polygraph test and never brought up my salary. I assumed he knew that I would be coming in as a GS-9. His answer to my problem was: "You goddamn fool, we would have given you anything you asked for" and a laugh.

My answer: "You SOB. You sat with me for almost an hour and never said a word."

I think the chief read me as someone who really wanted the job and would take anything they offered. His assessment wasn't far from wrong. More importantly, I believe that because I didn't fight for the grade I had been told I would get, I was seen as weak.

Before I started my polygraph training, I had to take an "Introduction to the CIA" course, during which I learned how very unpopular CIA's polygraph examiners were. That would be a constant throughout my career.

My polygraph training lasted five weeks, and in early August, I went on line and conducted my first test. All new examiners start out testing applicants and have to do five hundred tests before being considered for working in the operational arena, where they would be testing assets recruited by CIA case officers.

I was doing two tests a day, most of which were pretty

run-of-the-mill, and enjoying the work. In early September, I obtained my first big admission when an applicant admitted to having participated in a gang rape during a graduation party the previous June. Getting admissions is one of the harder parts of the job, and there is often an emotional high concomitant with a successful interrogation. This test was one of those occasions, and I was elated. I wrote up my report and submitted it.

The next day, my supervisor told me that I would have to delete that information about the gang rape because it was "kid stuff." I asked him if he would see the gang rape as kid stuff if it had been his daughter who was raped, and he said, "Look, John, the Office of Personnel doesn't want this kind of information. Just take it out."

In my hubris, I saw myself as a "toiler in the vineyards of truth and justice," and what was going on here was contrary to what I saw as my role as an examiner. I told my supervisor that if he wanted the information about the gang rape deleted from my report, he would have to sign it, because I wouldn't. The information about the gang rape stayed in my report. The applicant wasn't hired, and although I won the battle, I lost the war, as I was seen as not being a team player who followed orders.

Life was pretty lonely. I had found an apartment, wasn't dating and didn't have a car. That made for a lot of TV watching and reading. When I finally heard from Judy, she asked me to meet her plane from Russia in New York and then said she would come to Virginia for the weekend.

In late August, I went up to JFK to meet Judy's plane. The weekend was short but very sweet. On the ride back to Virginia, Judy told me that their group took a bus from Moscow to Vienna and that the roads were filled with Russian tanks moving west. As it turned out, the tanks were the vanguard of the Soviet invasion of Czechoslovakia. When I took her to the airport on Sunday, our relationship was definitely more serious than it had been when we last saw each other, and I foresaw it getting even more so.

The next week I tested someone who had been on the same trip as Judy. He had graduated from MSU the previous June, applied for a job with the CIA, and arranged to come in for his polygraph when he came back from Russia.

When I asked him about any contacts he had made while in Russia, he pulled out the letter from the CIA advising him as to the date of his polygraph test. His Russian contact had written his name and address on the back of the letter. The young man did well on his test, but he wasn't hired.

I was calling Judy several times a week and writing to her on the days when I didn't call. In October, she came up for a visit, and all was going well. For Christmas, I sent Judy a very nice pearl ring. She called to thank me but also told me that she had been hoping for another kind of ring.

In April of 1969, even though I hadn't done the required five hundred cases, the powers that be decided I was ready to do operational tests. I went on my training trip with a senior examiner. The trip went well, and that, in conjunction with the fact that I was the only single examiner in the office, made me the examiner of choice for trips outside the DC area. After completing my training trip, I was on the road constantly, loving the work, and making good money.

My first solo trip was to Latin America, and as soon as I got back, I was sent on a rather long TDY (temporary duty) assignment to Laos.. That trip began a career-long infatuation with the men and women working in the Special Operations Group (SOG). They were some of the best people I worked with during my career.

My job in Laos was to debrief the Road Watch teams we sent out to monitor the Ho Chi Minh trail. One day, one of the teams radioed this message back to the base: "Please send more opium. We are addicted to near dead." I thought that a bit humorous, but seeing two of those young boys, brought in from a mission and lying on the tarmac with their legs nearly blown off sobered me up.

We worked seven days a week and I lost track of time. The food was, to me, very good and I was enjoying the work, but there was a problem: no Coca Cola. If ever I had an addiction, it was to Coca Cola. I had gone more than two weeks without a Coke when a plane brought two cases of Coca Cola in. I had two cans of it and curled up on the floor with severe cramps.

When I got back from Laos, there were trips to Europe, Miami, New York, and San Francisco. I not only liked the work but thought it was important. I was weeding out bad applicants, as well as fabricators, and earning my pay.

The only fly in the ointment was that I was very lonely, and during a visit to Judy and her family in August, we got engaged. I had never been happier.

After a trip abroad in October, I rerouted my flight to Detroit and visited Judy in East Lansing. Things didn't seem quite right, and when we said good-bye, I had a sense that I wouldn't be seeing her again.

A week before Thanksgiving, I had to go to Europe. Judy's parents had invited me to spend Thanksgiving with them, and I was looking forward to the visit. I was scheduled to fly from Frankfurt to Detroit on the day before Thanksgiving, but I got a letter from Judy the day before I was to leave telling me that she wouldn't be able to see me over Thanksgiving. She gave no reason.

My flight back to D.C., on Thanksgiving Day, was less than joyous. I got home at about nine in the evening and had just gone to bed when Judy called to tell me that she had met someone else and it was all over. True love had once again eluded me.

Early in December, I took a female colleague to a Redskins football game, after which there were a couple of more dates. All was not lost. When I was sent on a trip to Latin America in

January, she took me out to Dulles, and we parted with warmth and affection.

This trip included three stops, and I arrived at my third stop early on a Friday afternoon. My instructions had been to check in to a hotel that had been arranged for me and call the office. The girl who answered the phone had a lovely voice. She told me I wouldn't have to come in until Monday but also invited me to a picnic on Sunday afternoon.

That Sunday, January 25, 1970, is a day I will never forget. Someone from the office picked me up at the hotel and drove me to a *finca*, a few miles outside the city. I was talking with one of the officers when a vision in a yellow pantsuit approached us and said to me, "I'm Lee."

I said, "I am John." What I didn't say was, "I think I am in love." Lee was Leonor Estela Tijerina. She was from Laredo, Texas, and the chief secretary at our office.

On the following Thursday, we had our first date, and on the following Sunday our second. I was enthralled, Lee much less so. I took her to lunch the next day, just before I left, and asked her if I could write to her. Lee said she was not much of a writer, and I took that as a rejection.

When I walked into the office on Tuesday morning, the ops supervisor said, "John, you have to go right back. Something big has come up, and they have asked for you."

I was on a plane Wednesday morning. The case I handled was a big one, but more importantly, I saw Lee every day for the next week. On the way back, the plane stopped in Houston, where I bought some very unique and rather beautiful greeting cards. Over the next few months, I wrote to Lee daily and sent many of the cards.

Lee and I didn't see each other until the Fourth of July weekend. Her station was the second stop on what would be a two-month trip. She subsequently joined me at another stop, where I asked her to marry me and she said yes. Coincidentally, on the day Lee said yes, I got a cable requesting that I add another stop to my itinerary. The added stop was one of the Caribbean paradises, and I suggested that it we be a great place for a honeymoon. On August 29, 1970, we were married.

The night before the wedding, I hired three troubadours to serenade Lee under her balcony. Her boss gave Lee away and hosted a great wedding reception. It poured rain that day, but I hardly noticed.

We had a working honeymoon, in that I had to do a case before we could go to the resort for our honeymoon. We were going to use the office secretary's house for the test, and the case officer took Lee and me out to see if the house was suitable. The house was in a cul-de-sac containing three houses. The case officer took us into one of the houses, and I deemed it suitable. We were sitting in the living room when a maid came downstairs and asked if she could help us. We were in the wrong house.

After the test, Lee and I flew up to a resort to begin our honeymoon. Lee had to wait for her replacement to arrive before she joined me in Virginia. In mid-November, I went to Laredo to meet Lee's family and bring her back to Virginia. Lee had four brothers and three sisters, all of whom welcomed me with open arms. As soon as we got back, Lee began working, and life was better than it had ever been.

Later that month, the chief asked me, "How would you and your wife like to go to Europe?"

I checked with Lee, and she said, "Fine." I told my boss we would go. When January came and I hadn't heard anything about processing for our assignment to Europe, I asked my boss when would we begin processing for our assignment.

"Oh, that's off. How would you two like to go to Vietnam?" Again, Lee and I said we would go. Two weeks later, I received a call asking why I hadn't begun my processing to go to Vietnam. I told the lady with whom I was speaking that I had been waiting for a call to tell me to start and then asked her, "What about my wife?" Then it got nasty.

"We have no information about your wife accompanying you, and as far as we are concerned, you will be going alone."

My answer was, "No Lee, no me." My refusal to go without Lee generated an interview with the number-three man in OS, who told me, "You will be letting down the office if you don't go."

I replied that I wasn't asked if *I* would go, but if "you and your wife" would go. It was a matter of principle.

"I have seen a lot of people in this office hurt their careers on matters of principle" was his response.

"Well, just put me down as one of those" was my answer.

In another case of winning the battle but losing the war, Lee went to Vietnam with me, but I was seen as not being a team player. We spent four years there and saved a lot of money, and our older son, John, was born there. But in the long run, my time in Vietnam was not career-enhancing.

I loved Vietnam, but our tour got off to a very rocky start. On our first day there, a Sunday, we were at the swimming pool at the top of the Duc Hotel, where we were staying. Someone Lee had known from another station introduced us to the chief of support, Rex Graves, the number-three man in the station. He was a bit drunk but pleasant enough.

"We've got a house all set up for you two. It is in Cho Lon, the Chinese section of Saigon, and we are using it for an operation. You will like it."

I said, "I am going to be on the road more than half the time I am here, and I don't know that I want Lee in such a situation.'

"The decision has been made, and if you don't like it, you can catch the next plane back home" was Graves's slurred answer.

"I think I can manage that" was my reply, and that is how we left it.

When I went in to work the next morning, Jack Gardiner, the

chief of security and my boss, told me, "I heard about your set-to with Rex yesterday. Don't worry about it. You and Lee can live wherever you want." Thus began a wonderful four years.

Saigon was a busy station, and I worked every day for my first eighty days in Vietnam. I didn't do a test every day, but counting travel time and report writing, I didn't have much free time.

Lee was working for the chief of finance and enjoyed her job very much, and we thought we had made the right choice in going to Vietnam.

My first reminder that there was a war going on occurred on a trip to Quang Ngai, a hamlet in I Corps, near where the My Lai Massacre took place. The case officer with whom I would be working was Paul D., a young man I had polygraphed when he entered on duty. He was a paramilitary (PM) officer whom I ran into on our first day in Vietnam. He told me he had a lot of work for me.

About two months after we arrived, Paul made a request to have me come up to Quang Ngai and test a source who claimed to have seen an American prisoner of war. Next to information on an imminent attack, information on POWs was our highest priority. When I arrived in Quang Ngai, Paul had gone out with his troops to bring his source in. I was waiting in the house when his troops came in and told us Paul had stepped on a mine and been killed.

Over the next four years, I would get shot at or come under fire on five occasions, see some men die, and get a feel for war that I never had while serving in the army. I was living out a childhood fantasy. Those experiences also gave me what I saw as a broad as well as unique perspective on the war that has served me well in my post-CIA lectures.

The first of those occasions was in MR/4. We had just taken off, in a Pilatus Porter/STOL aircraft, when three green streaks went by the port-side wing. The pilot took evasive action, and it was an exciting moment. I knew it was enemy fire because the streaks were green, indicating Viet Cong or North Vietnamese ammunition.

On another occasion, I had caught a ride with a U.S. Army Air Cavalry unit in one of their helicopters. The pilot of the lead helicopter told me that they would have to do a mission, looking for NVA tanks in the Michelin rubber plantation in III Corps, before returning to Saigon. I said that was fine with me. We had just come over a tree line when a VC hiding under a tree fired on us with his AK-47. We circled around and went down pretty low looking for him but couldn't find him.

I was in a house out in the boondocks doing a test when the house began to shake. Windows broke, and plaster fell from the walls and ceiling. We were a little too close to a B-52 strike.

The worst incident occurred in February of 1975, in Cambodia. I had been doing a test in a police station, at night, when a mortar attack took out the local power plant. We couldn't continue the test and decided to postpone it until the next day. The two case officers with whom I was working took me to a deserted old guest house. They told me to find a bed and said they would pick me up the nest morning.

I had just dozed off when the shooting started. It was like the Fourth of July. AK-47s, machine guns, mortars, and M-16s were exchanging fire. I don't know how close the fighting was, but I could hear men scream as they were hit and knew the action was closer to me than I liked. I was scared out of my wits.

For someone who had never heard a shot fired in anger during five years in the army, this was pretty exciting, as well as dangerous. This was not one of my Walter Mitty fantasies. There were other such events, but they were part of the job, and I am grateful that I came out of the experiences safely.

My last day in Cambodia was also the occasion of a close call. I was in our office in Phnom Penh when sirens sounded and rockets began falling. I was told to get out to the airport, and on the ride out, I saw a rocket hit a VW beetle. When I got to the airport, I immediately got on a C-47 that had been waiting for me. We were waiting for clearance to take off when the rockets started falling. Shrapnel fell all over the plane, and we had to deplane.

I was squatting under a wing when I saw a small shed take a direct hit and an arm in a short, white sleeve go flying in the air. The barrage didn't last long, and we took off. I still have a piece of the shrapnel that fell that day.

Compared with the combat experiences of soldiers and marines, these experiences pale, but I could have been wounded or killed. I didn't want to die for any reason, but I had determined that our cause in Vietnam was lost, and if I were going to die, I would prefer it not to be for a lost cause and in vain.

There was one other incident that I recall as being the first time I was sure that I was going to die. I had gone up to a small Vietnamese fishing village with a case officer to do a test. The plane dropped us off in a meadow, and we told the pilot to come back in five hours.

It was pouring rain when he came back, and visibility was pretty poor when we took off. I don't know how high up we were when it seemed as though a huge fist hit the plane. The motor stalled, and the pilot sent an SOS. I thought a crash was imminent and just started reading a book, waiting to see what happened. The pilot got the plane out of its stall, and we went back to Can Tho with another war story to tell.

In Vietnam, I worked with some of the best as well as some of the worst CIA officers, including honorable, competent, and dedicated officers as well as drunks, lechers, and total incompetents. One of the worst, of the latter category, was the examiner I replaced in Vietnam. When he left Vietnam, he did a lateral transfer to another Asian post. About a year after he left Vietnam, he wrote to me and asked me to request him to come and help with my case load. By then there were three examiners in Saigon, and we didn't need him, nor would we ask for him even if there was a need.

During his tour in Vietnam, every test he conducted was favorable. He did forty-five tests in one day, and many of the officers with whom I worked expected me to do likewise, making my job much more difficult. When he took me on my first trip up country, he got knee-walking, commode-hugging drunk on the first night of what was to be a week-long trip and had to return to Saigon the next day. During my first six months in Vietnam, I identified five subjects who had beaten him when he tested them. More important than all of these was that I didn't like him and had no respect for him.

Shortly after I rejected his request, his boss came to Saigon to see me. He asked me why I didn't want my predecessor's help. I told him, chapter and verse, and in so doing seriously damaged my career.

During that first tour, Lee and I took vacations to Hong Kong, Katmandu, and Malaysia at practically no cost. We were also saving a lot of money, and our time in Vietnam allowed us to build a nest egg that gave us some real financial security, a very new sensation for me.

Our tour was for two years, and because we liked it so much, we decided to ask for another tour. IRB, which had by then become Interrogation Research Division (IRD), approved the request.

Before starting our second tour, we were allowed forty-five days of home leave and spent most of it in Laredo with Lee's family. During that visit, Lee found out that she was pregnant, and we rejoiced.

I took some time to visit Bill, in Albany, and then went to Langley to check in with IRD. They were glad I was willing to take another tour, because no one else wanted to go.

On our way back to Vietnam, we spent a couple of days in Monterey, where I visited some of my Russian teachers, and a couple of days in Hong Kong. Once we were back, it took one day to pick up where we left off.

Of the many things I wanted to be—doctor, athlete, priest, teacher—being a husband and father trumped all of them. On December 4, 1973, the birth of our son John fulfilled that dream. Only time would tell how well I would perform as a father, and I looked forward to finding out. John was born in the Seventh Day Adventist Hospital in Saigon, and the VC welcomed his birth with a rocket attack on a huge ammunition dump at Nha Be, less than two miles from the hospital.

With the withdrawal of American combat troops from Vietnam, things began to deteriorate rapidly. President Thieu and most of the South Vietnamese leaders knew that the United States would never live up to the promises it made when the Paris Peace Accords were signed and that it was only a matter of time before the North Vietnamese won the war.

When the NVA began their final offensive, I told my boss, Art Sullivan, that I wanted Johnny and Lee out of Vietnam. He laughed at me, telling me that the current offensive was just "saber rattling." I insisted, and they left. Two weeks later, I took the station files out. I accompanied the files from Saigon to Palo Alto, California, after which, and without any sleep, I flew to Washington with a letter from Tom Polgar, the COS in Saigon, to Headquarters.

The next morning, I flew to Laredo. I got out of the taxi, a short distance from the Tijerina house, and walked to the back door. Johnny was getting a drink of water at the sink. I didn't say anything but just waited for him to see me. When he did, he let out a shout, "Daddy!" and ran to me. That was one of my life's all-time highs.

In January 1975, I contacted a former colleague who was a real estate agent in Northern Virginia and asked him to have some houses to show us in April, when our tour was up. Within two weeks of getting back to Virginia, I had my first driver's license, had bought a house and a car, and was doing polygraph tests. While I was in Vietnam, IRD had become Polygraph Division (PD), and that would be my home for the next twenty-four years.

As did all OS employees returning from overseas, I had an interview with Bob Gambino, The D/OS of the Office of Security. He asked me what I wanted to do, and I told him, "Stay in PD." He said that was fine, and that was it.

On my first day back in the office, Don Carpenter, one of the new examiners, invited me into his room and told me that the powers that be in IRD, as well as some of the hierarchy in OS, were *very* pissed at me for blowing the whistle on my predecessor in Vietnam. Don turned out to be right.

I had been away from PD for four years. All of the supervisors who had been there when I left were gone, and as a result of my work in Vietnam, I knew more people in the DO than in the Office of Security.

Les Fannin was the chief of PD, and one of the first things he did after I got back was to send me for Spanish language training. It was only eleven weeks, but it was pretty intensive, and with Lee to help me, I did very well. Her help and a lot of studying, as well as travel in Latin America, gave me another language in which I could communicate pretty well.

It was during this period that I conducted the best examination of my career. I tested a Czech agent that the FBI had been running for four years. He had been trained to beat the polygraph, but I caught him. Doing cases like this one was why I was a polygraph examiner.

Not one person in PD congratulated me on a job well done. If I had had any doubts as to my status in PD or OS, that lack of recognition removed those doubts. Catching a double agent is the holy grail of a CIA examiner, and I managed to catch seven of them during my career.

Doing operational tests was the best part of the job, but it was not of much importance to OS. They would rather PD catch homosexuals and drug users than double agents because they had no input in operations.

Not being promoted was a disappointment, but my home life more than made up for any workplace slights. Johnny was a beautiful little boy, and I couldn't get enough of him.

One of my more memorable moments occurred when Johnny was three years old. Lee wanted to take him to Laredo to visit her family, When I took them to the airport and Johnny realized that I wouldn't be going with them, he didn't want to go and began crying. He was still crying when I pulled away, and it was a long day.

As soon as I got home from work, I called Laredo. The first words I heard were, "I want my daddy." I had never been so happy, and sad, at the same time.

On August 19, 1977, our second son, Jimmy, was born. Both Lee and I were sure we were going to have a girl, and the last thing she said to me before going into the OR, was, "It's going to be a girl." I left Lee at the OR doors, and by the time I got to the waiting room, the PA system was telling me come see my son.

Not long after Jimmy was born, one of my colleagues with whom I had worked overseas asked me if Lee would be interested in working at home on contract. Lee was delighted, and for the next twelve years she was paid very well to work on a highly sensitive project for which she subsequently received two commendations.

Money was never a problem for us. We had one car and a mortgage payment of $267 a month, and we lived very comfortably.

When Johnny was six, we signed him up for soccer. The team needed a coach, and I offered to do it. I ended up coaching most of John's and Jimmy's athletic teams: soccer, basketball, and baseball. Johnny took to sports more than Jimmy, and I was living vicariously through Johnny's athletic successes. There were days when John had a soccer match, baseball game, and tennis match on the same day, and those days were hectic but reward-ing. Jimmy thought Johnny was a victim of child abuse.

There was a hitting wall at the tennis courts near our home, and when Johnny was nine, I took him to the wall to practice hitting. On his first attempt, he hit and returned the ball 209 times before he missed a ball.

Johnny ended up leading his high school team, South Lakes High School, to a state championship. He also was recruited by the Army, Navy, and Air Force Academies. He had had a bout with asthma as a child and was turned down by the Air Force Academy.

In February of 1992, I took John up to West Point for his interview. February is not a good month in which to visit West Point, and on the way home, John said, "Dad, there is no way I am going to spend four years here." He decided on the Naval Academy and did well, not only becoming captain of the tennis team but also company commander. His graduation day was one of the prouder moments of my life. Earlier this year, he was inducted into his high school's athletic hall of fame.

Jimmy's focus is music, and he and his wife Mary are both professional musicians living in Nashville. He and Johnny are as different as day and night, but both have given me moments that I wish for every father.

While these events were going on, work went on as usual. I still looked forward to going to work every day, but my travel had been pretty much curtailed, in part due to overexposure. I had spent 2011 days overseas, met more spies than anyone, including double agents, and was probably known to other services. In telling me that my future travel would be limited, the chief told me, "John, I wouldn't want to have to do a damage assessment if you were ever arrested or went missing."

I did get promoted to GS-14, but there came a time when I was the only line examiner who had not gone through PD's polygraph school and was perceived by some as an anachronism. Polygraph had changed, and I hadn't.

After the Aldrich Ames fiasco in 1992, PD became paranoid about missing another double agent. Examiners were being told that they hadn't done their jobs unless they obtained an admission, or were getting complaints. Another mantra chanted by PD management was, "Every subject who comes in here is lying, and it is your job to determine just how much they are lying."

I had always been an iconoclast in claiming that polygraph was much more art than science. That belief put me in the crosshairs of some of PD's managers, and that, along with the post-Ames paranoia, made my last few years in the division very uncomfortable.

As a member of the CIA's Retirement and Disabilities System (CIARDS), I had to retire at age sixty, and on August 30, 1999, that's what I did. I turned in my badge to the Special Protective Officer (SPO) and walked out the door. I was relieved and satisfied: relieved that I would no longer be involved in a process which I felt had been corrupted and satisfied that in conducting approximately five thousand tests, no complaint had ever been made against me.

Chapter 17

OUT TO PASTURE

To paraphrase General MacArthur, "Old spooks never die. They just retire, write books, attend funerals, and trade war stories with old colleagues."

I may have been retired, but so much of what I have done in retirement came about as a result of my CIA career that I was constantly being reminded of my CIA days. Jobs I was offered, books that I wrote, interviews and lectures that I gave, and former colleagues with whom I socialized were among those reminders.

In the first two months after retiring, I was contacted by eight prospective employers offering me jobs doing polygraph tests. One offer came from a former high-ranking CIA officer who wanted me to go into partnership with him to conduct polygraph tests in Latin America. We would be working out of Miami, and Lee was eager to go. Unfortunately for Lee, and my prospective partner, doing another polygraph test was not on my bucket list.

I had one man who had failed a polygraph test with another government agency come to my home, throw a hundred dollars on the table, and ask me to give him a "practice test." I declined.

On September 1, 1999, I began writing my first book, *Of*

Spies and Lies: A CIA Lie Detector Remembers Vietnam, and 366 days later, I submitted it to the CIA's Publications Review Board (PRB). It took less than three weeks for the review. They asked that eleven words be redacted, which I did, and the book was published in April 2002. It didn't come close to being a best-seller but did make me a public face for CIA polygraph, and in that capacity, I was doing a lot of lectures and media interviews.

There were no repercussions from the CIA or OS for Of Spies and Lies, but that was not the case with my second book, *Gatekeeper: Memoirs of a CIA Polygraph Examiner.*

In September 2002, I began writing *Gatekeeper.* My intention was to present a history of polygraph in the CIA, as I saw it, addressing the positive as well as negative aspects of the program. In doing the latter, I incurred the wrath of PD and OS. That wrath manifested itself on March 11, 2004, when I took a polygraph test in conjunction with a contract job for which I had applied. I was certain that I had passed the test, but the examiner told me otherwise. His behavior told me he was lying, and his refusal to show me the polygraph charts on which he was basing his call convinced me that I never had a chance of passing that test.

On February 14, 2005, eleven months after my test, I received a letter from OS telling me I was being denied access to classified material. It cited my polygraph test as the reason for the denial. The details cited in the letter were an egregious misrepresentation of what had occurred during the test, and I immediately appealed the decision.

After submitting my appeal, I consulted with an attorney whose specialty was cases such as mine. I had met him at an Association of Former Intelligence Officers (AFIO) luncheon, after I had given a talk on polygraph. I told him about the letter I had received and that I had appealed the decision. He told me the best evidence I could get to support my appeal was a transcript of my polygraph examination, which was exempt from a

Freedom of Information request. He also told me that the process could take years and would be very expensive, and my chances of winning the suit were slim.

Appeals of OS denials of access to classified information are rarely upheld, but three months after filing my appeal, I was notified that my appeal had been upheld. According to the notification letter, information had come to light that supported my appeal. Included in that information was that proper procedures had not been followed, and most of that information came from the supervisor of the examiner who had tested me. That supervisor became my "Deep Throat" and told me:

1. A key question had not been properly asked.

2. My examiner's supervisor had rewritten the examiner's report, making significant changes with which the examiner didn't agree, and also coerced the examiner into signing the revised report..

3. The charts of my test, which, according to "Deep Throat," would have supported a favorable call, were withheld from a Quality Assurance Review.

4. The CIA entity to which I had applied for a job was told that I had withdrawn my application, which I hadn't done.

. In every venue of which I am aware, when an appeal is upheld, the appellant is awarded something for having won—damages in a civil suit, yardage in a football game, release from prison, and so on. Not so with CIA. Having my appeal upheld meant that if I could get a prospective employer, who was doing contact work with the CIA, to offer me a job and request a security clearance from the CIA, I would be given the privilege of going through the security screening process again.

The problem was that without a security clearance, attending many job fairs or even getting an interview for jobs requiring a CIA security clearance was almost impossible.

Having won my appeal, and being aware of the misconduct on the part of PD, I again sought legal redress. I filed suit in June of 2005. A year and more than twenty thousand dollars later, one of the lawyers handling my case called to tell me, without forewarning, that they had withdrawn the suit, as the case was not winnable. He did assure me that the CIA would not be countersuing me. Somehow, that did not assuage my anger and disappointment.

During the pressing of the suit, my lawyer had missed a filing date and on three occasions had requested me to send copies of documents that I had already sent to him. When I asked him what he had done with the documents I had sent him, he said, "I put them in a box until I need them."

A couple of weeks before withdrawing the suit, my lawyer asked me what the terms of our contract had been. We had never signed a contract. As much as I liked my lawyer on a personal level, I came away from that experience feeling that I had not been well served by him.

Still being the eternal optimist, and having been handed a rather large lemon, I decided to make lemonade, that being a book about my suit against the CIA. I was working on the book sporadically when, in August of 2006, I submitted my resume and a list of the topics on which I would like to lecture to Elder Hostels. My offer was accepted, and I began giving lectures to Elder Hostels groups.. I would give six or seven lectures each year, and I loved the audiences. The pay was minimal, but I was having fun.

Lee had done all the typing for my first two books, and I couldn't have written them without her. Each night, after I went to bed, Lee would review and correct everything I had written that day and leave the computer ready for me to pick up where I left off the night before. She was doing the same with my third book, but with much less enthusiasm.

"John, this book is eating you up. I can see you getting angry as you work on it, and it isn't healthy."

That's where we were in October of 2009, when Lee got a

call from our son, John. It was just a call to say hello, and few minutes later, Lee asked me, "Who just called?" She also seemed disoriented.

It got worse, and I called John. He came over and said, "Dad, we have to get Mom to the ER." Two days later, she was diagnosed with stage four colon cancer.

Three years before, Lee had a bad experience with a colonoscopy and refused to go back for another one. She would only take half the prescribed medication for her Type II diabetes, to save money, and in general was a very bad patient. It came to pass that Kaiser Permanente, our health care provider, sent Lee a letter telling that if she wouldn't follow their advice, there was nothing they could do for her.

Dealing with bad news is not something I do well, and I was devastated. Lee's younger brother, Dennis, was in town for a training course at that time, and I can remember sitting with him at our kitchen table while we both cried.

Lee's family was incredible throughout Lee's and my ordeal. When I could no longer care for her, we put her in a hospice. Her older brother, Rolando, came up for two weeks to sit with her when I couldn't, and when he had to go back to Corpus Christi, two of Lee's sisters, Diana and Cindy, came up to spell me.

The three of us were in the room when Lee passed away. Cindy had been holding Lee when Diana said, "Cindy, let me hold her for a while." Diana held Lee in her arms and was whispering to her when Cindy said, "She's gone." She was.

My first call was to Kristen, my daughter-in-law. Her response was above and beyond anything I could have expected. She immediately came over and, in a very good and compassionate way, took over. Kristen scheduled a funeral Mass as well as the cremation and was there 24/7. I could not have made it through that ordeal without her.

Father Mark Moretti, one of the two best priests I have ever met, said the funeral Mass and did a great job. Katie and

Andrew, our grandchildren, took the gifts up to the altar during the Offertory, and Andrew cried his eyes out. That was my most poignant memory of that event.

Cindy scheduled another service in Laredo for early January. John, Kristen, Katie, Andrew, Jimmy, and his wife, Mary, all went with me to the funeral in Laredo.

Lee was one of eight children, and if just her immediate and extended families had attended the funeral, it would have been crowded, The church was packed and the service beautiful.

At the grave site, Cindy provided me with my life's most poignant memory. In addressing the crowd, Cindy said, "There is a family story about John's hiring three troubadours to serenade Lee under her balcony the night before their wedding. I have hired two Mariachi singers to help us celebrate Lee's life before we bid her adios." Then the two Mariachis sang *"Amor Eterno"* (Eternal Love). Their rendition of the song was moving, and I completely lost it. Five years later, I can't hear that song without crying.

Our house was pretty big, and rattling around it at night, I was lonelier than I had ever been. The worst part was that I was forever doing things that would remind me of Lee. I can remember two occasions while driving home from a school where I had substituted, being at a stop light, and thinking, "Lee won't be there when I get home." On both of those occasions, I cried. Going home to an empty house was a real downer, and I thank God that I wasn't a drinker.

There were positives during this time, none more so than Mrs. Young Hee Cho. She was a widow and the proprietor of Young's Tailor Shop, which was located near my office. I had known her, and most of her family, for more than twenty-five years. Young would practice her English with me, and we became very good friends. She was an outstanding student, and I loved practicing English with her. About three months after Lee passed away, Young suggested that I take up line dancing. She was, and still is, a line dance instructor, and told me about a class at the YMCA. I enrolled in the class, and for the first time in my life, I began to dance.

Subsequently, I began doing lectures on Royal Caribbean Cruise Line ships. Young and I have gone on four cruises and are looking forward to doing more. As I mentioned earlier in the book, not learning how to dance had been one of my life's big regrets. Line dancing classes were followed by ballroom classes, and Young and I have been dancing ever since.

Life was good, and I decided to make it better. I stopped working on my third CIA book. Lee was right; it was eating me up, and I just stopped. It wasn't only that it was angering and depressing me, or that I no longer had Lee to help. I had come to realize that no one cared. I wouldn't be telling the powers that be in the CIA or Office of Security anything that they didn't know or condone, and I would just be another lonely voice, crying in the wilderness. If I had thought the book would have even a minimum positive effect, I would have kept on. The time had come to stop crying and start singing.

In November 2007, *Eye Spy Magazine,* a British publication, published an interview they had conducted with me based on my latest book and entitled it "CIA Gatekeeper." The article gave me some exposure and ultimately led to me being featured on a German version of *60 Minutes.* Propeller Productions, a Berlin-based television production company, filmed me over two days in Washington DC, and subsequently the program was shown throughout Europe. I was pleasantly surprised when a former colleague called me from Paris to tell me that he was watching me on TV.

I was also getting some exposure on the home front. On a Saturday morning in April 2007, I received a call from one of my college classmates, Jim Clavell, telling me that there was some guy on Book TV talking about his book *Enter the Past Tense,* in which he claimed to have been an assassin for the CIA. When I tuned in to Book TV, I heard Roland W. Haas, the author, claim that when he was nineteen, he was recruited while at Purdue University, by the CIA, to be an assassin. As he went on, it became clear to me that his story was fiction.

Haas's book and my *Gatekeeper* both were published by Potomac Press, and I called my editor to ask her why I hadn't been asked to check Haas's manuscript for authenticity. "We thought his story was believable" was her answer.

Many of my former colleagues publicly challenged Haas, but I was the most visible of his detractors, and he wrote a full-page attack on me that was published in his local paper. His diatribe was as inaccurate as his book, and in it, he identified me as someone who had challenged him at one of his lectures. He referred to me as a "desk jockey, James Bond wannabe." I hadn't attended the lecture to which Haas referred, nor had I ever met him.

I was discussing Haas with Pete Earley, the best-selling author of *Confessions of a Spy, Family of Spies,* and several other books, when he told me that what I was doing could be dangerous. That hadn't entered my mind, but in retrospect, maybe it should have.

Haas had been doing very well on the lecture circuit, and there was serious talk about a movie, based on his book, when I first called him out. As our dispute became more public, the public's interest and belief in Haas went up in smoke.

On October 24, 2013, Haas "accidentally" killed himself when he shot himself in the leg and hit his femoral artery. That same day, an AP reporter called and asked me if I felt in any way responsible for Haas's death. Even if I believed that Haas had committed suicide, I don't think I would have felt any guilt. I believe he deliberately shot himself but had no intention of dying and that the accidental aspect of the shooting was that he hit the femoral artery.

For me, it is not a stretch to posit that Haas was planning to give himself a flesh wound and claim that someone had tried to kill him. He was a fraud right up untilo the end, and although I feel a modicum of sympathy, I don't feel an ounce of guilt.

At the time I was doing battle with Haas, I applied for a job teaching a course on the American Intelligence Community at a local community college, and think the exposure I got from the Haas dispute might have helped me get the job. As much as I enjoyed teaching the course, I was shocked and concerned about how poorly educated some of my students were. One semester was about all I could take.

I subsequently filled out applications to teach in the Fairfax County public school system as well as in Paul VI Catholic High School in Fairfax, Virginia. Based on my college transcripts as well as my year of Russian at Monterey, I was deemed qualified to teach social studies, English, Russian, German, Spanish, and business education.

Langley High School (LHS) is, academically, one of the best if not the very best public high schools in Fairfax County, and it is the only school in the county that has a Russian program. There are two Russian teachers at LHS, Valentin Cukierman and Rhonda Salem, and both are outstanding teachers. In 2011, Mr. Cukierman was named the best high school Russian teacher in the United States. Substituting for them has been the best of my substituting experiences.

Being able to communicate in Spanish has turned out to be a real blessing, and I have never had any trouble with the Latino students. On my first substituting assignment, the teacher for whom I was subbing left me a note saying that his second-period class was the "Class from hell: The kids don't want to be there and are very unruly. Good luck."

Almost half the students were Latinos, and when I took the attendance, I spoke some Spanish with each of them. I had no problems with the class and enjoyed it. After the class, one of the Latinos approached me and said, "Mr. Sullivan, you are the first f—ing teacher who has tried to speak our language. Thanks."

I have substituted in nine public schools in Fairfax County and am hoping to be able to continue doing so until I am physically incapable of going on. In looking back, I have no regrets about my career choice, but I feel that I have done more to make the world a better place by teaching than I ever did as a polygraph examiner.

There have been three polygraph-related incidents since my retirement that have assuaged some of the guilt I have taken on over the years, including guilt about not trying to do more to stop the post-Ames excesses in PD and guilt about putting my job ahead of my family on a few occasions. The first of the three incidents occurred shortly after I retired.

I was contacted by a law firm asking me to review the polygraph charts of a test conducted on one of their clients. The lawyer with whom I spoke was the brother-in-law of a CIA colleague who had referred me to him.

Initially, the prosecutor had agreed to have the results of the polygraph test admitted as evidence, but then she reneged on her offer. Subsequently, the prosecutor backed off a little and said she would allow a statement admitted into evidence attesting to the fact that the client had passed his polygraph test. What the lawyer wanted me to do was review the charts of the test and let me know whether or not I agreed with the "no deception" call.

Without having a video of the test to go along with the charts, I was reluctant to do this. The charts produced during the test are only one, albeit critical, part of the equation in assessing the results of a test. Body language as well as verbal behavior are also factored into the assessment, and not having those diminishes the reliability of the assessment. That being said, and because of the connection with my former colleague, I agreed to do the review.

"How much do you charge?" was the next question.

"Nothing" was my answer. I then told the lawyer that if I took money, I would become, in effect, one of the firm's hired guns, and as such, my objectivity might be questioned.

"How about letting us send you a very good bottle of Scotch or box of cigars?" was his next offer.

I again declined, saying,"I am a red-nosed Irishman who neither drinks nor smokes, but thanks for the offer."

When I got the charts, I reviewed them and found no indications of deception therein, which is what I said in the e-mail I sent to the attorneys. The lawyers were pleased. Their client won the suit and was awarded significant monetary damages. Unfortunately for the client, the defendant was bankrupt. My last contact with the firm was when the law firm's secretary called me to buy two signed copies of my books.

More recently, I became involved in a case in which I was asked to testify as an expert witness. I was home one afternoon when I got a call from a man who identified himself as Antony Haynes, an attorney with Williams and Connolly. I recognized the name of the firm and knew it was one of the premier law firms in D.C.

Mr. Haynes then told me that Williams and Connolly would like to hire me as a consultant and expert witness in a suit their client (TC) was filing against an Other Government Agency (OGA). He went on to say that T.C. had taken a polygraph test in conjunction with his application for a job with the OGA, and had failed the test. Mr. Haynes also told me that the OGA examiner who tested T.C. claimed that TC admitted to having had unauthorized contact with a foreign intelligence agent.

TC vehemently denied having made such an admission and accused the examiner of lying. When I learned that the alleged admission had not been recorded, red flags began flying. I couldn't believe that the OGA had reported such a serious admission without anything other than the examiner's word as evidence.

TC subsequently passed an FBI polygraph test, and during the FBI's investigation, information was developed that cleared TC of having contact with a foreign intelligence agent. Had the OGA in question been the CIA, I would have turned down the

Williams and Connolly offer, but I did check with the CIA to see if they had any objections to my getting involved in the case. The CIA had no problems, and I so informed Mr. Haynes. He then asked, "How much do you charge?"

As with the previous case, I declined to take any payment, for the same reasons that I declined in the first case. I was told, "We have to pay you."

I said, "Okay, how about a hundred an hour?"

The counteroffer was, "How about three hundred an hour?"

At no time in my life had the thought of making more than a hundred dollars an hour crossed my mind, and as soon as I got over my surprise, I accepted Mr. Haynes's offer. I also recommended Bob Pickell, a former colleague, as a consultant, and they hired him.

There was another factor in my accepting the offer. When I paid more than twenty thousand dollars to sue the CIA, that money was, at least in my opinion, wasted, and I saw this as an opportunity to get some of it back.

As a victim of polygraph abuse, I also saw the Williams and Connolly offer as an opportunity not only to help right a wrong but also to focus some attention on polygraph abuse. Riding to the rescue is occasionally an element of a Walter Mitty fantasy, and that is how I assessed my role in this case.

Two days later I met with TC and the team of lawyers at the Williams and Connolly offices in DC. When I checked in with the receptionist, she said, "Yes, Mr. Sullivan, we have been expecting you. Please follow me to the dining room."

Once I was in the private, and very well-appointed, dining room, a waiter approached and asked, "Mr. Sullivan, what would you like for lunch?" W&C ran a first-class operation.

Over lunch, I met with the other lawyers. The lead attorney was F. Whitten "Whitt" Peters, the lead attorney in the case and a former Secretary of the Air Force. He was also one of the more down-to-earth people I have ever met. Antony Haynes was the second chair, and there was one more attorney at the lunch whose name I do not recall. With this array of legal talent on the case, I assumed that TC had very deep pockets. TC had been a presidential adviser on national security and was very well known in the upper echelons of the national security apparatus, He certainly outranked anyone I had ever tested, and I was looking forward to meeting him.

Mr. Haynes had sent me a copy of the OGA's report of the polygraph test, and although it was very heavily redacted, I got enough from reading it to conclude that the client had been victimized by the examiner who had tested him.

Prior to retiring, one of my colleagues and I observed a polygraph test conducted by a polygraph examiner of the OGA involved in the suit. During the test, I observed a very strong reaction to one of the relevant questions. The examiner did not address the question, and after consulting with a supervisor, terminated the session. My impression was that the examiner and supervisor wanted to work out a strategy for resolving the reaction before proceeding and didn't want my colleague and I to observe. That incident left me with a less-than-positive impression of the OGA examiner I observed.

The relevant questions that were asked during TC's first OGA test were included in the report Mr. Haynes had sent me, and after reading them, I was convinced that the examiner who had done the test had never tested an accused or suspected spy. The questions he asked almost guaranteed that TC would not pass the test.

When I was introduced to TC, he came on a bit confrontationally. He had *Gatekeeper* with him and had highlighted several passages in the book, which he pointed out and on which questioned me. He had done his homework and was not about to buy a pig in a poke. My initial impression of TC wasn't good, in that he was a bit of a hard charger and, at least in my mind, might be very abrasive.

What came through most clearly during that discussions was TC's rage at his first OGA examiner. "That man blatantly lied when he said I admitted to him, after the test, that I had had met with a foreign intelligence officer! That never happened and I never admitted to any such thing!" These were not the protestations of a liar who had been caught, but rather the emotional responses to an injustice by a righteously indignant man. There was no doubt, at least in my mind, that TC was telling the truth, and I left that meeting looking forward to helping clear him.

On court day, W&C sent a chauffeur-driven limousine to pick me up, and I couldn't help but think, *If only Mom could see me now.* In the corridor outside the courtroom, I ran into two of our witnesses, both of whom I had tested while I was with the agency. One of them was a very high-ranking officer in the CIA's Directorate of Science and Technology. He approached me and said, "John, I haven't seen you since you tested me in 1986." I didn't remember him but was flattered that he remembered me.

He then told me that he had recently taken his reinvestigation polygraph test and said, "You don't ever want to tell a CIA examiner that you have read John Sullivan's book." I had heard that many times before, from former colleagues still with the CIA as well as from people I met at AFIO luncheons who had undergone CIA polygraph tests. According to those with whom I spoke, they were accused of reading my book(s) in an attempt to learn how to beat a polygraph test.

I did remember the second of my former subjects, as he did me. My test of him had led to his being asked to resign from the CIA, but he didn't seem to have any hard feelings. He had worked with TC and was going to testify on his behalf.

The OGA examiner who had done TC's last polygraph examination was the first witness to be called. The government's attorney objected to my being present during his testimony, but he was overruled by the judge. However, the judge did say that I could only observe.

In my observation, the first thing I noticed was how very nervous the examiner was. He mumbled many of his answers, many of which were, "I don't know," "I don't remember," or "I don't recall." For a minute, as I listened to him, I thought I was watching John Dean during the Watergate hearings. It was very clear to me that he was an unwilling participant in the proceedings. I almost felt sorry for him.

When Mr. Haynes reviewed the examiner's qualifications, the examiner acknowledged that he had never caught a spy, conducted any espionage cases, or been involved with any counterintelligence activity and that most of his tests were focused on drug use.

As high-profile as this case was, I was very surprised that an examiner with such a lack of experience had been chosen to do TC's test. It also occurred to me that this may have been why he was chosen: His lack of experience and seniority might make him more malleable and easier to coerce, if that became necessary.

One of the questions I suggested that Mr. Haynes ask the OGA examiner was whether or not he had talked with the examiner who had done TC's first OGA test, or reviewed the charts of that test before he did TC's second test. When Mr. Haynes asked the question, the examiner said, "I can't recall."

There was absolutely no reason for the examiner not to have talked with the previous examiner and many reasons, as well as a protocol, to have done so. More importantly, it is beyond belief that the examiner would not recall such a discussion, if it happened. The examiner's body and verbal language were indicative of deception, and I nudged one of our attorneys and whispered, "He's lying."

During my career, I have done many retests and have never performed one without discussing the test with the previous examiner and reviewing the charts of the test, with one exception. That exception occurred when an examiner was suspected of fabricating a test, and I was asked to retest his subject without consulting or notifying him. I did the test and found out that the examiner had fabricated the results of his test. That examiner was my last supervisor in PD.

There are only two reasons I can come up with as to why an examiner assigned to do a retest would not consult with the previous examiner or review the charts of the test: one, the examiner is not available, and two, the results are a foregone conclusion. The examiner who had done TC's first test was in the courthouse that day.

When I was called to testify, Mr. Haynes was reviewing my qualifications when the defense attorney interrupted to say, "We acknowledge Mr. Sullivan's expertise."

Mr. Haynes asked me what would have been done in the CIA's polygraph program if an examiner had claimed an admission had been made but not recorded. My answer was that the admission would not have been acknowledged in any part of the report. Also, and depending on the seriousness of the admission, the examiner might be polygraphed. I also said that if the examiner were found to have misrepresented what occurred during the test in his report, he or she would, at the very least, never conduct another CIA polygraph test.

Mr. Haynes then asked me, "What was it about the test, itself, that concerned you?"

My answer was, "The questions." I went on to say that a cardinal rule of question formulation for polygraph test is that the examiner doesn't use pejorative words in the questions, for example, using "take" instead of "steal" and "have sex" or "make out" instead of "rape." The philosophy behind this is that a subject will admit to taking something but not stealing or having sex, but not raping. The examiner used the word "spy" in four of the questions. The other questions were ambiguous and designed to make sure TC didn't pass his test.

In my final remarks, I pointed out that the OGA could not possibly be objective or afford to have TC pass his second test.

If TC had been deemed truthful on this second test, that could only mean that he had been honest on his first test and unjustly vilified. The OGA could not and would not allow that to happen. That put an undue amount of pressure on the second examiner to make sure that TC did not pass his test. Under no circumstance should the examiner be under more pressure than the subject, as it changes the whole dynamic of the test.

Some might see having another agency's examiner do the test as a good alternative, but to do that the OGA would most likely have to show the new examiner the polygraph charts of TC's test. I am sure that those charts, if read by a competent examiner, would not support a call of "deception indicated."

The judge seemed to agree and ordered TC's clearances reinstated. As I saw it, my testimony was significant, but so too was the testimony of the OGA's examiner. The judge didn't believe him.

I was paid $14,700 for forty-nine hours' work and would have done the job pro bono. Mr. Whitten sent me a very complimentary letter thanking me for my efforts. I still have the letter and consider working on this case to be the most satisfying professional experience I ever had.

My experience with CIA's insidious appeals process dramatically enhanced the satisfaction I got from helping win one for the good guys. The last time I saw TC, it got even better.

A little over three months ago, I took my son John to an AFIO luncheon honoring a former colleague and very good friend. During the intermission between speakers, TC, whom I hadn't known was there, sat down at our table next to John and began talking with another guest at our table.

When TC finished talking, I reached across John, tapped TC on the shoulder, and said, "TC, I would like you to meet my son."

TC's response was to say, "I have to stand up to shake hands with you. You saved my life." He then asked John if he were in the "family business," and we had a brief conversation. There aren't many opportunities for people of my pedigree to impress their children, and to have someone of TC's stature say something very complimentary about me in front of my son was as good as it gets.

The third incident involves an author who has been asked to write a book about a man who is currently in prison after having been convicted of murder. The Innocence Project has taken the case, and the author asked me to look over the man's polygraph test before he made a decision as to whether or not he would write a book about the case. When I reviewed the polygraph report, I assessed the test as being flawed.

This case is ongoing, and if my participation helps get an innocent man out of jail, I would be more than delighted. At age seventy-five, I don't expect to have any more such moments. I spend more of my time reveling in my past pleasures and enjoying my current ones than I do looking forward to the future.

A part of all our futures is passing away, and I neither look forward to nor fear that event. I cite Luke 12:48 for this outlook, to wit: "To whom much has been given, much shall be required." It raises the question, is the converse also true? To whom little has been given, shall little be required? I don't think there were any expectations for me that I didn't exceed, and I see myself as having made the most of whatever gifts I have been given. When I meet my maker, and if he has a sense of humor, I should get a pass. With a closing glance back, and in summing up the last seventy-five years, I conclude that my life has been a fairy tale, still in progress, and made possible by being well raised by a village that cared.

ACKNOWLEDGEMENTS

Raised by a Village is a book of my memories over the last seventy-plus years. On many occasions, when my memory faltered or I needed more details on specific events and people, there were many on whom I called for help. To them I owe my sincerest thanks, as well as a public acknowledgment for their contribution to whatever success the book may have.

Primary among them is Bernie Heaney. Long before I ever thought about writing *Raised by a Village*, Bernie was my go-to person who would keep me current on what was happening in Greenport as well reminding me of events in Greenport's past. He has an almost encyclopedic knowledge about Greenport's history and was an invaluable asset.

Tom Breese is the Breese family historian and was particularly helpful with helping with my chapters on Coach Jackson and the 1953 championship season. Former teammates Dick Breese, Reg Tuthill, and Harry Bubb made sure that I got it right regarding specific game details.

Bill Pell, another former teammate and mayor of Greenport, was an invaluable asset for information on Greenport's political climate. There are many others, too numerous to mention, who helped and encouraged me. I hope they, and the aforementioned, find *Raised by a Village* an accurate presentation of the information they provided me and that their encouragement wasn't misplaced.

The biggest problem I had with writing *Raised by a Village* was that I no longer had Lee to help me. As computer illiterate as I was and still am, I had a lot of problems with this book. I would accidentally erase material and have problems with formatting. My brother-in-law, Frank "Rick" Aguilar, turned out to be the answer to my prayers. Rick's computer proficiency is only exceeded by the generosity with which he dispensed it to me.

Initially, Rick created an app for my book that made it easier to pull the manuscript up, and since I began the manuscript, he has done everything, except write the words, to help me. On at least four occasions, I locked myself out of the computer, and he got me back online. Within the next couple of days, Rick will paginate the manuscript, make sure all of the print is the same font size, and do anything else necessary to make the manuscript suitable for submission. Just as I couldn't have written my first two books without Lee, I could not have written *Raised by a Village* without Rick. My regret over my lack of computer competence is only surpassed by my gratitude to Rick.

CPSIA information can be obtained at www.ICGtesting.com
Printed in the USA
BVOW02*0139221215

429925BV00001B/1/P